PREFACE

ALL students of seventeenth-century poetry are indebted to J. M. Berdan's *The Poems of John Cleveland*, which first presented the poet to an American audience, and to Saintsbury's edition in *Minor Poets of the Caroline Period*, which first made the poems available to a modern English reader. The present edition is intended to continue and to elaborate the work so well begun by our predecessors. Our aim has been threefold: to supply an accurate text of Cleveland's genuine poems, establishing the canon and the transmission of the printed texts; to offer a critical account of the poetry and the vagaries of its literary reputation; to provide such a commentary as will initiate and support an informed reading of the poems themselves. A few poems are printed here for the first time; a larger number, appearing in previous editions, can now be dismissed from the canon and assigned to their true authors.

A work of this kind necessarily incurs great debts of gratitude to both institutions and individuals. We are grateful to the Research Board of the University of Reading, for a grant to facilitate work in American libraries in the summer of 1963, and to the American Association of University Women, for the New York State Endowed Fellowship, 1964–5. All the libraries in which we have worked have afforded notable courtesies, and it would be invidious not to distinguish the staffs of the British Museum, the Bodleian, the Henry E. Huntington Library, and the New York Public Library, in which a great deal of the work has been done. Dr. Helen Gardner, Dr. James M. Osborn, and Dr. Alice Walker have maintained a vigilant and helpful surveillance over a number of years; they have not only saved us from error, they have taught us the way we should go. For particular help of many kinds our thanks are due to Professor Philip Brockbank, Mrs. Jean Bromley, Dr. Harold Brooks, Dr. W. J. Cameron, Miss M. C. Crum, Professor Herbert Davis, Mr. Gordon Jones, the late J. B. Leishman, Dr. J. G. McManaway, Mr. D. H. Merry, Mr. D. G. Neill, Miss Lois Spencer, the late Colonel C. H. Wilkinson and Professor F. P. Wilson, and Dr. D. H. Woodward. For our errors we are content to blame each other.

York   B. R. M.
New York   E. M. W.

CONTENTS

POEMS PROBABLY BY CLEVELAND

LIST OF SIGLA

1. *The printed editions of Cleveland's poems*

D1	The Character of a London-Diurnall, with severall select Poems by the same Author, 1647. The First Edition.
D1A	The Character of a London-Diurnall, with severall select Poems by the same Author, Optima et Novissima Editio, 1647. The First Edition with additional material.
D2	The Character of a London-Diurnall, with severall select Poems by the same Author, 1647. The Second Edition.
D2A	The Character of a London-Diurnall, with severall select Poems by the same Author, Novissima et castigatissima Editio, 1647. The Second Edition with additional material.
D3	The Character of a London-Diurnall, with severall select Poems by the same Author, 1647. The Third Edition.
D4	The Character of a London-Diurnall, with severall select Poems by the same Author, Optima et novissima Editio, 1647. The Fourth Edition.
D5	The Character of a London-Diurnall, with severall select Poems by the same Author, Optima et novissima Editio, 1647. The Fifth Edition.
D6	The Character of a London-Diurnall, with severall select Poems by the same Author, Optima et novissima Editio, 1647. The Sixth Edition.
P1	Poems, by J. C., With Additions, 1651. The Seventh Edition.
P1A	Poems, by J. C., With Additions, 1651. The Seventh Edition with additional material.
P2	Poems, by J. C., With Additions, 1651. The Eighth Edition.
P3	Poems, by J. C., With Additions, 1651. The Ninth Edition.
P4	Poems, by J. C., With Additions, 1651. The Tenth Edition.
P5	Poems, by J. C., With Additions never before Printed, William Shears, 1653. The Eleventh Edition.
P6	Poems, by J. C., With Additions never before Printed, William Shears, 1653. The Twelfth Edition.
P7	Poems, by J. C., With Additions never before Printed, William Shears, 1654. The Thirteenth Edition.
P8	Poems, by J. C., With Additions never before Printed, William Shears, 1654. The Fourteenth Edition.

P9   Poems, by J. C., With Additions never before Printed, William Shears, 1656. The Fifteenth Edition.

P10   Poems, by J. C., With Additions never before Printed, William Shears, 1657. The Sixteenth Edition.

P11   Poems, Characters, and Letters. By J. C. With Additions never before Printed, 1658. The Seventeenth Edition.

P12   Poems, Characters, and Letters. By J. C. With Additions never before Printed, 1658. The Eighteenth Edition.

P13   Poems. By John Cleavland. With Additions never before Printed. William Sheers, 1659. The Nineteenth Edition.

P14   Poems. By John Cleavland. With Additions never before Printed, John Williams, 1661. The Twentieth Edition.

P15   Poems. By John Cleavland. With Additions never before Printed, William Shears, 1662. The Twenty-first Edition.

P16   Poems. By John Cleaveland. With Additions never before Printed, John Williams, 1665. The Twenty-second Edition.

P17   Poems. By John Cleaveland. With Additions never before Printed, John Williams, 1669. The Twenty-third Edition.

CV   Clievelandi Vindiciae, or Clieveland's Genuine Poems, Orations, Epistles, etc., Printed for Nathaniel Brooke, 1677. The Twenty-fourth Edition.
Variant imprint. Printed for Obadiah Blagrave, 1677.
Another Issue. Printed for Robert Harford, 1677.

W   The Works of Mr. John Cleveland. Obadiah Blagrave, 1687. The Twenty-fifth Edition.
Another Issue. Printed for O. B., 1699.
Another Issue. Printed for J. Brown, J. Midwinter, J. Clarke, 1742.

CR1   J. Cleaveland Revived: Nathaniel Brook, 1659.

CR2   J. Cleaveland Revived: Nathaniel Brooke, 1660.

CR3   J. Cleaveland Revived: Nathaniel Brook, 1662.

CR4   J. Cleaveland Revived: Nathaniel Brooks, 1668.

2. *Printed editions of individual poems*

AD   Ayres and Dialogues For One, Two, and Three Voyces, by Henry Lawes, 1653.

DD   The Decoy Duck: Together with the Discovery of the Knot in the Dragons Tayle calld &c., 1642.

H1   The Hue and Cry after Sir John Presbyter, 1649 (B.M. shelfmark 669. f. 14 (25)).

H2	The Hue and Cry after Sir John Presbyter, 1649 (B.M. shelfmark 669. f. 14 (64)).
H3	The Loyal Livery-Mens Hue and Cry after Sir John Presbyter 1683.
IC	Irenodia Cantabrigiensis, 1641.
J	Justa Edovardo King, 1638.
K1	The Kings Disguise, 1647 (B.M. shelfmark E.372 (2)).
K2	The Kings Disguise, 1647 (Harvard shelfmark EC 65. C. 5993. 647K).
PR	On the most Renowned Prince Rupert, n.d. (B.M. Luttrell broadside i, 126).
S	The Scots Apostasy, 1647 (B.M. shelfmark 669. f. 10 (117) and B. M. Luttrell broadside ii, 200).

3. Manuscripts containing poems by Cleveland

A2	British Museum, Add. MS. 22602.
A3	British Museum, Add. MS. 22603.
A24	British Museum, Add. MS. 24863.
A27	British Museum, Add. MS. 27879 (The Percy Folio MS.).
A30	British Museum, Add. MS. 30982.
A37	British Museum, Add. MS. 37719.
Ash36	Bodleian Library, Ashmole MS. 36, 37.
Ash38	Bodleian Library, Ashmole MS. 38.
Ash47	Bodleian Library, Ashmole MS. 47.
Ash78	Bodleian Library, Ashmole MS. 788.
B50	Bodleian Library, Ballard MS. 50.
C42	Cambridge University Library, Add. MS. 42.
CT5	Cambridge, Trinity College, MS. R5. 5.
Don	Bodleian Library, MS. Don. e. 6.
Douce	Bodleian Library, Douce MS. 357.
E20	British Museum, E.206 (9) (MS. leaf in printed book).
EG24	British Museum, Egerton MS. 2421.
EG27	British Museum, Egerton MS. 2725.
EP24	Bodleian Library, English Poetical MS. f. 24.
EP25	Bodleian Library, English Poetical MS. f. 25.
EP50	Bodleian Library, English Poetical MS. c. 50.
Firth	Bodleian Library, Firth MS. e. 4.
Fol	Folger Shakespeare Library, Washington, MS. V. a. 169.

H17   British Museum, Harleian MS. 6917.
H18   British Museum, Harleian MS. 6918.
H35   British Museum, Harleian MS. 3511.
H493   British Museum, Harleian 4931.
HE70   Harvard College Library, Eng. MS. 703.
L22   British Museum, Lansdowne MS. 223.
Loan   British Museum, Loan MS. 35.
O   MS. Owned by Dr. James Osborn, Yale University.
R   Rosenbach 193 (239/22).
RD10   Bodleian Library, Rawlinson MS. D. 1099.
RP26   Bodleian Library, Rawlinson Poetical MS. 26.
RP71   Bodleian Library, Rawlinson Poetical MS. 71.
RP84   Bodleian Library, Rawlinson Poetical MS. 84.
RP116   Bodleian Library, Rawlinson Poetical MS. 116.
RP117   Bodleian Library, Rawlinson Poetical MS. 117.
RP142   Bodleian Library, Rawlinson Poetical MS. 142.
RP147   Bodleian Library, Rawlinson Poetical MS. 147.
RP173   Bodleian Library, Rawlinson Poetical MS. 173.
S14   British Museum, Sloane MS. 1467.
SP16   Public Record Office, SP. Dom. 16, vol. 480.
T306   Bodleian Library, Tanner MS. 306.
T465   Bodleian Library, Tanner MS. 465.

ABBREVIATIONS

THE following abbreviations have been used for works frequently cited:

Berdan	*The Poems of John Cleveland*, ed. J. M. Berdan, Yale, 1903.
BNYPL	*Bulletin of the New York Public Library.*
DNB	*Dictionary of National Biography.*
ELH	*A Journal of English Literary History.*
Macray	Clarendon, *History of the Rebellion*, ed. W. D. Macray, 6 vols., 1888.
MLN	*Modern Language Notes.*
MLR	*Modern Language Review.*
MP	*Modern Philology.*
NQ	*Notes & Queries.*
OED	*Oxford English Dictionary.*
PMLA	*Publications of the Modern Language Association.*
PQ	*Philological Quarterly.*
RES	*Review of English Studies.*
Saintsbury	*Minor Poets of the Caroline Period*, ed. G. Saintsbury, Oxford, 1905–21.
Sayle	*The Works of Sir Thomas Browne*, ed. C. Sayle, 3 vols., Edinburgh, 1904–7.
STC	*Short-Title Catalogue of Books printed in England &c. 1475–1640*, ed. Pollard and Redgrave, 1926.
Tilley	M. P. Tilley, *A Dictionary of the Proverbs in England in the Sixteenth and Seventeenth Centuries*, Ann Arbor, 1950.
Wing	*Short-Title Catalogue of Books printed in England &c. 1641–1700*, ed. Donald Wing, 3 vols., New York, 1945–51.

INTRODUCTION

I. THE LIFE OF JOHN CLEVELAND

1. *Summary Biography*[1]

JOHN CLEVELAND was born at Loughborough, and baptized on 20 June 1613. He was the eldest son of a country clergyman, Thomas Cleveland, who had been educated at St. John's College, Cambridge. In 1621 the family moved to Hinckley, where John received his early education from Richard Vines, who later became a prominent Presbyterian.[2] On 4 September 1627 Cleveland was admitted as a lesser pensioner at Christ's College, Cambridge.

Although one of his ballads seems to have brought down the wrath of the University authorities (see the headnote to 'How the Commencement grows new', p. 147), his career at Cambridge was uniformly successful. In 1629 he was chosen to deliver the Latin address of welcome to the Chancellor of the University and the French Ambassador (with his suite, among whom was Rubens), and while he was probably still an undergraduate he, like Milton, officiated as 'Father' of the Cambridge Revels. He proceeded B.A. in 1631 and M.A. in 1635. On 27 March 1634 he was elected to the Hebblethwaite Fellowship in his father's college, St. John's. Wood informs us that in 1637 Cleveland was incorporated Master of Arts at Oxford, 'not that it appears so in the public register, but from the relation of a certain person who was then a master of this university'.[3] Whether this is true or not must remain doubtful, but Cleveland's life at Cambridge seems to have followed the expected pattern. As a Fellow, he directed the work of undergraduates in his charge, and among his pupils were John Lake and Samuel Drake, who, some forty years later, were the compilers of the 1677 edition of his

---

[1] The standard biography of Cleveland is contained in Berdan.

[2] In 1643 Vines became a member of the Westminster Assembly, which Cleveland satirized in 'The Mixt Assembly', and he was employed by Parliament in all their treaties with the King. See J. Nichols, *The History and Antiquities of the County of Leicester*, 1795, III. ii. 913–16.

[3] Anthony Wood, *Fasti Oxonienses*, ed. Bliss, 1813–20, i, col. 498.

b

Works.[1] Between 1635 and 1637 he was made Rhetoric Reader, and his Oration on this occasion, like the various letters he wrote on behalf of the College, displays the same light, extravagant wit as we find in his poems. Within the University Cleveland was probably better known as a disputant than as a poet, and in his fifteen years at Cambridge he contributed to only two of the University miscellanies. Yet many of his best-known poems were written at this time. 'How the Commencement grows new', 'On Princess Elizabeth', the Elegies on Edward King, 'A Dialogue between two Zealots', 'Epitaph on the Earl of Strafford', 'Smectymnuus', 'The King's return', 'To P. Rupert', and 'Upon Sir Thomas Martin' all belong to this period, and one can probably add 'Square-Cap' and many of the other non-political poems to the list. Clearly, he was deeply concerned with the political issues of the time, and the remark recorded by Lake and Drake in the preface to the 1677 edition may well indicate the quality of his involvement:

When *Oliver* was in Election to be Burgess for the Town of *Cambridge*, as he engaged all his Friends and Interests to oppose it, so when it was passed, he said with much passionate Zeal, That single Vote had ruined both Church and Kingdom.[2]

Cambridge, in the early 1640's, was no place for such opinions, and it is not surprising that soon after the outbreak of the Civil War Cleveland left the University and joined the King's camp at Oxford. The latest certain reference to Cleveland at Cambridge is in June 1642,[3] but he probably stayed there until the spring of 1643, since 'Upon Sir Thomas Martin' refers to events in Cambridgeshire, and must be dated later than March 1643. While he was at Oxford Cleveland composed what is probably his most famous poem, 'The Rebell Scot', and also wrote and published *The Character of a London-Diurnall*, a prose pamphlet which aroused great hostility among the

[1] Lake fought in the Royalist army, and received steady preferment after the Restoration until he became Bishop of Chichester in 1685. Drake fought at Newark, under Cleveland, and was made Vicar of Pontefract after the Restoration. See John Walker, *Sufferings of the Clergy*, 1714, pp. 150 and 294, and A. G. Matthews, *Walker Revised*, Oxford, 1948, pp. 40 and 230.

[2] CV, sig. A6ᵛ.

[3] See S. V. Gapp, 'Notes on John Cleveland', *PMLA*, xlvi, 1931, pp. 1075–86. This article corrects and supplements Berdan on some points.

Parliamentarians. Mr. Gapp has suggested that Cleveland was in London in February 1645, to look after the publication of the third edition of the *Character*, but the evidence for this is not conclusive.

By 27 May 1645 Cleveland had been appointed Judge Advocate to the garrison at Newark, under Sir Richard Willis.[1] Here he wrote 'The Kings Disguise', and he seems to have been known as the official spokesman or letter-writer for the garrison.[2] But during Cleveland's stay at Newark the King's cause had been lost, and on 5 May 1646, at Southwell, near Newark, Charles surrendered himself to the Scots army, who demanded the immediate surrender of the garrison. The King agreed, and the surrender was made on the following day. The story that, at the surrender, Cleveland was tried by the Scottish commander, David Lesley, and dismissed with contempt, may or may not be true,[3] but if it took place at all it must have happened on the 6th or 7th of May 1646, since Lesley left Newark immediately after its surrender.

It is impossible to say with any certainty what happened to Cleveland after the fall of Newark. Like so many other Royalists he probably wandered about the country depending upon his more fortunate friends. It has been suggested, by Gapp and others, that Cleveland was in London between 1647 and 1649, concerning himself with the publication of various Royalist Mercuries, and this may very well be so. Thorn-Drury has shown, from the evidence of two poems by the Earl of Westmorland, that Cleveland was staying in Manby, at the house of Stephen Anderson, in or about 1651.[4] But these are only glimpses. For nearly ten years after the fall of Newark Cleveland disappears from sight, and in this decade fourteen separate editions of his Poems were published.

---

[1] See Cornelius Brown, *The Annals of Newark-upon-Trent*, 1879, pp. 168–9. Some of Brown's statements are unsubstantiated. For example, 'When besieged in Newark, he was not idle. He composed a volume entitled *The Muses' Mistress, a storehouse of rich fancies, written at succedaneous hours, during the action at Newark.*' See *BNYPL*, lxii, May 1963, pp. 326–7 for reasons why this work could not be Cleveland's.

[2] See *Mercurius Britannicus*, no. 128, quoted by Gapp.

[3] It is first recorded in *The Critical Review*, xxvii, 1769, pp. 426–7, in a review of Granger's *Biographical History of England*.

[4] G. Thorn-Drury, *A Little Ark containing Sundry Pieces of Seventeenth-Century Verse*, 1921, pp. 16–18.

On 10 November 1655 Cleveland was arrested at or near Norwich, and sent to imprisonment at Yarmouth. The letter preserved in the Thurloe State Papers (MS. Rawl. A. 32, f. 331) describes him as 'John Cleveland of Norwich', and says that he admitted coming to Norwich from London 'about a yeare since'. He accounted for his presence in Norwich by saying that he was employed by a Mr. Edward Cooke, to help him in his studies. The accusations made against Cleveland are not very substantial, and the catalogue of his offences ends 'Mr. Cleveland is a person of great abilities and soe able to doe the greater disservice'. After some three months in prison Cleveland wrote a letter to the Lord Protector asking for his release, or, as Lloyd describes the incident, 'he composed an Addresse to the Pageant Power at *Whitehall* of so much gallant Reason, and such towring Language, as looked bigger than his Highness, shrinking before the Majesty of his Pen . . .'.[1] The petition seems to have been granted, although no precise date can be given for his release. He seems to have continued his wanderings until, as the Preface to *Clievelandi Vindiciae* says, 'After many intermediate Stages (which contended as emulously for his aboad, as the seven Cities for *Homer's* Birth) *Grays-Inn* was his last'. Unfortunately, Cleveland's name is not entered on the Gray's Inn Register, but Berdan's statement 'I think we are safe in saying that he spent the fall of '57 in Gray's Inn, London' is probably as near the truth as one is likely to get. According to Wood, he found there 'a generous Maecenas', who has been identified by Dymock-Fletcher and Berdan as 'John Onebye' of Hinckley, and who was admitted to the Inn on 14 June 1651.

Cleveland died of an intermittent fever on 29 April 1658. His body was carried to Hunsdon-house, and he was buried in the parish church of St. Michael Royal, on College-Hill, on 1 May. The burial service was performed by the Revd. Edward Thurman, and the sermon preached by Dr. John Pearson, who was a contemporary of Cleveland's at Cambridge, and subsequently became Bishop of Chester.[2] The church of St. Michael Royal was destroyed by fire in 1666.

[1] David Lloyd, *Memoires*, 1668, p. 618.
[2] See Walker, *Sufferings of the Clergy*, p. 67, and Matthews, *Walker Revised*, p. 340.

2. *Four Contemporary Accounts*

1. Fuller, *The History of the Worthies of England*, 1662, pp. 135–6 (Leicestershire).

JOHN CLEVELAND was *born* in this *County* at *Hinckley* (where his *Father* was Vicar) and bred therein under Mr. *Ricard Vines* his School-master; he was afterwards Scholar of *Christs*, then Fellow of S. *Johns* in *Cambridge*, and during the late Civil Wars was much conversant in the *Garison* of *Newark*, where (as I am informed) he had the place of *Advocate General*.

A General Artist, Pure Latinist, Exquisite Orator, and (which was his *Master-piece*) *Eminent Poet*. His *Epithetes* were pregnant with *Metaphors*, carrying in them a *difficult plainness, difficult* at the *hearing, plain* at the *considering* thereof. His lofty Fancy may seem to stride from the top of one Mountain to the top of another, so making to it self a constant *Level* and *Champian* [sic] of *continued Elevations*.

Such who have *Clevelandized*, indeavouring to imitate his Masculine Stile, could never go beyond the *Hermophrodite*, still betraying the weaker Sex in their deficient conceits. Some distinguish between the *Veine* and *Strain* of Poetry, making the former to flow with facility, the latter press'd with pains, and forced with industry. Master *Cleveland's Poems* do partake of both, and are not to be the less valued by the Reader, because most studied by the Writer thereof. As for his Anagram *John Cleveland Heliconean Dew*. The difficult trifle I confess, is rather well endevoured then exactly performed. He dyed on *Thursday* morning the 29. of *April* 1658. at his Chamber in *Greys Inne*, from whence his Body was brought to *Hunsdon House*, and on Saturday being *May day*, was buryed at *Colledge Hill Church*, Mr. *John Pearson* his good friend preaching his Funeral Sermon. He rendred this reason why he cautiously declined all commending of the party deceased, because such praising of him would not be adequate to any expecta-tion in that Auditory, seeing such who knew him not, would suspect it far above, whilest such who were acquainted with him, did know it much beneath his due desert. The self same consideration, shall put a period to my pen, in his present Character, only this I will adde, that never so *eminent* a *Poet*, was *Interred* with fewer (if any remarkable) *Elegies* upon him.

I read in an excellent[1] Authour, how one *Joannes Passerativus*, pro-fessor of the Latine Tongue in the University of *Paris*, being no bad

[1] Marginal note, *Thuanus de Obit. virorum Illustrium anno* 1602.

Poet, (but *Morose* and conceited of himself) forbad by his dying words, under an Imprecation, *That his Herse should be burthened with bad funeral Verses*, Whereupon out of fear to offend his Ghost, very few Verses were made upon him, too much the modesty and charity of Mr. *Cleveland*, by any such Injunction to obstruct his friends, expressing their affection to his memory. Be it rather imputed to the *Royal party*, at that juncture of time generally in restraint, so that their fancies may seem in some sort to sympathize with the confining of their persons, and both in due season may be inlarged.

Of such Verses as came to my hand these were not the worst, made by my good[1] Friend since deceased.

> *Ye Muses do not me deny*
> *I ever was your Votary,*
> *And tell me seeing you do daigne,*
> *T'inspire and feed the hungry brain,*
> *With what choice cates? with what choice fair?*
> *Ye* Cleevelands *fancy still repair.*
> *Fond man, say they, why dost thou question thus?*
> *Ask rather with what Nectar he feeds us.*

But I am informed, that there is a Book intended by the Poets of our age, in the Honour of his Memory, who was so eminent a Member of their Society.

2. Edward Phillips, Eminent Poets among the MODERNS, *Theatrum Poetarum*, 1675, pp. 104–5.

John Cleaveland, a Notable Highsoaring Witty Loyalist of *Cambridge*, whose Verses in the time of the Civil War begun to be in great request, both for their Wit and zeal to the King's cause, for which indeed he appear'd the first, if not only, Eminent Champion in Verse against the *Presbyterian* Party; but most especially against the *Kirck* and *Scotch* Covenant, which he prosecuted with such a Satyrical fury, that the whole Nation fares the worse for it, lying under a most grievous Poetical Censure. In fine, so great a Man hath *Cleaveland* been in the Estimation of the generality, in regard his Conceits were out of the common road, and Wittily farfetch't, that Grave Men, in outward appearance have not spar'd in my hearing to affirm him the best of English Poets, and let them think so still, who ever please, provided it be made no Article of Faith.

---

[1] Marginal note, Mr. *Edward Martin* of *London*.

3. John Aubrey, *Brief Lives*, written *circa* 1680, edited Andrew Clark, 1898, i. 174–5.

John Cleveland was borne at . . . (quaere Mr. Nayler) in Warwickshire. He was a fellow of St. John's Colledge in Cambridge, where he was more taken notice of for his being an eminent disputant, then a good poet. Being turned out of his fellowship for a malignant he came to Oxford, where the king's army was, and was much caressed by them. He went thence to the garrison at Newark upon Trent, where upon some occasion of drawing of articles, or some writing, he would needs add a short conclusion, viz. 'and hereunto we annex our lives, as a labell to our trust'. After the king was beaten out of the field, he came to London, and retired in Grayes Inne. He, and Sam. Butler, &c. of Grayes Inne, had a clubb every night. He was a comely plump man, good curled haire, darke browne. Dyed of the scurvy, and lies buried in St. Andrew's church, in Holborne, anno Domini 165 . . . (quaere Mr. Nayler, of . . .).

4. *Funerall Elegies. Or The Sad Muses in Sables* . . . . Written by S. H., 1655.

On the death of the High-priz'd Poet JOHN CLEAVELAND, Esq;

> What, are all silent! are the Sons of Art,
> Afraid to mention this dead *Ascapart*?
> This *Colbrand* of *Castalia*, he whose strength,
> Takes up nine Acres at the least in length:
> Like *Titius*, every line of his might well,
> Serve *Faustus*, or *Agrippa* for a Spell;
> Nor durst the Romanist his Numbers mind,
> Till with the Cross he had his fore-head sign'd;
> Thou great Gargantuan, huge Colossian Bard,
> Who shall dare sing thy worth unlesse prepar'd
> With Sack and Sulphure, every word should pierce
> Like Thunder through the wond'ring Universe;
> Although thou art inhum'd (to fancy Fate)
> Yet still to us thou dost tonitruate,
> Thy words want each an *Atlas*; we can Rant,
> 'Tis true, but not like thee (our Termagant)
> Whose every syllable a sentence is,
> Each word an Axiome, thou hast searcht Abysse,

(The Muses *Hercules*) and shown to us,
That triple-headed bandog *Cerberus*,
So by the Magick of thy haughty Rhimes,
The Powers celestiall cringe to mortall crimes:
No marvell thou couldst cramp so many Pens,
Whose face and belly were as big as *Bens*:
Gyant of Wit as well as Bulk, thy Quill,
(That Maule of minds) rests on the Muses Hill
A sacred Trophey; ye small Wits bow down,
Give worship to this Bashaw of the Gown;
Grand Vizier to *Apollo*, the Vice-King
Of fair *Castalia*, when thy Soule took wing,
Why didst thou not appoint who should succeed?
Who now shall dare to wear thy Regall weed?
To put the Lawrell on, or to give Law
In Verse that would keep *Lucifer* in awe;
Like *Alexanders* Captains, wanting thee,
We now shall quarrell for Supremacie;
For thou hast left a world of wit behind,
For those to share whom blessings cannot bind;
Thus like some mighty Potentate that dyes
Without an Heir, those Laws and Liberties
So oft confirm'd by Phoebus Parliament,
Shall be made void, yet on thy Monument
We will presume this Epitaph to grave,
Here Cleveland *lyes, whose Wit went wondrous brave.*

II. THE CANON

Cleveland's poems were not, so far as we can judge, published under their author's supervision or even with his consent. A few were printed separately as anonymous pamphlets or broadsides, but the seventeen poems which were published in 1647 as *The Character of a London-Diurnall: With severall select Poems By the same Author* (D1) mark the first attempt to collect a number of Cleveland's poems. This edition was reprinted five times in the same year without further ascription. In the reprinting new poems, some of them demonstrably spurious, were added sporadically, the fifth and sixth editions relegating some new and some which had appeared in all

previous editions to a section headed 'Additionall Poems by uncertain Authors'. The derivative editions of 1647 (D1A–D6) added
eight poems to the original seventeen, bringing the total to
twenty-five.

The first suggestion of Cleveland's authorship comes in the first
edition of 1651 (P1), which was set up from two of the editions of
1647. Its title-page reads, 'Poems. By J.C. With Additions', and it
reprinted twenty-two poems and added four. Several of the first nine
editions deriving from it added further poems without distinguish-
ing between new and old. By 1658, the year of Cleveland's death,
the number attributed to 'J.C.' had risen to forty-one, when two
new editions appeared (P11 and P12), which relied partially upon
manuscripts, and added a further nine poems bringing the total to
fifty. In 1659 P13, which marked the resumption of reprints deriving
from P1, included thirty-three more poems in a section headed
'Additions', and these were reprinted in the last four editions of the
series (P14–P17), so that the total stood at eighty-three.

The year 1659 also saw the first edition of *Cleaveland Revived*, a
collection of poems which had no connexion with the series deriving
from P1. It carried thirty-seven poems, and its title-page promised
'Poems, Orations, Epistles, and other of his Genuine Incomparable
Pieces, never before publisht. With Some other Exquisite Remains
of the most eminent Wits of both the Universities that were his
Contemporaries'. In its epistle to the reader, dated 'Newark,
Novemb. 21. 1658', one E. Williamson conceded that Cleveland had
written comparatively few poems; but,

> It was my fortune to be in Newark, when it was besieged, where
> I saw a few manuscripts of Mr. *Cleavelands*, amongst others I have
> heard that he writ of the Treaty at Uxbridge . . . the intimacie I had
> with Mr. *Cleaveland*, before and since these civill wars, gained most
> of these papers from him;

Most of the 'former printed Poems' Williamson declared genuine,
though not those 'lately added, to make up the Volume'. Some
additional papers 'from one of M. Cleavelands neere Acquaintance'
had been read hastily by a friend of the poet at Gray's Inn, who
thought them genuine. Williamson decided to publish the poems

he had, together with others 'such as the Reader shall find to be of such persons, as were for the most part Mr. *Cleavelands* Contemporaries'. Despite these rambling evasions the poems seem to have been widely accepted as Cleveland's during three reprintings. CR2 (1660) had twenty-five new poems, apparently added by the 'Stationer' who says in his Preface that the success of the first edition encouraged him 'to use my best diligence to gain what still remained in the hands of the Authors friends'. These 'remains', lacking even the doubtful authority of Williamson, reappeared in the last two editions of CR.

With the publication of CR4 (1668) 145 poems had been printed more or less uncritically as Cleveland's. Not until 1677 did two of his old pupils, John Lake and Samuel Drake, attempt to 'edit' the collection, promising on the title-page of their *Clievelandi Vindiciae* (CV) only 'Clieveland's Genuine Poems, Orations, Epistles, &c. Purged from the many False and Spurious Ones Which had usurped his Name. . . . To which are added many Additions never Printed before . . .'. Addressing the Master and Fellows of St. John's College, Cambridge, the editors attacked CR:

We know you have not without passionate resentments beheld the prostitution of his name in some late Editions vended under it, wherein his Orations are murthered over and over in barbarous Latine, and a more barbarous Translation: and wherein is scarce one or other Poem of his own to commute for all the rest. At least every Curiasier of his hath a fulsom Dragooner behind him, and *Venus* is again unequally yoaked with a sooty Anvile-beater. *Clieveland* thus revived dieth another death.

The Vindicators retained only twenty-nine of the previously printed poems, fourteen of which had been in D1. They added two, to bring the total of poems attributed to Cleveland to 147.

The *Works* of 1687, however, defeated their efforts. Its first section was a reprint of CV; its second included all but twelve of the poems rejected by Lake and Drake in the editions of the P and CR series; and its third was the prose piece 'The Rustick Rampant'. Reissued in 1699 and 1742, this edition made no editorial judgements, and is fittingly called by Saintsbury the 'omnium gatherum' of poems ascribed to Cleveland.

With no surviving holograph, the printed editions must be the basis from which to distinguish the genuine, the spurious, and the doubtful among 147 poems ascribed to Cleveland. As a guiding principle we may accept as genuine any poem printed as Cleveland's during his lifetime, which is not questioned in any subsequent edition, which is not ascribed elsewhere to any other author, and which is not strikingly unlike the great majority of poems which fulfil these conditions. Corroboration is provided if the poem is included in CV, and strengthened if it also appears in the Osborn manuscript. This manuscript, like D1 and CV, represents a deliberate collection of Cleveland. It contains many of his poems, letters, and orations, and nothing by any other author. It is of great value in establishing the canon since no other manuscript presents a comparable range or amount of Cleveland's work, nor is any other devoted wholly to him.[1]

In D1 the following ten poems are, on these grounds, immediately acceptable:

'Upon Phillis', 'Upon a Miser that made a great Feast', 'A young Man to an old Woman Courting him', 'To Mrs. K. T.', 'A Faire Nimph scorning a Black Boy Courting her', 'A Dialogue between two Zealots', 'The Mixt Assembly', 'The Kings Disguise', 'The Rebell Scot', 'To P. Rupert'.

Three not fulfilling these conditions are equally certain. In H493 (f. 17) 'Smectymnuus, or the Club-Divines' is ascribed to 'Mr Cresswell', and on the verso an inferior satire, 'Smectymnuus, Bellua multorum capitum', is given to Cleveland. But the first poem is in all the seventeenth-century editions of Cleveland except CR, four manuscripts either ascribe it to him or initial it 'J.C.', and it is in O. The attribution in H493 must be a scribal error.[2] 'Upon an Hermophrodite' and 'The Authour to his Hermophrodite' are related poems; the first appeared in the 1640 and all subsequent editions of Randolph's poems, and both were printed in the 1653 edition of the poems of Beaumont, which has been accurately

---

[1] For fuller discussion see pp. l-li. All the poems attributed to Cleveland are discussed by E. Withington, 'The Canon of John Cleveland's Poetry', *BNYPL*, lxvii, May 1963, pp. 307–27, and June 1963, pp. 377–94.

[2] For further discussion see *BNYPL*, lxvii, June 1963, pp. 377–9.

described as 'a "dumping-ground" for odds and ends of all kinds'.[1] It is quite certain that the second poem is Cleveland's protest against the inclusion of the first in Randolph's poems. Thirteen of the seventeen poems in D1 are therefore genuine.

'A Song of Marke Anthony' and 'The Authours Mock-Song to Marke Anthony' are first printed, as a single poem, in D1A, and first separated in D5; as no other author has ever been suggested for the 'Mock-Song' it may be accepted as genuine. D5 added three other poems, and two of these, 'Square-Cap' and 'Upon the death of M. King' (already printed as Cleveland's in *Justa Edovardo King*, 1638), have never been claimed for any other author. Thus, sixteen of the twenty-five poems in the series D1–D6 are indisputable.

Of the four poems added to P1 Cleveland's claim to three—'The Senses Festival', 'The Hecatomb to his Mistresse', and 'Upon Sir Thomas Martin'—has never been questioned; all three are ascribed to 'J. C.' in H18, and 'The Senses Festival' is mentioned in an Elegy on Cleveland by 'T. P., Gen. Norfolciensis', 1658.[2] P1A added two more genuine poems: 'The Hue and Cry after Sir John Presbyter', whose first line is quoted as Cleveland's in *Memoirs of the Life of Colonel Hutchinson*,[3] and 'The Antiplatonick', which, although included in the notorious 1653 edition of Beaumont, is ascribed to Cleveland in three contemporary manuscripts, RP116, RP147, and H18, and headed 'by I. C.' in Thomas Jordan's *Claraphil and Clarinda* (*c.* 1650).

In the last three editions of 1651 two of the four new poems are certainly genuine. 'How the Commencement grows new' is in O and ascribed to Cleveland in RP147, T465, and C42; in H18 it is given to 'J. C.' and followed by an attack, 'Saltmarsh of Magdal: against Cleuelands new commencement', and a defence 'by Wilde of S^nt Johns'. 'Fuscara', never ascribed to another poet, is mentioned in the preface to CV and printed as its first poem; it is also in O and ascribed to 'Cleaueland' in RP116.

Between P5 (1653) and the last edition certainly published in Cleveland's lifetime (P10) six poems were added to the collection,

[1] Saintsbury, iii. 28.
[2] *An Elegie Upon the Never Satisfactorily deplored Death of that Rare Column of Parnassus, Mr. Iohn Cleeveland.* B.M. shelfmark C. 20. f. 2 (22).
[3] Written by his Widow Lucy, Everyman's Library, 1908, p. 95.

but only 'To Julia' can be genuine. It has never been claimed for any other author, and is in both CV and O.

One more poem belongs in the list of certainties. 'Upon the Kings return from Scotland' was first printed in *Irenodia Cantabrigiensis: Ob paciferum Serenissimi Regis Caroli e Scotia reditum*, Cambridge, 1641, where it was signed 'John Cleveland, Fellow of St Johns Colledge';[1] though it does not appear in the series D1–P17 it is in O and reprinted in all the editions of CR and CV. Thus of the poems in print as Cleveland's before his death twenty-five form the core of the canon, against which doubtful poems may be tested.

A large number of poems may be rejected without lengthy discussion. There is a prima facie case that if a poem is attributed to two writers, one well known and popular and the other obscure, the attribution to the popular writer is the wrong one. In addition to poems demonstrably by other authors we may reject with confidence those poems attributed to Cleveland in posthumous editions which had been printed as the work of other men, or ascribed to them in manuscript. We may also reject poems for which no other author can be found, but which are ascribed to Cleveland only in an unauthoritative edition. One hundred and seven poems come within this formula.

Six by other authors were printed as Cleveland's during his lifetime. 'On I.W. A.B. of York', an attack on John Williams, appears in D1 and regularly thereafter, though in the 'Uncertain Authors' section of D5 and D6 and not in CV. It was also printed in Thomas Weaver's *Songs and Poems of Love and Drollery*, 1654, and Weaver's claim is corroborated by its appearance in MS. Rawl. Poet. 211, a holograph collection of his work.[2] Two poems, 'Britanicus his Blessing' and 'Britanicus his Welcome', appear only in the reissue of the second edition (D2A); both were published in Sir Francis Wortley's *Characters and Elegies*, 1646, and may confidently be

---

[1] See Alberta Turner, 'The University Miscellanies: Some Neglected Early Texts of Cleveland and Cowley', *MLN*, lxiv, June 1949, pp. 423–4.

[2] David Lloyd, in his life of John Williams, says: '... the very wretch that writ the Satyr upon him, Printed with *Clevelands* Poems, owing his heat to the wine in his Cellar; and his Vein, to his Gold. For receiving twenty pieces of him, and despairing of more, to please his new patrons in the next Ale-house, vomited this libel on his old one. A libel nothing would be guilty of, but *Poetry*, and *Beggery*,' (*Memoires*, p. 380).

ascribed to him. In P1 a second elegy on Edward King is demonstrably spurious. It is the last fourteen lines of W. More's elegy
printed immediately after Cleveland's in *Justa Edovardo King*,[1] and
was probably included by P1's printer merely to fill up his sheet. Of
the elegies on King Charles in P6 (1653) two can certainly be assigned to other authors. 'Chronostichon Decollationis Caroli Regis'
had appeared in print three times before.[2] The anonymity of these
interregnum versions is understandable, but in 1661 a broadside
edition made the following ascription: 'Written many yeares since
by Major P. F. and at the instance of Friends reprinted, M.DC.LXI'.
The author must be Payne Fisher (1616–93), Cromwell's 'poet
laureate' and one of the age's most notorious turncoats. 'Major P.F.'
is the title-page ascription on several books known to be by him,
and 'Chronostichon' is strikingly like some of his other poems.[3] The
other elegy, an even clearer case, is followed by the printed ascription 'Montrose' and the comment 'Written with the point of his
sword'.[4]

The second group of rejections includes poems by other authors
ascribed to Cleveland only in derivative posthumous editions.
'Humane Inconstancie', added to P11, was also ascribed to Montrose
in an eighteenth-century broadsheet,[5] but in *Chronicles of the Frasers*,
a manuscript composed over a period from 1666–99, James Fraser
says that George Wishart, Montrose's chaplain, wrote 'the noble
poem . . . of which the famous English poet Cleveland averrs that
he would renounce all his art of poetry providing he were master of
these 30 lines. . .'.[6] 'The Four-Legg'd Elder', earlier published as
a broadside,[7] and added to P12, is ascribed to Sir John Birkenhead

---

[1] See Saintsbury, iii. 26.

[2] In *Vaticinium Votivum, or Palaemon's Prophetick Prayer*, 1649; as a broadside (B.M.
669. f. 14 (24) with the manuscript date 'Aprill 30 1649'); and in *Monumentum Regale*,
dated by Thomason 'June 14th. 1649'.

[3] A considerable collection of these is in B.M. Add. MS. 19863.

[4] For other contemporary ascriptions of this poem to Montrose see *Poems of James
Graham, Marquis of Montrose*, ed. J. L. Weir, 1938, pp. 45–46 and 60–61.

[5] See Sir James Ferguson, *The Green Garden*, Edinburgh, 1946, p. 172, and C. V.
Wedgwood, 'Poems of Montrose', *Essays and Studies*, New York, 1960, pp. 61–63.
L22 and RP84 have this poem in sections containing poems by Cleveland and others;
collations show that they are too closely related to P11–12 to be an independent
witness to authorship.   [6] Ed. Wm. Mackay, *Pub. Scottish Hist. Soc.*, xlvii. 363.

[7] The B.M. broadside, 669. f. 11 (70), bears the manuscript date 1 September,
1647; it was reprinted in 1677 [B.M. C. 40. M. 11 (57)].

in Wood's *Athenae Oxonienses* (ed. Bliss, 1820, iii, col. 1205) and in two eighteenth-century miscellanies.[1] Of the thirty-three poems added in P13 thirty-one had been printed in R. Fletcher's *Ex Otio Negotium*, 1656; the section in which all but one of them ('The Sigh') are printed is headed 'Additions', and no poem is elsewhere attributed to Cleveland. They may safely be dismissed.

Thirty-four of the thirty-seven poems in CR1 can be assigned to other authors. The following eleven were first printed in John Hall's *Poems*, Cambridge, 1646:

'Upon a talkative woman', 'On an ugly woman', 'On a little Gentlewoman profoundly learned', 'On Parsons the great Porter', 'To Cloris a Rapture', 'Upon Wood of Kent', 'To his Mistresse' [Come (dearest Julia) thou and I], 'On one that was deprived of his Testicles', 'The Flight', 'On a Burning-glasse', 'Not to Travel'.

There is every reason to believe Hall the author of these poems, but differences in text and in several titles suggest that the copy for CR was a manuscript and not the printed edition of Hall's poems.

Six poems had appeared in various miscellanies of the period as the work of Jasper Mayne, a Christ Church man whom Cleveland may have met at Oxford:

1. 'To the King recovered from a fit of sicknesse'.
2. 'To the Queen upon the birth of one of her Children'.
3. 'An Elegie upon Ben. Johnson' ('As when the Vestal hearth went out, no fire').
4. 'In Nuptias Principis Auranchii & D. Mariae filiae Regis Angliae'.
5. 'To the King' ('The Prince hath now an equall').
6. 'To the Queen, upon the birth of her first Daughter'.[2]

Three more poems from the miscellanies are the work of Richard West:

1. 'An Elegie on Ben. Johnson' ('Poet of Princes, Prince of Poets, wee').

---

[1] *Wit and Mirth: or Pills to Purge Melancholy*, 1707, iii, and *Songs Compleat, Pleasant and Divertive*, 1719, v.

[2] No. 1 in *Musarum Oxoniensium Pro Rege Suo Soteria*, Oxford, 1633, pp. 13–14; no. 2 in *Flos Britannicus Veris Novissimi Carolo & Mariae Nata*, Oxford, 1636, where it is the second of the English poems; no. 3 in *Ionsonvs Virbivs*, 1638, pp. 29–33; no. 4 in Προτέλεια *Anglo-Batava*, Oxford, 1641, sig. A2ᵛ–A3; nos. 5 and 6 in *Vitis Carolinae Gemma Altera*, Oxford, 1633, printed consecutively, with Mayne's name, after no. 6.

2. 'Upon the marriage of the Prince of Orange &c.' (' 'Tis vain to wish them joyes; nor is it meet').

3. 'To the Queen' ('If Poets could be born as oft as you').[1]

Two poems, 'To his Mistresse' ('What mystery is this? that I should finde') and 'The Puritan', may be assigned to Strode,[2] and two more, 'On the May Pole' and 'Upon Tom of Christ-Church', are Richard Corbett's.[3] The ten remaining poems are each by a different author:

1. 'Rebellis Scotus' (a translation of 'The Rebell Scot') is by Thomas Gawen.[4]

2. 'Upon the Birth of the Duke of York', on sig. K4ᵛ–K5 of *Vitis Carolinae Gemma Altera*, 1633, is by Josias Howe.

3. 'An Epitaph' ('Stay gentle Reader and shed o're'), on sig. G2–G2ᵛ of *Parentalia Spectatissimo Rolando Cottono Equiti Aurato Salopiensi*, 1635, is by Dudley Digges.

4. 'An intertainment at Cotswold' on sig. B2ᵛ–B4 of *Annalia Dubrensia*, 1636, is by William Durham.

5. 'To the Queen' ('Whom tumults lessen not, whose wombe, we see'), on sig. b2 of *Horti Carolini Rosa Altera*, is by Martin Lluellin.

6. 'An Elegy on Ben. Jonson' ('Who first reformed our stage with justest laws') in *Ionsonvs Virbivs* is by James Cleyton.[5]

7. 'Upon the Marriage of the young Prince of Orange with the Lady Marie' ('We are no longer Iland, speedily'), on sig. b1–b1ᵛ of Προτέλεια *Anglo-Batava*, is by Richard Paynter.

8. 'An Epitaph on Ben. Johnson' ('The Muses fairest light in no dark time'), on p.27 of *Ionsonvs Virbivs*, is by Sidney Godolphin.[6]

---

[1] No. 1 in *Ionsonvs Virbivs*, 1638, pp. 55–58; no. 2 in Προτέλεια *Anglo-Batava*, Oxford, 1641, sig. b3–b4ᵛ; no. 3 in *Horti Carolini Rosa Altera*, Oxford, 1640, sig. a3ᵛ–a4ᵛ.

[2] Both are in the Strode autograph MS., CCC. E. 325, the first on f. 73ᵛ, the second on f. 114. A manuscript version of 'The Puritan' entitled 'The Towne's new teacher' is in the library of St. John's College, Cambridge (James, 542), and was tentatively ascribed to Cleveland by G. C. Moore Smith.

[3] See *The Poems of Richard Corbett*, ed. Bennett and Trevor-Roper, Oxford, 1955, especially pp. 130–31 and 165–6. For other attributions, none to Cleveland, see *BNYPL*, lxvii, May 1963, p. 311.

[4] See Wood, *Athenae Oxonienses*, iv, col. 131, and also MS. Rawl. Poet. 246 (f. 17).

[5] See Herford and Simpson, *Ben Jonson*, Oxford, 1952, xi. 429, 451.

[6] See *BNYPL*, lxvii, May 1963, pp. 316–17; also *The Poems of Sidney Godolphin*, ed. William Dighton, Oxford, 1931, pp. xxxviii and 68.

9. 'To a Lady that wrought a story of the Bible in needle-work' is by William Cartwright.[1]

10. 'Upon Sheriffe Sandbourn' is by Benjamin Stone.[2]

Thus thirty-four of the thirty-seven poems in CR1 that Williamson claimed were based on Cleveland's own papers can be assigned to other authors. The 'papers' could have been in Cleveland's hand and still have represented not his own poems, but his commonplace-book. Cleveland would naturally be interested in the work of John Hall, even though he left Cambridge before Hall came up; the poems by Oxford men could have been collected during Cleveland's stay there.

Thirteen of the twenty-five new poems in CR2 (1660) can be ascribed to other authors. 'News from Newcastle' and 'On the Inundation of the River Trent' are by Thomas Winnard. They are the first two poems in CR2, and are also associated in three manuscripts: Rawl. Poet. 246 (f. 31), Rawl. Poet. 65, and Rosenbach 232/14 (ff. 19–26).[3] Two more poems, 'For Sleep' and 'Against Sleep', are attributed to 'The Reverend M^r. Tho: Sharp of Leedes' in the B.M. Add. MS. 4276 (f. 114), an attribution corroborated by Calamy.[4] A further two, 'A sad Suit . . . to his Patron' and 'A Time-Sonnet', are by Thomas Jordan; a broadside version of the first appeared in 1663 with the ascription 'T.J.', and the second is in Jordan's *A Royal Arbor of Loyal Poesie*, 1664 (sig. Aa5^v) as 'Rebels Market. 1646'. The seven remaining poems are each by a different author: 'Against Ale' is ascribed to Thomas Bonham in two Bodleian MSS., RP147 (pp. 153–4) and Sancroft 53 (pp. 28–29); 'A Relation of a Quaker' is by Sir John Denham;[5] 'A Song of Sack' is in the manuscript of Charles Cotton's poems in the Borough Library at Derby, and printed in *Cotton's Poems on Several Occasions*, 1689; 'The Parliament' is ascribed

---

[1] See *The Plays and Poems of William Cartwright*, ed. G. Blakemore Evans, Madison, Wis., 1951, pp. 459, 691.

[2] See *Parnassus Biceps*, ed. G. Thorn-Drury, 1927, p. 170, and C. F. Main, 'Notes on Some Poems Attributed to William Strode', *PQ*, xxxiv, October 1955, p. 448.

[3] Rawl. Poet. 246 deals with events from 1620 to 1660, and was probably compiled by a Cambridge man; Rawl. Poet. 65 may be dated 1680–90, and is concerned with St. John's College, Oxford, of which Winnard was a member; Rosenbach 232/14 is described in *BNYPL*, lxvii, May 1963, p. 322 n.

[4] See *The Nonconformist's Memorial*, revised by Samuel Palmer, second edition, 1803, iii. 421.

[5] See *The Poetical Works of Sir John Denham*, ed. Banks, Yale, 1928, pp. 91–94.

to Sir Henry Moody in MS. Tanner 466 (f. 60); 'The Schismatick' is in MS. Rawl. Poet. 211, the holograph collection of Thomas Weaver's poems, and printed in his *Songs and Poems of Love and Drollery* (pp. 16–20), as 'The Rotundos'; 'An Answer to the Storm' is by Sir William Godolphin;[1] 'A zealous Discourse between the Parson of the Parish and Tabitha' is given in Ash 36 (f. 204) to 'Sr Clifford Clyfton upon Mr Justice Charleton's wife who dwelt at Nottingham'. A total of eighty-six poems can thus be ascribed to other authors.

The third group contains twenty-one poems which cannot be so ascribed but which are attributed to Cleveland only in unauthoritative editions. 'A New Letanie for our New Lent', a burlesque litany printed only in the 'Uncertain Authors' section of D6, had already appeared in an abbreviated form.[2] Totally unlike Cleveland's genuine poems, it is accompanied in the Bodleian copy of D6 (Vet. A3e. 7) by an interleaved Latin translation in manuscript of the complete poem, over the signature 'Henricus Stapleton'. Also in this group are four of the nine poems added to P11 and P12: 'On a Scratch on a Ladies Arme', 'On a Gentlewoman that Died in the Night, Snow falling the next Morning', 'Englands Jubile', and an untitled poem beginning 'Some Christian people all give ear | Unto the grief of us'. Nowhere else is any of these independently attributed to Cleveland.[3] Two poems, 'Praelegenda to . . . The Wife-Hater' and 'Vituperium Uxoris', added to P13, later appeared separately in miscellanies, but always anonymously.[4] They are ascribed to Cleveland only in P13 and its reprints, and are unlike his genuine poems.

Since only one of the thirty-seven poems in CR1 is genuine, and

---

[1] It is ascribed to him in MSS. Rawl. D. 258, Rawl. Poet. 173, Eng. poet. e. 4, Rawl. C. 556, and Locke. e. 17—all in the Bodleian Library.

[2] B.M. 669. f. 10 (120), dated by Thomason 'March 15th. 1646'; it is reprinted in *Political Ballads of the Seventeenth and Eighteenth Centuries*, annotated by W. Walker Wilkins, 1860, i. 23–27.

[3] Copies of the first three in a section of RP84 headed 'Cleulands Poems' are too close to the printed text to be an independent witness. The fourth, entitled 'The Fire on London Bridge', is in *Merry Drollery Compleat, 1691*, ed. J. W. Ebsworth, Boston, Lincs., 1875, pp. 87–90; it was first printed in *The Loves of Hero and Leander*, 1651, and according to Ebsworth in *Choice Drollery*, Boston, Lincs., 1876, pp. 376–7, refers to a fire on 13 February 1633.

[4] The 'Praelegenda' in *Pecuniae obediunt Omnia*, second edition, 1698. For 'Vituperium Uxoris' see Day and Murrie, *English Song-Books, 1651–1702*, 1940, Index of First Lines, s.v. 'He that intends to take a Wife'.

thirty-three can be assigned to other authors, we may safely dismiss the two remaining poems, 'On Christ-Church windows' and 'Upon one that preach't in a Cloak'.[1] For the same reason we may also reject the following twelve poems attributed to Cleveland only in CR2 and its reprints:

'On his going by Water, by the Parliament-House'; 'Upon coming into a Chamber called Parnassus'; 'The Old Gill'; 'The Antiplatonick' ('Fond Love, what dost thou mean'); 'The poor Cavalier, in memory of his Old Suit'; 'A sight of the Ruines of St. Pauls'; 'The second Part of the Scots Apostacy'; 'The Definition of a Protector'; 'Upon the new Invention of Flying with Chymical Magick'; 'The Coach-man of St. James'es'; 'On Black eyes'; 'On O. P. Sick'.[2]

Adding the twenty-one poems of this group to the eighty-six assigned to other authors, we may reject as spurious 107 of the 147 poems attributed to Cleveland in the various printed editions. Since we have already accepted twenty-five as genuine, this leaves fifteen uncertainties.

The poems requiring discussion include those in the 'Uncertain Authors' section in D5 and D6, those which, though like his style, are attributed to Cleveland only in the later editions, and those in which his authorship is contested by an equally strong claimant.

For the 'Epitaph on the Earl of Strafford' external evidence is inconclusive. It is in D1, but in the 'Uncertain Authors' section of D5 and D6, and not in CV. Saintsbury admits it, with reservations, while Berdan prints it among the 'Poems attributed to Cleveland' and finds it 'internally unlike his manner'. A popular poem, it is in fifteen manuscripts, but not in O. Only two manuscripts ascribe it to Cleveland, and though eight contain other poems by him none places this in a significant series of his work.[3] A version in H35 adds at the end lines 5–8 of the Elegy on Edward King printed in P11 (see p. 155), and there is evidence (see p. 80) that Cleveland sometimes reworked early lines into his later poems, though usually with

---

[1] Both are in *Parnassus Biceps*, 1656, and G. Thorn-Drury, in his edition of that miscellany, shows that they are about events in Oxford considerably earlier than Cleveland's known writings (see pp. 168 and 191).

[2] The events in this last poem took place after Cleveland's death.

[3] See *BNTPL*, May 1963, pp. 318–19; the version in the State Papers mentioned on p. 318 proves to be not a broadside but another unsigned manuscript in a collection of loose leaves relating to Strafford's trial.

greater subtlety. The Epitaph is unlike any of his genuine poems, but considering the extreme tact enjoined by the event upon a Fellow of St. John's not yet irretrievably committed to the King's cause, it is what one might expect: a trail of consciously clever antitheses, half-shielding and sophisticating the pathos of bloody 'riddles'. That Cleveland felt the full shock of the trial is evident from other allusions to Strafford scattered throughout his works,[1] especially the 'Answer to a Pamphlet written against the Lord Digby's Speech concerning the Death of the Earl of Strafford', in CV and O. His claim is certainly stronger than that of his only rival, the Revd. Thomas Forrester, episcopal clergyman at Melrose.[2] That ascription is late, putative, and uncorroborated, and until a better case appears, the Epitaph may be regarded as at least possibly Cleveland's.

The Latin Epitaph on Strafford, immediately following the English in D1, is not really a poem, but one of the 'Carmina Lapidaria' developed in the sixteenth century and exploited in the seventeenth.[3] Cleveland's claim to this 'Epitaphium Thomae Comitis Straffordii' rests on its appearance in D1, since it is excluded from CV and O. Three manuscripts—Tanner 227 (f. 14ᵛ), Add. 29975 (f. 123), and Egerton 2982 (f. 171)—carry no ascription, and EG 27 (f.39b), which contains signed or initialled copies of many poems by Cleveland, says firmly 'Anonymus'. In Tanner 88 (f. 8b), written in the hand of Archbishop Sancroft, the Latin is given to 'Dr. Gray of Eton', i.e. Nicholas Gray (1590–1660).[4] Only a few poems by Gray have survived, and he was not known as a poet. Why should this have been attributed to him, if he did not write it? And why should we expect the printers of D1 to be more scrupulous about the authorship of Latin companion pieces than Lake and Drake, who included Thomas Gawen's 'Rebellis Scotus' in CV? Gray's case is stronger than Cleveland's, and removes the 'Epitaphium' from the canon.

---

[1] Ibid., pp. 319–21.

[2] See Adam Milne, *A Description of the Parish of Melrose*, Edinburgh, 1743, p. 41. There is a brief account of Forrester in *DNB*.

[3] For the development of this genre from inscriptions on tombstones and triumphal monuments see Emmanuele Tesauro, *Cannocchiale Aristotelico*, Torino, 1654.

[4] See *Etoniana*, No. 119, 1966, and *Neophilologus*, L (1966), 346–52.

What may be another 'companion piece', 'A Song of Marke Anthony', first appears together with its 'Mock-Song' in D1A, and is in all later editions except CR1–4. However, RP147 (p. 219) attributes its version to 'S. Briggs' (identified as Sampson Briggs in the Bodleian first-line index) and places it with fifteen other poems by him in its last forty pages. Five other manuscript copies carry no ascription, and of these only H35 contains a number of Cleveland's poems. O has the 'Mock-Song' without its model, but the preceding leaf, which did contain writing, has been torn out. It is futile to speculate whether that leaf contained the 'Song', or, if so, whether its excision was intentional. Nor will inclusion in CV provide the usual corroboration, since 'Rebellis Scotus' implies that the editors were as careless about the authorship of association pieces as the compilers of Rochester's *Poems* (1680).[1] For explanatory purposes the poem must precede the 'Mock-Song', but Cleveland's authorship is far from certain.

'On the Archbishop of Canterbury', another of the poems in D1 relegated to the 'Uncertain Authors' section in D5 and D6, is in CV and O, and has never been claimed for anyone else. Lloyd prints it as Cleveland's, and as one of the two 'monuments' interred with Laud when the body was removed from London to St. John's College, Oxford in 1663.[2] It may seem 'almost a caricature of our author's more wayward and more fantastic manner',[3] but one of the characteristics of his style is the increased grotesqueness in satires inspired, like 'The Kings Disguise' and 'The Rebell Scot', by highly emotional public events. The elegy belongs with them in the canon.

'The Scots Apostasie' first appears in the 'Uncertain Authors' section, and regularly thereafter, though it is not in CV and O. It also circulated as a broadside, the Thomason copy inscribed in Thomason's hand 'March 10th 1646 [1647] Cleaulands'. An answer entitled 'The Scots Constancy. Or, An Answer to Cleveland's Scots Apostacy' has on the Thomason copy the manuscript note 'Aprill. 1st. 1647. written by Robin Bostock the Stationer'.[4] It begins 'Is

---

[1] See David M. Vieth, *Attribution in Restoration Poetry*, New Haven, 1963, chap. 8.
[2] *Memoires*, p. 256 (i.e. sig. Ll 4ᵛ).　　　　[3] Saintsbury, iii. 68.
[4] For Robert Bostock see H. R. Plomer, *A Dictionary of Booksellers and Printers . . . 1641–1677*, 1907, p. 28. For another verse diatribe by him against Cleveland and the Royalists see *BNYPL*, May 1963, p. 317.

Cleveland new in print? Is this the fume | Of his last cup of Sack?' and later makes reference to lines 19–20 of the 'Apostasie'. Clearly, Bostock believed Cleveland wrote this poem, as did Lloyd in 1668.[1] Their attributions make it probably Cleveland's.

'An Elegy upon Dr. Chaderton' and 'Maries Spikenard', which first appear in P2 (1651), are rejected by CV and not ascribed to Cleveland in any manuscript.[2] The 'Elegy' consists of a string of lightly-linked conceits, his basic formula; but the conceits are too simple, and there is too much plain writing like the following:

> Thine ears after an Hundred year,
> Might now plead Custom for to hear:
> Upon thy head that reverend snow,
> Did dwell some fifty years ago,
> And then thy cheeks did seem to have
> The sad resemblance of a grave.
>
> (lines 13–18)

'Maries Spikenard' reads like a weak imitation of Crashaw, a contemporary of Cleveland's for more than ten years at Cambridge. It is possible that on this solitary occasion Cleveland produced an imitation, but this poor pastiche is not the extravagance one would expect. Both poems may safely be rejected.

The first edition of 1653 (P5) adds only 'To the Hectors'. This is nowhere else ascribed to Cleveland, nor has it been claimed for any other author. Saintsbury does not think it Cleveland's, and Berdan, with masterly evasion, finds it 'like his manner, but not sufficiently so to be included in this edition'.[3] The opening, a string of vocative phrases, is analogous to that of 'Smectymnuus', 'The Mixt Assembly', or 'The Authour to his Hermophrodite', but the rest of the poem does not display Cleveland's gift for loading one ingenious conceit upon another. Passages of simple statement are common:

---

[1] *Memoires*, p. 618.

[2] The 'Elegy' is in Ash 36 (f. 263), and 'Maries Spikenard' in Add. 29921 (f. 46b).

[3] *Berdan*, p. 249. Since the subject of the poem, Mr. Henry Compton, was killed in a duel on 10 May 1652 (see C. H. Firth, *The House of Lords during the Civil War*, 1910, p. 233) the 1653 edition is the first in which it could have been included. For other references to the duel see *BNTPL*, May 1963, p. 324, and Lloyd's *Memoires*, pp. 363–8.

> Then y'have the gift of fighting, can discern
> Spirits, who's fit to act, and who to learn,
> Who shall be baffled next, who must be beat,
> Who killed—that you may drink, and swear, and eat.
>
> (lines 13–16)

This is so foreign to Cleveland's style that the poem cannot be kept in the canon.

Two elegies on King Charles added in P6 have already been rejected; the other two require discussion. 'An Elegie upon King Charles the First, murthered publikely by His Subjects' appeared in *Monumentum Regale*, 1649, and in *Jeremias Redivivus: or an Elegiacall Lamentation on the Death of our English Josias, Charles the First*, 1649. On the Thomason copy of the latter is the manuscript note 'said to by [*sic*] written by Walther Mountacute'.[1] This is probably Walter Montagu, the Roman convert and author of *The Shepheard's Paradise*,[2] though the opening lines do not look as if they were written by a Catholic:

> Were not my *Faith* boy'd up by sacred blood,
> It might be drown'd in this prodigious flood;
> Which reasons highest ground doth so exceed,
> It leaves my *soul* no Anch'rage but my *Creed*:

The statement in lines 20–21 that this crime has 'left but privation | In *Church* and *State*' would also come more readily from a Protestant. Internal evidence does not favour Montagu, but the flat didactic tone of the following lines does not suggest the author of the elegy on Laud:

> Let *Christians* then use otherwise this blood,
> Detest the Act, yet turn it to their good;
> Thinking how like a *King of death* He dies;
> We easily may the world and death despise:
>
> (lines 43–46)

'An Elegie on the best of Men and meekest of Martyrs, Charles the First' is even less like Cleveland. It is printed in *Monumentum Regale*,

---

[1] Laurence Hanson noted this ascription in 'Points in the Bibliographies of John Cleveland and Alexander Brome', *RES*, xviii, July 1942, pp. 321–2.

[2] See the article on Montagu in *DNB*, and S. R. Gardiner, *The History of England, 1603–1642*, 1894, iii. 139.

but ascribed to him only in three untrustworthy manuscripts: Ros. 239/18 (p. 12), a commonplace-book with many misattributions for fragments from miscellanies of the 1650's; RP173, an eighteenth-century collection which follows W in assigning poems by R. Fletcher and John Hall to Cleveland; and Cambridge University Library's Add. MS. 79, where its grouping, on ff. 24–26, with Cleveland's Petition to Cromwell, the 'Chronostichon', and the last four lines of 'Were not my *Faith*' suggests derivation from some printed collection. The low-powered transparency of statement in both poems discredits their claim to belong in the canon.

Three of the additions to P11 (1658) require brief discussion. Several lines in 'Parting with a Freind upon the Rode' reappear in 'Upon the Kings return from Scotland' which, we have seen, is genuine. Probably the 'Parting' is a genuine early poem used to provide material for the later welcome. The eight-line poem 'On Princess Elizabeth' bears no obvious signs of Cleveland's style. The decisive evidence is its inclusion in CV and O, and it may be regarded as genuine. The third poem, another elegy on Edward King, beginning 'Whiles Phebus shines within our Hemisphere', provides four lines for a variant of the Strafford epitaph in H35, and in lines 13–14 it echoes lines 7–8 of 'The Authour to his Hermophrodite'. In *Justa Edovardo King* it preceded the elegy ascribed to Cleveland. It is the only unsigned poem in the volume, and probably Cleveland contributed two poems over one signature.

'The General Eclipse' and 'Epitaphium Thomae Spell' appear first in CV. The former is not in O, and its first four stanzas make up the anonymous 'Antiparode' facing Wotton's 'You meaner beauties of the Night' in Ash 78 (f. 22). The first, second, and fourth stanzas, entitled 'Beauties Eclyps'd', are set to music in Henry Lawes's *Ayres and Dialogues* (1653, i. 35), and indexed as the lyrics of 'Mr. Francis Lenton'. Perhaps the poem is a hybrid, with Cleveland contributing only the last three verses.[1] On the meagre evidence it may still be regarded as at least possibly or partially his. The 'Epitaphium' is a 'carmen lapidarium' in memory of a Fellow of St. John's College, Cambridge, who served as President from 22 January

---

[1] See *BNYPL*, May 1963, p. 314.

1636 until his death on 13 December 1640.[1] Cleveland, therefore, was in the right place at the right time to be the author. The deciding factor in admitting this piece to the canon must again be its inclusion in CV and O.

Of the fifteen poems requiring discussion we may now accept four as genuine, five as probably or possibly genuine, and reject six. Of the 147 attributed to Cleveland in the various printed editions we preserve thirty-four and reject 113.

Outside the printed editions twenty-seven more attributions may be found. The evidence for and against these poems is set out fully in *BNYPL*, May–June 1963, and from the conclusions reached there we may dismiss the following eighteen poems:

J. C., 'A Declaration of the Frontispiece (Before you travel to the Holy Land)' in Thomas Fuller's *Historie of the Holy Warre*, Cambridge, 1639 and later editions;

eight poems or poetic fragments in *The Character of a Moderate Intelligencer* With some select Poems Written by the same Author J.C.;

a ballad beginning 'When as we liv'd in peace (God wot)' quoted by J. B. Williams [Joseph George Muddiman], *History of English Journalism*, 1908, p. 8, from *Mercurius Pragmaticus*, 14–21 Sept. 1647;

two ballads:—'The Poore Committee-Mans Accompt, Avouched by Britanicus [August 26th, 1647]' and 'The Committee-Mans Complaint and the Scots Honest Usage [August 26th, 1647]'[2]— in *Political Ballads Published in England During the Commonwealth*, ed. Thomas Wright, Percy Society's Early English Poetry, Ballads . . . iii, 1841, pp. 55–59;

two poems in *The Muses Mistress: or, a Storehouse of Rich Fancies, by J. C. Written at Succidanious hours during the Action at Newark*, ascribed to Cleveland in Cornelius Brown's *Annals of Newark-Upon-Trent*, 1879, p. 168;

'Newarke', a ballad from A27, ascribed to Cleveland by Bishop Percy;

---

[1] See Venn and Venn, *Alumni Cantabrigienses*, Cambridge, 1922–54, pt. i, iv. 130, and *Letters of Archbishop Williams, with Documents Relating to him*, ed. John E. B. Mayor, Cambridge, 1866, pp. 79–80.

[2] A ballad in A3 (f. 67) initialled 'M.I.', which the B.M. first-line index thinks may be for Jasper Mayne, has the same opening line, but is otherwise very different.

'Upon his Ma:^{ties} sickness and happy recovery' ('What meant that strange distemper wch of late'), found in Lambeth Library by R. J. Roberts (see *NQ*, November 1958, p. 486);

'Smectymnuus Bellua multorum capitum. By Cleveland', in H493 (f. 17b);

'A Gentlewoman walking in a frosty morning' ('In Nonage of a winters day'), in Ros. 239/18, p. 43.

The other nine poems may be included as possibly or probably Cleveland's. 'Mr Cleauelands reply from Belvoir to the 3 Newarke Poets' was discovered by Berdan in EG27, a manuscript whose ascriptions to Cleveland were made with considerable care.[1] The translation of Lovelace's 'Why shouldst thou say I am foresworne' appears only in RP147, where it is attributed to Cleveland. Since he would not be an obvious choice for anyone seeking an author for a piece of Latin verse, his claim may well be good, though based on a single witness. The poem we have entitled 'To his Mistress' appears only in Fol, where it is ascribed to 'J: Cleveland'. The manuscript, *c.* 1650, contains many seventeenth-century lyrics, but only this ascription.[2] The poem itself, though less polished than his published works, is what one would expect of Cleveland's early love lyrics. 'On the Pouder Plot' appears only in L22 (f. 134), next to the lines on Princess Elizabeth in a section containing twenty-one poems described in the Lansdowne Catalogue (1812) as 'by Mr Cleveland and others: some of them printed'. Six poems are by him, seven have been attributed to others elsewhere and never to Cleveland, and seven are totally unlike his style.[3] This poem resembles his style enough to be an early academic exercise by him, or one of his journalistic efforts just before Charles's execution. It contains many echoes of his indisputably genuine poems.

Five of the six hitherto unpublished poems in O are probably genuine. The exception is Henry Stephan's Latin version of Εἰς τὸ δεῖν πίνειν, carelessly copied from his edition of Anacreon (1554

---

[1] See *BNYPL*, May 1963, pp. 315–16.

[2] The manuscript is in two parts: f. 1–f. 45 contains numerous lyrics; on f. 46 begins 'The successions of the Dukes and Earles of this Kingdome from the Conquest vntill the 12th yeare of the Raigne of K: James the first'. The manuscript was purchased from Mr. F. Wheeler in March 1914, when he was resident in New York.

[3] For a description of this manuscript see p. liv, and *BNYPL*, June 1963, pp. 381–6.

or later). It precedes an English version, which is as succinct and colloquial as one would expect from Cleveland and is probably genuine.[1] Both poems are written on the first leaf of O, where the scribe also sets down playfully some couplets in English and Latin, which appear again in EG27, though without ascription.

Two other poems, 'News, news, News' and 'On an Alderman who married a very young wife', carry the heading 'Juvenilia not enterd', but since the 'News' is the fall of Newcastle in October 1644, this was probably a diplomatic way of explaining why obviously inferior work was to be suppressed in preparing a printed edition. The last two poems, 'No Hubbub surnamd Hue & cry' and 'Upon Lee & Owens Fencing, a Dr Roan & a Jeffray', are similarly examples of Cleveland's balladeering. Although they are not ascribed to Cleveland elsewhere there is no other claimant for their authorship, and they may be admitted on the strength of their presence in O and their echoes of his genuine work.

III. THE EDITIONS

The twenty-five editions of Cleveland's Poems printed between 1647 and 1700 testify to his popularity. They also present the bibliographer with what Saintsbury ruefully described as 'a terrible tangle'.[2] The transmission is complicated, but a general picture shows three stages. Firstly, there are the six editions and two re-issues which appeared in 1647 (D1–D6), which are so closely related and interwoven that no complete time sequence can be established. Secondly, there is the long series of reprints appearing from 1651 to 1669 (P1–P17), interrupted only by the two editions of 1658 (P11–P12) which rely to some extent on an authority outside the printed editions. Finally, there is *Clievelandi Vindiciae*, 1677, and its reprints, where the previous printed editions are for the most part rejected, and the text is set up, as far as possible, from manuscript sources.

[1] Compare the versions ascribed to Sir John Cotton in B.M. Add. 10307 (f. 5), Abraham Cowley (*Poems*, 1656), and Charles Cotton (*Poems on Several Occasions*, 1689).

[2] The full bibliographical evidence for the relationship of the editions is set out by Brian Morris, 'The Editions of Cleveland's Poems, 1647–1687', *The Library*, vol. xix. For descriptions of the individual editions and issues see Brian Morris, *A Bibliography of the Poems of John Cleveland*, Bibliographical Society, 1966.

The editions and reissues of 1647 are not easy to distinguish.[1] Not one of them gives either the place of publication or the name of printer or publisher, and in none of them does Cleveland's name appear on the title-page. The first three editions (D1–D3) have a page-for-page correspondence, and almost certainly precede D4–D6, since each of the latter three states on its title-page that it is 'Optima & novissima Editio'. It seems probable, for two reasons, that D1 is the earliest edition. Firstly, it is the best produced. It uses good type, it is attractively set out and printed, and there are comparatively few literal errors. D2, and to a lesser extent D3, look like rushed jobs. They use old type, punctuate carelessly, and introduce a considerable number of literal errors. Secondly, the British Museum copy of D1, in the Thomason collection, has the manuscript date on the title-page 'Feb: 13th, 1646' (i.e. 1646/7), so that it must have been in existence by 13 February of the year in which all six editions were published. It is clear from the evidence of shared errors in pagination that D2 was printed from a copy of D1, and the textual evidence shows that D3 also derives from D1, so that the first two reprints are independent of one another, and do not form, as one might expect, an ancestral series.

The reissues, D1A and D2A, need separate consideration. As reference to Table 1 (p. xliv) will show, both contain considerable portions of previous editions. D1A uses the same setting of type as D1 for gatherings D to G, and has its own setting for gatherings A and C (its setting of A appears again in D4 and D5, and its setting of C in D4). D1A compresses the whole of 'The Character of a London-Diurnall' into gathering A, and uses the space thus saved (B1 and part of B2ʳ) to print the poem called 'A Song of Marke Anthony' for the first time. The remainder of the gathering (B2–B4ᵛ) is printed from the same setting of type as D2.

D2A is more complicated. The standing type of D2 was used to print the inner forme of gathering A (plus the single page A4ᵛ), both formes of gathering D, the outer formes of gatherings E and F, and the single page G2. The remaining formes and pages are new

[1] Each of them prints the poems as a group after the prose piece 'The Character of a London-Diurnall', which had appeared alone in 1644. See F. Madan, *Oxford Books*, 1912, ii. 373, and Wing, C4659–61.

settings of type. D2A adds a final gathering (H) containing the 'Marke Anthony' poem and two new poems on 'Britanicus'. The setting of 'Marke Anthony' is the one which appeared as B1–B2 in D1A; the signatures only are changed. Both reissues were clearly called for before the type set for the first two editions had been distributed, which suggests that the first appearance of Cleveland's poems in print was a greater commercial success than had been anticipated.

The other three editions of 1647 (D4–D6) form an ancestral series. D4, which uses D1A's setting of type for gatherings A to C and has its own setting for D to G, corresponds page for page with D1–D3, and the textual evidence shows that it was set up from a copy of D1. D5, on the other hand, is not a page-for-page reprint. It appears to be a definite and careful revision in which attention has been paid to neatness of presentation. The Harvard copy has the manuscript note on the verso of the title-page 'I bought this booke at Rotharam the 10:th of May 1647 it cost one shilling', which gives an idea of the speed of printing; five editions were published within twelve weeks. D6, a cramped, cheaply produced book, is the worst printed of all the 1647 editions. It contains the accumulated errors of D1–D5 and adds many of its own.

The table on p. xliv shows the make-up of each edition and reissue. Each letter represents a new setting of type, and the diagram shows how the reissues, in particular, make use of type already set. In describing D5 and D6 the symbols π and δ have been used to stress that these editions are not page-for-page reprints as the others are.

The next ten editions (P1–P10) form two ancestral series, P1–P4 and P5–P8, linked by P5's dependence upon P3. The last two editions, P9 and P10, do not depend upon their immediate predecessors.

The first four (P1–P4) appeared in 1651, and represent a change in the presentation of Cleveland's poems.[1] Each title-page reads 'Poems, By J.C., With Additions', the phrase 'With Additions' covering both the ten poems which appear for the first time in 1651, and the 'Letters' and 'Character of a Country-Committee-man' which, together with the 'London-Diurnall', are placed at the end

---

[1] There is one reissue (P1A) which cannot be accurately placed in the time sequence. It uses the same setting of type as P1, and adds two new poems in a gathering of two leaves signed ★.

of the poems. The reorganization suggests that by 1651 Cleveland's readers were more interested in his poems than in his Royalist pamphlets. The printer of P1 is not known, but he appears to have been aware that additions were made to the collection as the editions of 1647 were published, since he uses both D1 and D5 to set up his text, and so reprints twenty-two of the twenty-three poems which appeared in D1–D6.

TABLE I

	Sig. A	Sig. B	Sig. C	Sig. D	Sig. E	Sig. F	Sig. G	Sig. H
D1	a	a	a	a	a	a	a	
D1A	x	$B_1-B_2 = x$ $B_2-B_4^v = y$	x	a	a	a	a	
D2	y	y	y	y	y	y	y	
D2A	(i) = y (o) = c$[-A_4^v = y]$	y $[-B_1^v = c]$	c	y	(i) = c (o) = y	(i) = c (o) = y	c	$H_1-H_2 = x$ $H_2-H_3^v = c$
D3	m	m	m	m	m	m	m	
D4	x	$B_1-B_2 = x$ $B_2-B_4^v = y$	x	b	b	b	b	
D5	x	π	π	π	π	π	π	π
D6	δ	δ	δ	δ	δ	δ	δ	

The second ancestral series (P5–P8) consists of the editions published in 1653 and 1654. In appearance they are very like the 1651 editions, and the only new claim made on their title-pages is that their 'Additions' were 'never before printed'. P5 is the earliest edition giving any information about its publisher. Both P5 and P6 print William Shears's title-page ornament, a Bible with clasps, and in P5 the ornament contains the initials 'W. S.' Shears had shops in various parts of London between 1625 and 1662, and published many of the poets of the period, including Brome, Phineas Fletcher, Thomas May, and Francis Quarles.

The last two editions of this group, P9 and P10, were not printed from their immediate predecessors. The textual evidence demonstrates conclusively that P9 was printed from a copy of P7; this means simply that the 1656 edition (P9) was set up from the earlier of the two 1654 editions rather than the later. Slightly more unusual is the fact that the 1657 edition (P10) was printed not from the edition which appeared in 1656, but from the later of the 1654 editions (P8). The ten editions published between 1651 and 1657 are thus wholly derivative. They have no textual authority except for those poems which appear in one or other of them for the first time, and a study of the transmission reveals a steady deterioration in the text.

The two editions of 1658 are markedly different from the earlier ones. They are duodecimos, they have redesigned title-pages, they interpolate prose pieces into the sequence of the poems, and they add a number of poems to the collection, some genuine, some spurious. Both are very carelessly printed, and since 1658 was the year of Cleveland's death, it may be that they were rushed through the press to catch a particular market. It is quite clear that P12 was printed from P11. All but five of the variants in P11 are reproduced in P12,[1] which adds a further forty-four of its own, and in many cases both editions agree in an obvious error which has never appeared before. The copy for P11 cannot be so easily established. It is a conflated text, and does not descend from any one of the previous editions. Many of the readings appearing for the first time in P11 are too distinctive to be printing-house corrections; often they agree with manuscript versions of the poems in the commonplace-books of the period. Yet the order in which the poems are printed is very like the order in P3–P10, though not identical with any one of them, and this is not likely to be the result of chance. An examination of the variants in P11 shows that different editions were used to set up different sheets. Three previous editions were used—P3, P6, and P9, and the resulting text seems then to have been corrected against a manuscript or manuscripts. Apart from the poems which it prints for the first time P11 has slight textual authority, and even where its readings agree with other surviving manuscripts, its evidence can be no more than supplementary. It is, in such cases, only the witness to an unknown manuscript.

The five editions which follow (P13–P17) continue the series interrupted by the editions of 1658. P13, published in 1659, is the first edition to bear the name of its publisher in full on the title-page. The imprint reads 'Printed for *W. Shears* at the Bible in *Covent-Garden*, and in the *New-Exchange* at the Black Beare. 1659'. It was set up

---

[1] All five exceptions are cases of error in P11 which P12 has corrected.

from a copy of P9, and like all the other editions it corrects some of the errors of its copy-text while retaining others and introducing its own. It adds, in a section headed 'Additions', a large number of poems not previously published as Cleveland's. The vast majority are by the virtually unknown poet R. Fletcher, the author of *Ex Otio Negotium. Or, Martial his Epigrams* which Shears had published in 1656. With one exception (P15) each of the five editions was printed from its immediate predecessor. P15, which was set up from a copy of P13, was the last edition to be published by Shears, and P14, P16, and P17 were the work of John Williams, at the sign of the Crown, or the Crown and Globe, in St. Paul's Churchyard.

From P1 (1651) to P17 (1669) seventeen separate editions in eighteen years show that Cleveland was still read even after the Restoration had removed the principal object of his satires. Apart from P11, which relies to some extent on manuscripts, each of the editions in this series can be shown to depend on one or another of its printed predecessors.

One other series of publications requires mention, before we come to the first 'edited' edition, *Clievelandi Vindiciae*. In 1659 there appeared the first edition of *Cleaveland Revived* (see above, p. xxiii, for detailed discussion), which claimed to present hitherto unpublished material by Cleveland. The poet had died in the previous year, his work was still popular, and it is perhaps not surprising to find that of the thirty-seven poems in CR1 only two are genuine. The first reprint of *Cleaveland Revived* (CR2, 1660) included twenty-five new poems, added not by Williamson, but by the 'Stationer', whose brief Preface cannot give any of them even the authority of Williamson; none of them is accepted as genuine. The last two editions of *Cleaveland Revived* are reprints of CR2, which add nothing to the collection.

Two of Cleveland's Cambridge pupils, John Lake and Samuel Drake, brought out their *Clievelandi Vindiciae* in 1677 to free their old tutor's name from the indignities they felt had been heaped upon it by the *Cleaveland Revived* series. Their Preface is addressed to the Master and Fellows of St. John's College, Cambridge (see above, p. xxiv). The edition may well have been a large one, for there are three different title-pages, though the rest of the book is printed from one setting of type and there is no evidence of press-correction. The title-page, in each case, makes three claims. It states that the edition is purged from 'Innumerable Errours and Corruptions in the True Copies'. If 'True Copies' means the earlier printed editions then the claim is true, since the errors which accumulated from D2 to P17 are not found in CV. Secondly, each title-page claims that the edition is one 'To which are added many Additions never Printed before'. This is an exaggeration, for only two small poems and a few unimportant prose pieces appear here for the first time. The third claim, that the edition is 'Published according to the Author's own Copies', is the most interesting, since it implies that the text was set up from the holograph. It seems possible, in view of the relationship between the editors and the poet. Unfortunately, the textual evidence does not support the claim. The variants reveal that the text of CV is not one and indivisible, and that its sources are of more than one kind. Most of the poems have been set up from manuscript, but in several cases it is clear that the manuscript must lie at several removes from the holograph. On the other hand, three poems at least were set up from one of the printed editions in the P1–P17 series. In those poems where CV relies on a manuscript source its readings are sometimes inferior to those of the first printed edition (D1), but sometimes they are manifestly better, and in one poem CV preserves several lines not found in D1. Yet everywhere, between CV and the holograph stand the 'editors' themselves. There is abundant evidence of editorial intervention, especially in the elucidation of Cleveland's often gnarled syntax; brackets are introduced, or existing brackets are altered, and complicated grammatical structures are frequently repunctuated, sometimes creating slight shifts in the sense. The 'editors' obviously considered it their duty to 'improve' Cleveland where they thought he needed it, and this must throw suspicion on some of CV's peculiar readings. The title-page claim that the edition was published 'according to the Author's own Copies' cannot be accepted. It is perhaps significant that CV is not the first edition to make it. The second edition of CR (1660) contains on its title-page the statement 'Now at last publisht from his Original Copies, by some of his intrusted Friends'. The claim is absurd, but it may well have been in the minds of Lake and Drake, especially in view of their savage attack on CR. The most likely hypothesis is that CV was printed from a manuscript containing for the most part good texts of a large number of poems, though these texts lay at various removes from the holograph, and that the manuscript was supplemented by the use of printed editions for those poems known to be genuine which it did not contain.[1]

CV was reprinted ten years later, in 1687, as part of *The Works of Mr. John Cleveland . . . Collected into One Volume With the Life Of the Author*. This edition gathers together almost everything previously printed as his. It is in three parts, distinguished by separate title-pages. The first section reprints CV, correcting a few misprints and creating a few more. The second section contains virtually all the poems which had appeared in the CR series, interspersing among them the 'Additions' which had first appeared in P13. It also gathers in some poems from the earlier printed editions which had been rejected by CV. The compilation is inclusive but careless, since one poem, 'To P. Rupert', appears in both the second section and the first. The third section contains only the prose piece 'The Rustick Rampant'.

The 1687 *Works* was reissued in 1699, with a fresh title-page emphasizing the presence of 'The Rustick Rampant' at the expense of both poems and prose. Finally, in 1742, the sheets of the 1687 edition (now fifty-five years old) were issued again under the imprint of three publishers, Brown, Midwinter, and Clarke, whose title-page describes the author as 'The Late Ingenious and Learned Mr. *John Cleveland*'. It is hard to believe that, in the age of Dr. Johnson, Cleveland would have found either a large or a sympathetic public.[2] He was essentially a poet of his age, and that age was long past.

As no holograph of any poem by Cleveland has survived, and as none of the existing manuscript copies can be shown to pre-date the earliest printed text, the importance of the editions in establishing the text of Cleveland's poems is paramount. From the bibliographical

---

[1] For discussion of the relationship between CV and the Osborn manuscript see pp. l–li.

[2] Only two copies of this edition are known: one in the London Library, the other in the possession of Professor Arthur Johnston, University College of Wales, Aberystwyth.

and textual analyses it is clear that only three editions have any textual authority: D1, the first edition, P11, because of the readings it introduces from a source outside the printed transmission, and CV, because of its manuscript sources. For the majority of poems

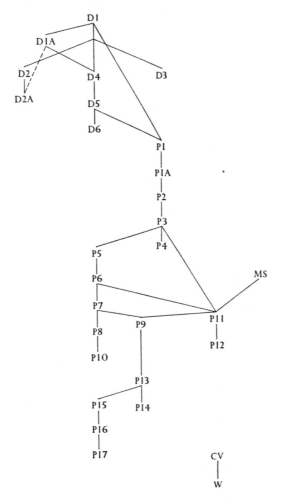

D1 preserves a text that is much better than that of any other witness, and it is probably as close as we can get to the words Cleveland wrote.

IV. THE MANUSCRIPTS

Nearly all the manuscripts containing poems by Cleveland are commonplace-books of no authority. No holograph is known to exist, and only one manuscript (see below) represents a deliberate collection of Cleveland's work.

The commonplace-books are the surviving witnesses to a tradition in which Cleveland's poems circulated in manuscript about a circle of unknown radius. Most of them contain only two or three of Cleveland's poems, but H18 has fifteen, EG27 twelve, and H35 nine; in each manuscript the poems are scattered in small groups. H35 usually preserves a fairly good text, while H18 varies considerably and the poems in EG27 are full of corrupt readings: its text of the 'Epitaph on the Earl of Strafford', for example, is almost certainly a memorial reconstruction, and a bad one. No relationship can be proved between any one of the commonplace-books and another,[1] and the *stemmata* which can be constructed for poems occurring in two or more manuscripts illustrate the random way in which they must have been compiled. The value of the commonplace-books for an editor lies in the check they provide upon the text of D1 and the other editions in which a poem appears for the first time. Their agreement with CV will frequently reveal an error in the copy-text which might otherwise have gone unsuspected (see the Commentary on 'A Faire Nimph', p. 101).

The most important manuscript is undoubtedly O, in the possession of Dr. James Osborn of Yale University. It contains a large number of Cleveland's letters and orations, together with twenty-two of his certainly genuine poems, and some others which are not attributed to him elsewhere. The manuscript is clearly related in some way to CV; both contain prose as well as verse, all twenty-two genuine poems in O appear in CV, though in a different order, and in the texts of most poems they share many readings against all other witnesses. The textual evidence shows that O was not copied from CV, and it seems unlikely that O is the manuscript which lies

---

[1] The only possible link is between H18 and Firth, but since Firth contains only two of Cleveland's poems it provides no decisive evidence.

immediately behind CV. CV relies on the printed editions for its text of the following poems:

'A Song of Marke Anthony', 'The Authours Mock-Song to Marke Anthony', 'Square-Cap', 'Upon the death of Mr. King', 'Upon Sir Thomas Martin', 'The Hue and Cry After Sir John Presbyter', 'How the Commencement grows new'.

O omits four of these poems, but contains perfectly good texts of 'The Authours Mock-Song to Marke Anthony', 'Upon the death of Mr. King', and 'How the Commencement grows new', which the editors of CV would hardly have ignored. In some poems the texts of CV and O are closely connected, as in 'To Mrs. K.T.',[1] 'The Kings Disguise', and 'To P. Rupert'; in others, like 'Smectymnuus' and 'The Rebell Scot', they are widely separated on the *stemma*, and in 'Upon a Miser' O appears to have been corrected by CV or a manuscript very like it. In individual poems the relationship can be stated fairly decisively, but no clear picture emerges of the general relationship between the manuscript and the printed book. The strongest clue is provided by the agreement between CV and O in the matter of the parentheses in lines 39–41 of 'Upon an Hermophrodite' (see *apparatus criticus*). This looks very like editorial intervention to clarify a difficult piece of syntax, and suggests that CV and O derive from a common original, perhaps even the miscellaneous papers which Lake and Drake assembled as the basis for copy for the printer of CV. It might well be that such papers would be brought together from various sources, including both holograph and printed texts, and this would account for both the agreements and the discrepancies between CV and O.

The British Museum manuscripts are described in the catalogues of the various collections in the Museum, and the Bodleian manuscripts in its *Summary Catalogue of Western Manuscripts*. The following list gives the approximate dates within which each was written, and additional notes on those asterisked:

[1] O is the only text which preserves her name, Katharine Thorold, which suggests that its compiler may have been one of Cleveland's circle. CV calls her simply 'Mrs. K. T.', which would be surprising if there were a direct descent from O to CV.

A2	1650–80	E20	*post* 1641	O	1640?–80?
A3*	*c.* 1650	EG24	1625–45	R	1600–60
A24	1640–60	EG27*	1640–50	RD10*	*c.* 1641
A27*	*c.* 1650	EP24	1630–60	RP26	1615–70
A30	1620–60	EP25*	1635–45	RP71	1640–50
A37*	1620–56	EP50*	1625–50	RP84	1650–70
Ash36	1640–90	Firth*	*c.* 1640	RP116*	1612–1725
Ash38*	1620–60	Fol*	*c.* 1650	RP117*	1630–90
Ash47	1640–50	H17*	1640–50	RP142	1630–50
Ash78	1620–60	H18*	1645–60	RP147*	1630–60
B50	1700–50	H35*	1640–50	RP173	*c.* 1705
C42	1636–42	H493*	*c.* 1642	S14	1640–60
CT5	1630–60	HE70*	1624–41	SP16	*post* 1641
Don	1632–60	L22*	1620–1670	T306	1620–1750
Douce	1640–85	Loan	1630–50	T465*	1640–50

Additional Notes

A3   This volume contains many seventeenth-century extracts from Herrick, Lovelace, Crashaw, Clement Paman, etc., and is in the same hand as MSS. Rawl. poet. 62 and 147. Several items are particularly concerned with events in Cambridge. See *The Poems of Richard Crashaw*, ed. Martin, Oxford, second edition, 1957, p. lxxx.

A27   This manuscript is printed as *Bishop Percy's Folio MS.*, ed. Hales and Furnivall, 1867.

A37   The commonplace-book of Sir John Gibson (1606–65) of Welburn, near Kirkby Moorside, Yorkshire, a Royalist prisoner in Durham Castle. The book is dedicated in a letter (f. 5b) dated March 1656 to his son, John Gibson. It contains Cleveland's Epitaph on Strafford.

Ash38 The commonplace-book of Nicholas Burghe, who was one of the poor Knights of Windsor in 1661. The first 165 pages were probably written before 1638 (see pp. 165–6), and the rest, including the Cleveland item, between 1640 and 1660. See *The Poems of Thomas Carew*, ed. Dunlap, Oxford, 1949, pp. lxx ff., and *The Poems of Richard Corbett*, ed. Bennett and Trevor-Roper, Oxford, 1955, p. lxiii.

EG27　A Poetical Miscellany, with a note of ownership (f. 179) by Sir Thomas Meres (of Kirton, Lincolnshire, knighted in 1660). It was written probably in the 1640's, and contains twelve of Cleveland's poems. None of these derives from the printed editions, and most are late and heavily corrupt copies from other manuscripts.

EP25　A notebook of University exercises at Cambridge, and copies of poems. Written probably by 'Edwardus Nately socius Regnalis' (f. 1), who was Fellow of Queens' College, 1635–44. It contains Cleveland's 'A Faire Nimph', 'A Song of Marke Anthony', and 'The Authours Mock-Song to Marke Anthony'.

EP50　A collection of nearly 250 poems copied by four hands. The book was owned during the seventeenth century by Peeter Daniell, whose initials are on the binding, and later by Bishop Percy. The contents are very fully described in the Bodleian catalogue.

Firth　See G. C. Moore Smith, British Academy Warton Lecture, 1927. On p. 1 of the manuscript is a poem dedicating the collection to Lady Harflete (d. 1664), wife of Sir Christopher Harflete of Canterbury.

Fol　The first part of this manuscript contains copies of numerous seventeenth-century lyrics, the second is a list of the Dukes and Earls of England from the Conquest until 1615. The poems were transcribed probably c. 1650, and 'To His Mistress' is ascribed to Cleveland on f. 40. We have not been able to consult this manuscript, and have relied on microfilm.

H17　See *The Poems of Richard Crashaw*, ed. Martin, Oxford, second edition, 1957, pp. lxxvi ff., *The Poems of Thomas Carew*, ed. Dunlap, Oxford, 1949, p. lxxiv, and *The Poems of Sidney Godolphin*, ed. Dighton, Oxford, 1931, pp. xxxiii ff. Martin suggests that the manuscript was transcribed 'somewhere between 1630 and 1645', and Dunlap says of the Carew poems in it 'the total impression is that of versions preliminary to those printed in 1640'. It contains Cleveland's 'The Authour to his Hermophrodite' and 'A young Man to an old Woman Courting him', the first of which cannot have been written before 1640 and was printed in D1 (1647).

H18   See *Crashaw*, ed. cit., pp. lxxvi ff., A. K. McIlwraith, 'The Virgins Character', *RES*, iv, 1928, pp. 64 ff., and R.G. Howarth, 'Some Unpublished Poems of James Shirley', *RES*, ix, 1933, pp. 24 ff. A commonplace-book belonging to Peter Calfe, it is probably slightly later in date than H17, and part of it was certainly written after 1641 (see Howarth). It contains fifteen of Cleveland's poems, including (f. 71) 'The Rebell Scot', which Cleveland wrote in the winter of 1643–4. On f. 40, after Cleveland's 'How the Commencement grows new', there is a poem called 'Saltmarsh of Magdalen against Cleveland's new commencement', followed by 'Answered by Wilde of St. Johns', which suggests that the scribe, or his source, was fairly closely connected with affairs in Cambridge.

H35   The commonplace-book of Arthur Capell (1631–83); fully described by Geoffrey Tillotson, 'The Commonplace Book of Arthur Capell', *MLR*, xxvii, 1932, pp. 381 ff. See also *The Poems of Thomas Carew*, ed. Dunlap, Oxford, 1949, p. lxxiv, and *The Poems of William Habington*, ed. Allott, Liverpool University Press, 1948, pp. lx and 164. It was written probably between 1640 and 1650, and contains nine of Cleveland's poems, at varying removes from the holograph.

H493   A miscellaneous collection of compositions in prose and verse, State Papers, and Parliamentary Reports, the State Papers referring chiefly to the years 1640 and 1641. It contains Cleveland's 'Smectymnuus' and 'Epitaph on the Earl of Strafford'.

HE70   A commonplace-book evidently compiled for or by Sir Henry Cholmley, brother of Sir Hugh, in various hands, 1624–1641.

L22   A volume of miscellaneous historical items. On f. 123 there is an 'Argument in the case of . . . the Portuguese Ambassador's brother' which is dated 1654, and ff. 133–8 contain, in a different hand, a number of poems including four by Cleveland.

RD10   Notes of debates and proceedings in the House of Commons from 22 May to 8 August 1641, in the hand of Sir John Holland. Cleveland's 'Epitaph on the Earl of Strafford' is at the end of the volume, on f. 190.

RP116   This volume is made up of four manuscripts (A–D). A was written in or soon after 1612, and C and D belong to the first quarter of the eighteenth century. B, which contains two of Cleveland's poems, is the commonplace-book of William Elyott (f. 16 'William Elyott his booke 1640'), and it was written between 1640 and 1655. 'The Antiplatonick' (f. 62) and 'Fuscara' (f. 63) are followed on f. 64 by a poem on the anagram 'Oliver: O I rule' which is dated 'Feb. 25th 1654/55.'

RP117   A commonplace-book owned and partly written by Christopher Wase (1625?–90). On f. 35 there is a poem called 'On Mayday 1644', and Cleveland's 'A Dialogue between two Zealots' is on f. 155.

RP147   Poems collected by a Cambridge man, and largely concerned with events in Cambridge, 1630–58. It includes 'How the Commencement grows new' (p. 48), 'The Antiplatonick' (p. 94), and 'A Song of Marke Anthony' (p. 219), the first two with 'Impressa' written in the margin. It also has the only copy of Cleveland's translation of Lovelace's 'Song'. Clement Paman's name appears on the index leaf, and there are many poems by him.

T465   A very large collection of Crashaw's poems. The manuscript is very fully discussed in Martin's edition (see above) on pp. lviii–lxxiii. It contains three of Cleveland's poems.

V. THE POETRY OF CLEVELAND

In his own age Cleveland was distinguished as a writer of 'strong lines'. The two poems in H18 which respectively attack and defend his 'How the Commencement grows new' mention this aspect of his art. John Saltmarsh writes:

> Can thy strong Lines, those mighty Cartrope things
> be twined, and twisted into fiddle strings?

and Robert Wilde replies:

> pray that the Satyrist be in that minde
> that thou art below his laughing at, tis kinde;
> his strong lines haue not yet so thinne a twist
> but thou maist finde them whipcord if he list:

Fuller, in his Life of Cleveland,[1] makes the same point when he says:

> His *Epithetes* were pregnant with *Metaphors*, carrying in them a *difficult plainness, difficult* at the *hearing, plain* at the *considering* thereof. His lofty Fancy may seem to stride from the top of one Mountain to the top of another, so making to it self a constant *Level* and *Champian* of *continued Elevations*.

and in one of the commendatory poems to Cartwright's *Comedies, Tragi-Comedies, with Other Poems*, 1651, John Leigh implores the publisher, Moseley, to

> Give us all Cleveland, all his gallant lines,
> Whose Phansie still in strong Expressions shines.

It is this very quality which Dryden censures in what was the first, and almost the final, critical judgement of Cleveland. In the course of *An Essay of Dramatic Poesy* he asserts that 'wit is best conveyed to us in the most easy language', and he castigates Cleveland in these words:

> . . . we cannot read a verse of Cleveland's without making a face at it, as if every word were a pill to swallow: he gives us many times a hard nut to break our teeth, without a kernel for our pains. So that there is this difference betwixt his *Satires* and doctor Donne's; that the one gives us deep thoughts in common language, though rough cadence; the other gives us common thoughts in abstruse words:[2]

The decisive quality of Dryden's dismissal, reinforced by Johnson's verdict in the 'Life of Cowley',[3] condemned Cleveland to an oblivion from which he is only now beginning to emerge. And yet it is a partial judgement, the stricture of a secure age upon the toys it had outgrown. Cleveland is censured for lacking a kind of poetic 'seriousness' to which he makes no claim, and his 'strength' is located too simply in the arrogance of his attitude to word and image. A modern judgement must be more complex, and must seek the answers to a different set of questions, by opening the proper historical perspective.

---

[1] The full context is quoted on p. xix.

[2] *Essays of John Dryden*, ed. W. P. Ker, Oxford, 1926, i. 52.

[3] Johnson quotes thirteen lines from 'To Julia' and says: 'Who would imagine it possible that in a very few lines so many remote ideas could be brought together?' See Johnson's *Lives of the English Poets*, ed. G. B. Hill, Oxford, 1905, i. 27.

The poems were written during and immediately before the Civil War, and had it not been for political events Cleveland would probably have remained a mere Cambridge wit, the Fellow most likely to deliver the Latin welcome to visiting dignitaries at St. John's; even there, Aubrey says, he was 'more taken notice of for his being an eminent disputant, than a good poet' (see p. xxi). Though a fellow graduate at Christ's, he could not have been one of the 'more timely-happy spirits' who gave Milton pause at the beginning of his twenty-third year. The early poems that can be dated with any assurance, 'On Princess Elizabeth . . .' and the elegies on Edward King, were both composed after Milton's sonnet, and though a few academic ballads may have predated it they would hardly have excited Milton's envy. Later compilers tried to make Cleveland the immediate heir to Randolph by attributing to him two of the best elegies in *Ionsonvs Virbivs*, but one of these was really by Sidney Godolphin and the other by James Cleyton (see p. xxx). There is no evidence that Cleveland's other witty pieces, even if written in the thirties, ever won him entry into the tribe of Ben. The first edition of Cleveland's poetry came two years after Milton's *Poems*, 1645, and its success was due to its political satire.

When Cleveland writes, on a conventional, 'literary' subject,

> For shame you pretty Female Elves,
> Cease for to Candy up your selves;
> No more, you Sectaries of the Game,
> No more of your calcining flame.
> Women Commence by *Cupids* Dart,
> As a Kings Hunting dubs a Hart.
> Loves Votaries inthrall each others soul,
> Till both of them live but upon Paroll.
>   ('The Antiplatonick', 17–24)

he is standing in the long shadow of Donne, and writing late 'Metaphysical' poetry for the sheer fun of the game. This has its attractions, but it is very different in tone and purpose from his political verse, which the following lines may illustrate:

> Come keen *Iambicks*, with your Badgers feet,
> And Badger-like, bite till your teeth do meet.

Help ye tart Satyrists, to imp my rage,
With all the Scorpions that should whip this age.
Scots are like Witches; do but whet your pen,
Scratch til the blood come; they'l not hurt you then.
Now as the Martyrs were inforc'd to take
The shapes of beasts, like hypocrites, at stake,
I'le bait my *Scot* so; yet not cheat your eyes,
A *Scot* within a beast is no disguise.
                        ('The Rebell Scot', 27–36)

Here the savagery is controlled by contempt, and the whip of
burlesque keeps the top spinning until in the final couplet it is used
to inflict pain. When Cleveland writes like this his mentors are few,
and his poetry is prophetic rather than decadent.

The Civil War made Cleveland a satirist, and its progress deter-
mined the course his satire took. At the start Cleveland's scorn was
playful, and had not later military defeats pushed him toward the
iambic wrath of an Archilochus stripped of all other weapons except
personal invective, he might have evolved a very different satiric
persona from the scourger or barber-surgeon of Elizabethan and
Jacobean satire. In 'A Dialogue between two Zealots, upon the &c.
in the Oath' he let Sir Roger and his 'brother of the cloth' do the
cursing, and in 'Smectymnuus, or the Club-Divines' he remained
a Momus mocking the ineffective wrath of the Presbyterians' 'vain
satyrists',

                    the zealous Cluster,
        Which like a Porcupine presents a Muster,
        And shoots his quills at Bishops and their Sees.
                                    (11–13)

Assuming a pose of assured intellectual superiority, he refused at
first to stoop to naming individual enemies:

        I could by Letters now untwist the rable;
        Whip *Smec* from Constable to Constable.
        But there I leave you to another's dressing.
                                    (93–95)

Despite Berdan's statement,[1] personal abuse or English as opposed
to Latin satire did not originate with Cleveland; among others,

---

[1] Berdan, p. 61.

Skelton and the anonymous authors of the satires against Bucking-ham[1] had been before him, and compared with them he seemed re-luctant to resort to it. When he first did so in 'To P. Rupert', he showed how clearly he understood the advantages of amused con-tempt by apologizing elaborately to Rupert (ll. 87–94) for referring to him in the same breath with Wharton, 'splay-mouth'd' Elsing, 'Impotent Essex', and 'Isaac' Pennington.

The decline of Royalist fortunes, however, had a marked effect on Cleveland's tone. In the early pieces the occasionally burlesque rhymes and careless rhythms usually suggested the grotesque fury of Cleveland's opponents; in the shadow of defeat he himself called up the scorpions of the Celtic *file* and the Elizabethan scourger to give the 'keen Iambicks' of 'The Rebell Scot' the proper bite, and with this magical tongue-lashing he attempted to bait and flay. So long as each lash told, it mattered little which was first or last. Each was laid on with more finesse than Marston or the Elizabethans had achieved, but with the force and speed of their anger.

> A Poet should be fear'd
> When angry, like a Comets flaming beard.
> And where's the Stoick can his wrath appease
> To see his Countrey sicke of *Pym*'s disease. . . .
>
>   ('The Rebell Scot', 7–10)

Probably Cleveland thought of Persius as the inconstant stoic, for this ominous comet had been Barten Holyday's emblem for the satirist in 'An Apostrophe . . . to his Authour Persius':

> Mount then, thou purer fire, and let thy heate
> Strongly exhale from their infectious seate
> Th' envenomed fogges of vice; And then inflame
> Them, that they may be lights to their Owne shame;
> Which, as a Comet, may affright the earth
> With horror, at its owne prodigious birth;
> And with its darting taile threatening dread
> Vengeance, point out to wrath each guilty head.[2]

---

[1] See esp. 'Upon the Naming of the D. of B. in the Remonstrance in Parliament, 1628', *Poems and Songs Relating to George Villiers, Duke of Buckingham*, ed. Frederick W. Fairholt, Percy Soc. Early Eng. Ballads . . . , xxix, 1850, pp. 24–28.

[2] *Aulus Persius Flaccus His Satires Translated into English*, Oxford, 1616, E2ᵛ. Cleveland might have used the third edition, 1635, sig. F7ʳ⁻ᵛ.

Dryden was to be impressed with the consistency of Persius' stoicism,[1] but Holyday's Preface emphasized the terror of Persius' momentary heat:

> . . . when a Satyrist, through the heate of his loue to Vertue, is set on fire to see the desperate securitie of prophanenesse: the furie of his passion doth so transport him, that there is no time left for the placing or displacing, choosing or reiecting of some particular word; but as most commonly their passions are vneuen, rough and furious: so is that also which they write being in this poeticall perturbation. ('To the Reader', 1635, A5.)

'Vneuen, rough, and furious' recalls the old derivation of satire from 'satyr' which Casaubon and Dryden rejected. The old spelling 'satyrist' appears in all seventeenth-century editions of Cleveland and in O, but since even Dryden allowed the form in his own 'Discourse . . .' too much significance can be attributed to it. Cleveland did not revert completely to old-fashioned 'satyre' in the course of the War, but he did discover almost overnight his talent for a special kind of 'satyric' indignation. The technique and its rationale are well described in the poem 'On the Pouder Plot' from L22 (f. 134) which Cleveland himself may have written:

> Satyres run best when Classhing tearms do meet,
> And Indignation makes them knock their feet.
> To bee methodicall in Verse, & rhime
> In sutch inuectiues is the highest crime.
> Who Euer saw a firy passion breake
> But in abruptnes? thus my pen must speak
> Make at Each word a period, which may show
> As Cornes of pouder, & then fire the row
> With sharp artic'late blasts, which breathing on
> Those lines, may 'nflame each hot expression.

As the enemy grew more powerful, impervious to Olympian ridicule, Cleveland's wrath had little time to cool. One hot word led to another, and verbal compression set off a series of explosions. Staccato effects were not new to satire. *Ingenioso* had spoken of

---

[1] 'A Discourse Concerning the Original and Progress of Satire. . . 1693', *Of Dramatic Poesy and Other Critical Essays*, ed. George Watson, Everyman's Library, 1962, ii. 122–4.

Juvenal's 'ierking hand' as early as 1601 in *The Return from Parnassus*.[1] Earlier, the follies and knaveries listed at such length in Elizabethan satire had tumbled forth in curt Senecan phrases. But Cleveland never employed such lists, and the abrupt questions and exclamations opening 'Smectymnuus', 'The Mixt Assembly', and 'The Rebell Scot' were hardly so numerous as those in many satires on Buckingham. With a few he would capture attention, but to hold it he counted on setting off a chain reaction of strong lines and epigrams chosen and arranged to command respect for his rhetorical variety and verbal agility.

In his satires Cleveland's 'strength' depends not solely on his attitude toward language but also on the quality of his engagement with the political event. He begins as the notable defender of authority and due order, and ends as the snarling critic of mob-rule. His language struggles to preserve the former in precise, perspicuous couplets whose Augustan quality has often been noticed; but it succumbs as often to the temptation to hold up the mirror of satirical imitation to the latter. In attempting to resolve this conflict Cleveland's special forte becomes 'wit stenographied', a wit that depends upon the neatly placed polysyllable for much of its emphasis and upon clench and catachresis for much of its coherence. Take, for instance, the earlier unrevised version of 'The Kings Disguise':

> The Sun hath mew'd his beames from off his lamp,
> And Majesty defac'd the Royall stamp.
> Is't not enough thy Dignity's in thrall,
> But thou'lt transmute it in thy shape and all?
> As if thy Blacks were of too faint a dye
> Without the tincture of Tautologie.
> Flay an Egyptian from his Cassock skin,
> Spun of his country's darknesse, line't within
> With Presbyterian budge, that drowsie trance,
> The Synods sable, foggy ignorance;
> No bodily nor ghostly Negro could
> Rough-cast thy figure in a sadder mould:
> This Privie-chamber of thy shape would be
> But the Close mourner of thy Royaltie.   (11–24.)

---

[1] Part II, I. i. 86. *The Three Parnassus Plays*, ed. J. B. Leishman, 1949, p. 225.

Here the link between the passages ending with 'Tautologie' and 'Royaltie' seems at first to be the heraldic connotations of 'Blacks' and 'sable' awakened by 'transmute' and 'tincture'; the next minute we see that the clothing image is still dominant in the comparison of Charles's disguise to the black clothes of churchmen ('Cassock skin', 'Presbyterian budge') and Close mourners. Changing 'transmute' to 'transcribe' muffles the heraldic overtones only to release the ink-and-paper image in 'Blacks', which reminds us that ink in Cleveland's day was made of lampblack. This is squinting wit. What justifies it in political satire? For one thing, it could reflect the precarious, the ephemeral, the incongruous, the hypocritical in a power vacuum where words meant whatever the latest coalition wanted them to mean. We should not forget that Cleveland had been trained in Roman law at St. John's just at the moment when the sanctions of the prerogative were removed and Parliament's word became ordinance. Compared with the satires of a contemporary like Mildmay Fane[1] Cleveland's are not didactic, but a recurring theme in them is this subversion of law as he had known it and the subsequent corruption of language. We cannot be sure that Cleveland wrote the Epitaph on

> STRAFFORD, who was hurried hence
> 'Twixt Treason and Convenience,

but after Strafford's trial he did compose '*An Answer to a Pamphlet written against the Lord* Digby's *Speech concerning the Death of the Earl of* Strafford', and in this he supported Digby's contention that since Strafford had not been proved guilty of plotting to bring over the Irish Army, under the statute he could be guilty only of transgressing the law, not of subverting it; on the other hand, it was genuine treason—'The Assassination of the Monarchy'—to call Strafford a traitor for believing in Majesty's right 'to do what power will admit'.[2] With Strafford's execution Cleveland found himself in a world where 'Allegeance is Malignant, Treason Merit' ('To P. Rupert', 8), a paradox easily rationalized by '*The Literall* and

---

[1] E. Withington, 'Mildmay Fane's Political Satire', *Harvard Library Bulletin*, xi, Winter 1957, pp. 40–64.

[2] CV, pp. 130–42.

Equitable Sence' (ibid., 20) of Puritan consciences and their mental reservations.

> The state in *Strafford* fell, the Church in *Laud*:
> The twins of publike rage adjudg'd to dye,
> For Treasons they should act, by Prophecy.
> The facts were done before the Lawes were made,
> The trump turn'd up after the game was plai'd.
> ('On the Archbishop of Canterbury', 42-46)

In an age when the whole idea of party politics was even more foreign than it was to Dryden, it seemed to Cleveland that all that was left to hold society and his couplets together was either verbal quibbling or some travesty on order and harmony like the fitful dance that starts up in the middle of 'The Mixt Assembly', a dance where like does not find like or its complement but where 'every *Gibeline* hath got his *Guelph*' and only Selden is left without a partner —'a Galliard by himself' ('The Mixt Assembly', 87-88). The disparate objects of Cleveland's fancy—'all th' Adulteries of twisted nature' (ibid., 33)—are his comment on the unnatural marriages and strange bedfellows of political expediency. Since nothing develops naturally, there are no natural relationships, only violent yokings and abbreviations; but part of the appeal of this curt wit depends upon the true conservative's ability to recall the older, didactic expansions and clarifications of its conceits and emblems. Thus the dance of the Westminster Assemblymen (67-90) is far more sinister if one recalls the old cosmic dance as it had been distorted in Marston's satire on Curio's pride in dancing:

> His very soule, his intellectuall
> Is nothing but a mincing capreall.
> He dreames of toe-turnes, each gallant hee doth meete
> He fronts him with a trauers in the streete,
> Prayse but *Orchestra*, and the skipping art,
> You shall commaund him, faith you haue his hart
> Euen capring in your fist. A hall, a hall,
> Roome for the Spheres, the Orbes celestiall
> Will daunce *Kemps Iigge*. They'le reuel with neate iumps
> A worthy Poet hath put on their Pumps?

O wits quick trauers, but *sance ceo's* slow,
Good faith tis hard for nimble *Curio*.
Yee gracious Orbs, keepe the old measuring,
All's spoyld if once yee fall to capering.[1]

Mr. R. A. Brower has recently discussed Pope's use of what he
calls 'the allusive mode',[2] and Cleveland's satire can profitably be
considered in these terms. His method may be no more than a crude
prefiguration of Pope's, but Pope learnt from Dryden, and Dryden
in his early verse owes much to Cleveland. In its unrefined form
this 'poetry of allusion' acquires its tone and strength from the
quality of its indirections. Only the reader who has Marston's dance
in mind sees how far short the Assembly comes of being a mirror of
divine order, for unlike Kinsayder Cleveland left moralizing to the
Puritans; the anarchy of a State and Church cut loose from monarchy
made the moral for him self-evident. What he copied from Marston
was the trick of pivoting on a word like 'travers'; what he intensified
was the rapid fantastication which propelled satire into grotesque
dark lines too 'hard for nimble Curio'. When Cleveland is seeking
similitudes for the Westminster Assembly, that 'mixture' of laymen
and clergy, he finds them in a strange world:

> Strange Scarlet Doctors these, they'l passe in Story
> For sinners halfe refin'd in Purgatory;
> Or parboyl'd Lobsters, where there joyntly rules
> The fading Sables and the coming Gules.
> The flea that *Falstaffe* damn'd, thus lewdly shewes
> Tormented in the flames of *Bardolphs* Nose.
> Like him that wore the Dialogue of Cloaks,
> This shoulder *Iohn a Styles*, that *Iohn a Noaks*.   (37-44)

In these eight lines the poet moves like a grasshopper from a
University procession to a Catholic Purgatory, to a dinner table, to
the College of Heralds, to the theatre, and to a Law Court. All these
belong to a world which was jeopardized by the 'Mixt Assembly',
and Cleveland's allusions are both ridiculing this 'Fleabitten Synod'
and asserting the breadth and richness of the world it threatens.

---

[1] 'Satire XI, *Humours*, The Scourge of Villanie', *Poems of John Marston*, ed. Arnold
Davenport, Liverpool, 1961, pp. 167-8, ll. 23-36.
[2] *Alexander Pope, The Poetry of Allusion*, Oxford, 1959.

Although Cleveland displays a fondness for the abstruse, academic allusion he is by no means limited by it. Within ten lines of 'A Dialogue between two Zealots' he can refer to things classical, Biblical, topical, popular, and political (29–38). Here again it is the narrowness of the Puritan creed which is being successfully exploited by the rich profusion of the allusive mode.

Was this wit equally appropriate for both comic and tragic satire? Whereas the self-conscious Marston, exorcizing 'grim reproofe' in expansive apostrophes, never succeeded in convincing his readers that he was 'great with Mirth', Cleveland's stenographied couplets bestowed on all satire, bantering or bitter, a certain playfulness. This gave more poise to the scourger in 'The Rebell Scot' than Marston had managed for any piece in *The Scourge of Villainy*, but a poem like 'The Kings Disguise' hardly required any artful dissembling of passion. Here Cleveland found he could no longer play the whipper towering over his enemy; for Charles himself, traitor to his own sovereignty, now took on something like the role of the *adversarius* in Roman satire. It is therefore no coincidence that this poem is the most tortured with catachreses and paradoxes as it moves from the plea

> Oh for a State-distinction to arraigne
> *Charles* of high Treason 'gainst my Soveraigne. (5–6)

to

> But since w' are all call'd Papists, why not date
> Devotion to the rags thus consecrate ?   (85–86)

With the final sob,

> But oh! he goes to *Gibeon*, and renewes
> A league with mouldy bread, and clouted shooes. (123–4)

we realize that this has been Cleveland's most bitter, despairing work. Yet for many readers the realization will dawn late. After the lines 'To P. Rupert' even Charles's flight to the Scots may seem just one more excuse to display the extravagant courtly compliments that went with a University education and, along the way, to dispose of Marchamont Nedham who had sent out 'A Hue and Cry' after the King in *Mercurius Britanicus*. In reality, the true purpose is to convince the Royalists at Newark, that though it is hard to distinguish between Charles's blasphemy and Nedham's, a king still leaves his followers the shreds of a religion and a hope of resurrection. The satirist who would thus lay mines for Armageddon must make sure that he is not merely setting off a few squibs, but here the frustration created by Cleveland's total commitment to a dying cause is only superficially dispelled. Like the times, his cumulative hyperboles tend to belittle even what he venerates. In fact, much of the imagery in his darkest satires might confirm the current thesis that satire 'works directly against the ostensibly conservative function which it is said to serve. Instead of shoring up foundations, it tears them down.'[1] On the one hand we are commanded to regard the King's disguise as libellous, blasphemous, ridiculous ('Cloathes where a Switzer might be buried quicke'), and archaic ('As Temples use to have their Porches wrought | With Sphynxes, creatures of an antick draught'—); on the other, Charles's 'ruines' prove 'a religious house' and his 'dark mysterious dresse' is 'the Gospell coucht in Parables'. So far from the monarchy's becoming sanctified, religion itself is made quaint. Suddenly we do not seem many years away from Cleveland's friend Butler, whose *Hudibras* was to bury not only the Good Old Cause but a Cerberean 'Leash of Languages' (I. i. 104) and all the vulgar errors that go with an emblematic view of the world.

Within the small circle of Cleveland's initial influence his satires provided a bitter and fragmented age with its most sophisticated and deadly wit.[2] In satire of this kind we would expect the point to be taken only by those readers to whom the allusions are readily available; the *persona* is a pedant who addresses himself to an artificially restricted audience (all other readers are eavesdroppers), and his frame of reference and allusion makes no concessions to those who are outside a particular, and narrow, culture. Yet for some twenty years after the events they commemorated, Cleveland's poems continued to find an enthusiastic if ever-changing audience. In his first swaggering display of admiration for Rupert and scorn-

---

[1] Robert C. Elliott, 'The Satirist and Society', *ELH*, xxi, September, 1954, p. 248.
[2] The verdict is C. V. Wedgwood's (*Poetry and Politics under the Stuarts*, Cambridge, 1960, pp. 85–130).

ful bantering of 'Smec', Charles's followers at Oxford found the voice
and posture they tried so hard to maintain even after Marston Moor.
In 'The Rebell Scot' and 'The Kings Disguise' some of their genuine
bitterness found relief in the fusillade of conceits that assured them
of their continuing intellectual superiority even after Naseby. When
the majority of the poems were collected from manuscript sources
in 1647 they found in London a new audience, less responsive to
Cavalier bravado and academic wit but more susceptible now to
one of Cleveland's dominant themes: the monstrous reversal of the
natural order by unnatural alliances with zealots and Scottish
traitors. In an unsettled State where Charles was now 'playing the
part of both king and pawn'[1] in the struggle between Parliament
and Army, Erastians and Tolerationists, many Londoners were
already fearful of the Levellers and impatient with the discretion of
the controlled press. The new edition of the prose *Character of a
London-Diurnall* with 'severall select Poems' reminded them of the
very different climate only three years earlier when the same press
had circulated rumours of 'Plots, horrible plots' together with the
Parliament's Ordinances summoning 'Militia . . . without the con-
course of Royall Jupiter'.[2] To the ironic contrast implied by the
prose reprint, the appended poems added the suggestion that the
current power vacuum was due in part to the earlier failure to cope
with a nightmarish world where 'Ox and Asse go yok'd in the same
plough' ('The Mixt Assembly', 94). So Cleveland became the poet
of that larger Royalist party which eventually included in its fear of
'parity' English Presbyterians as well as Cavaliers, gentry as well as
London burghers. In the days of the Commonwealth Mildmay Fane,
the second Earl of Westmoreland, saw him as 'all great Arts
Leviathan':

> For now I shall no longer looke
> Whence Hobbs intiteled his booke
> Though surreptitious & by stealth
> Since thou'rt above all comonwealth
> Thy straines Monarkike, nor can bear
> Th' affront of a competitor

---

[1] Joseph Frank, *The Beginnings of the English Newspaper*, Cambridge, Mass. 1961,
p. 116.   [2] *The Character. . .*, A2ᵛ.

> Wher Science Liberall is who giues
> Not unto All prerogatiues
> Over yᵉ Tongue & Pen but brings
> Those best deserue to be her Kings.[1]

After 1660, as long as there was a generation whose support of monarchy could be summoned up by fears lest '1641 be come again', there was still an audience for Cleveland.

A political satirist, it is true, has ready-made enemies as well as ready-made friends. These, for a time, only underlined Cleveland's triumph. The prose *Character of a London-Diurnall* provoked a barrage of replies in 1645, the number alone a tribute to its success. Most were feeble attempts to dismiss Cleveland as a mere 'ballad-writer', the parliamentarian's favourite epithet for all pamphleteers.[2] Only the time-server Nedham, in an otherwise undistinguished piece, succeeded in impaling him and Aulicus as academics, 'things halfe made up between *Syllogisme* and *Sophistry*. . .'.[3] Later, when Cleveland was competing with Samuel Sheppard and Nedham for the title of Mercurius Pragmaticus, the opposition press chose to single him out as

the wittiest knave of the whole crew: (giue the devil his due,) he is the Court-jester, the Cavaliers fool, the chief squib-crack, arch pamphlet-puppy; if his Brethren (in iniquity) get him, the fools hug him, as the Papists doe a Dispensation, to eat flesh Fridayes; where with they are furnished with jests and jeers for a long time after.[4]

Along with such grudging compliments came the supreme one from the new régime at the Universities. When the Oxford muses were bidden to congratulate the Lord Protector on his peace with the Dutch in 1654, one Robert Mathew, Bachelor of Law and Fellow of New College, chose to address Cromwell as if he were Cleveland saluting Rupert:

---

[1] 'Verses addressed to John Cleveland by the Earl of Westmorland', *A Little Ark Containing Sundry Pieces of Seventeenth-Century Verse*, ed. G. Thorn-Drury, p. 17. The manuscript of Fane's Fugitive Poems from which this was taken is now in Harvard College Library.

[2] Hyder E. Rollins, *Cavalier and Puritan*, New York, 1923, p. 32.

[3] *Mercurius Britanicus*, no. 70, 17 February 1645, Bbbb.

[4] *Mercurius Anti-Mercurius*, A2. Thomason dated his copy 'Aprill 4th 1648'.

Nay, You calme *Seas* too, that as *Laplanders*
We may in *Egg-shells* waft our Passengers.
Black was the *Fate* of *Colliers*, their *Eyes*
Ran *Ink* enough to *write* their *Miseries*.
But *London Chymnies*, which, like *Green-sick-Girles*,
On *Coales* and *Ashes* made their cheifest meales
Have now their due Provision which is sent,
And are not sconc't by th' other *Element*.
This joyes the *Alderman*, who now appeares
Like *Four-leg'd-Watt* only in *Furr* and *Eares*,
His *Quakings* quite have left him; such o such
Is our *Agrement* that's made with the *Dutch!*
    Holland and *Wee* are reunited *Lands*
    Wee that have *shaken Armes*, do now *shake Hands*.[1]

It was, however, this vein of playfully extravagant academic compliment which destroyed the vogue for Cleveland. The culmination of decades of loyal panegyric art at the Universities, it was right for Rupert but hardly appropriate for Cromwell. An anonymous wit who set out to satirize the whole Oxford miscellany had the most fun with this 'bumbast Muse' of 'my *Cleavelandified* Mathew'.[2] A year later one 'S. H.' wrote as a climax to two other Royalist elegies a mock 'On the death of the High-priz'd Poet JOHN CLEAVELAND, Esq' (see p. xxi), and another elegy, even more extravagant and poker-faced, appeared in a broadside later claimed by Thomas Pecke on his title-page for *Parnassi Puerperium*, 1659.[3] A more straightforward indictment, 'Uppon Mr. J. C. a Famous Poet of our time', appears in B.M. MS. Add. 10307, f. 20^v–21^v, a collection of poems by Sir John Cotton:

Poet in bumbaste, whose conceptions bee
But Witts-impostumes, and a timpanie:
The race of the zamzummins only fitt
To bee the Midwifes of thy giant witt . . .

---

[1] *Musarum Oxoniensium 'ΕΛΑΙΟΦΟΡΙΑ*, Oxford, 1654, pp. 66–67.

[2] *Momus Elencticus* or a light Come-off upon that serious piece of Drollerie presented by the Vice Chancellor of Oxon in the name of all his Mirmidons, to expell the Melancholy of the Court, and to tickle its gizzard with a Landskip of dancing Fryars to their own Musick and Numbers, 1654, pp. 6–7. Madan attributes this (no. 2246) to '[Ireland, Thomas]'. The B.M. copy has no t.p.

[3] T.P. gen. Norfolciensis, '*An Elegie Upon the Never Satisfactorily deplored Death of that Rare Column of Parnassus, Mr. JOHN CLEEVELAND*', 1658.

Thy verses like the Cataracts of Nile
Disturbly rumble, and are heard a Mile
Before a man come at them, they who write
Thus, doe not please or proffit, but affright.
Virgil and Lucan though their numbers bee
As high as ever Roome was great, are free
From turgid two-foot wordes, and strained soe
As if a fed Oxe should to dancing goe . . . .

Though such criticism was ostensibly non-political, defenders often replied to it by emphasizing Cleveland's political integrity and inimitable masculinity:

It was not power, but justice made him write,
No ends could *May*-like, turn him Parasite.
The Cause by Candles-ends he did not rate,
When others Pens did Truth assassinate. . . .[1]

But even before Dryden the tide had turned. With the rise of neo-classicism and the utilitarian ideals of the new philosophy at court there came a non-partisan distrust of scholastic word-play. Nedham's old charge of academicism was made to stick. When John Evelyn warned the Chairman of the Royal Society's Committee for improving the English tongue against 'exotic words', he thought immediately of Cleveland as one who had 'lived long in Universities' and did 'greatly affect words and expressions no where in use besides. . . '.[2] When Dryden finally turned Fuller's praise into condemnation (see p. lvi of this edition) it is interesting that he put the famous objections in the mouth of Eugenius, who was supposed to uphold the moderns against the ancients. Cleveland failed because, like Plautus, he was too bold to satisfy an Horatian ideal:

to express a thing hard and unnaturally, is his new way of elocution. . . . But to do this always, and never be able to write a line without it, though it may be admired by some few pedants, will not pass upon those who know that wit is . . . most to be admired when a great thought

---

[1] J. M., '*An Elegy, Offered to the Memory of that Incomparable Son of Apollo, Mr.* John Cleveland', *Cleaveland Revived*, 1660, p. 4.

[2] 'Letter to Sir Peter Wyche, 20 June, 1665', *Critical Essays of the Seventeenth Century*, ed. J. E. Spingarn, Oxford, 1908, ii. 311–12.

comes dressed in words so commonly received that it is understood by the meanest apprehensions, as the best meat is the most easily digested. . . .[1]

After this the editors of 1677 might attempt a vindication by purging the Cleveland canon of the *spuria* and mistranslations in CR; they might preface it with a satirical reply To 'the grand Sophys' that 'will not allow him the reputation of wit at all' ('To The Right Worshipful and Reverend Francis Turner D. D. . . .', CV, sig. A4). But Lake and Drake wrote as his former students; their imitation of his satirical vein and their very dedication to the Master and Fellows of St. John's, Cambridge, only strengthened the impression that what had been mistaken for a party's and then for mankind's was really a college's. Ten years later the publishers of the *Works* felt Cleveland would need all the spurious stuffing from previous editions to recapture an audience now used to the wit of Rochester and Dryden.

The reissue of the *Works* in 1699 may have prompted Dryden to think once more of Cleveland; for there he would have found one of the commenders from CR still saying,

> We poor Retainers angle for a thin
> Fancy, his like a Drag-Net sweeps all in. . . .[2]

A famous passage in 'The Preface to the Fables' (1700) again turned this compliment into insult, and Robert B. Hinman[3] refuses to believe that it was intended for Cowley as annotators have heretofore assumed:

One of our late great poets is sunk in his reputation, because he could never forgive any conceit which came in his way; but swept like a drag-net, great and small. There was plenty enough, but the dishes were ill sorted; whole pyramids of sweetmeats for boys and women, but little of solid meat for men. . . . . for ten impressions which his works have had in so many successive years, yet at present a hundred books are scarcely purchased once a twelve-month. . . .

(*Of Dram. Poesy* . . ., ii. 280)

Yet the earlier summation of Milton's nephew Edward Phillips in his *Compendiosa Enumeratio Poetarum* appended to the seventeenth

---

[1] *Of Dramatic Poesy and Other Critical Essays*, i. 39–40.
[2] 'An Elegy on Mr. Cleveland, *and his Verses on* Smectymnuus', *Works*, 1699, p. 284.
[3] *Abraham Cowley's World of Order*, Cambridge, Mass., 1960, p. 10.

edition of Johannes Buchler's *Sacrarum Profanarumque Phrasium Poetarum Thesaurus*, 1669 would have been fairer and briefer: 'Joannes Clevelandius Inflato quodam Satyrae genere delectatur.'[1]

Like them or not, Cleveland's inflations were suited to political satire as he found it before 'Absalom and Achitophel'. The drag-net plenty of his dishes was apparently not due to any knowledge of Casaubon's derivation of Roman satire from *satura lanx*; in English criticism that was Dryden's discovery. Or, if Cleveland read Casaubon he did not follow him, as Dryden did, in applying Aristotelian dramatic principles to satire.[2] Instead the very pressure of events pushed him half-way back to Elizabethan conceptions of the satirist, encouraging him in occasional obscurity, ostentatious indifference to structure, and extravagant conceits. Yet in Cleveland's drag-net there will be found most of the traditional tricks of the age's invective, and in his couplets English satire is making a Cacus-like progress. Unlike John Collop, who stole a whole couplet from 'The Authour to his Hermophrodite',[3] or the author of 'An Epitaph upon James, Duke of Hamilton' in *Digitus Dei*, who borrowed another from 'The Rebell Scot' (cf. notes in Commentary to ll. 55–56), Cleveland could dredge up and strain out a miraculous draught of nourishing wit from a single cast. Trace the figure of the barnacles at the end of 'The Rebell Scot' (122–6) through Hall,[4] Marvell,[5] and Butler[6] and see how inflation and compression go together in his best work; only Cleveland milks the conceit of four different insults in five lines and succeeds in making them all sound like throw-aways.

This gift for compressed extravagance worked best in the lampoon because it suited the whipper's *persona*. Butler's burlesque, jogging along at a pace faintly reminiscent of Sir Thopas or Corbet's *Iter Boreale*, could exploit a dying era's *curiosa* once more but not Cleve-

[1] R. G. Howarth, 'Edward Phillips's "Compendiosa Enumeratio Poetarum" ', *MLR*, liv, July 1959, pp. 323, 327.

[2] Mary Claire Randolph, 'The Structural Design of Formal Verse Satire', *PQ*, xxi, October 1942, p. 381.

[3] *Poems*, ed. Conrad Hilberry, Madison, Wis., 1962, p. 90.

[4] Virgidemiarum, IV. ii. 140, *The Collected Poems*, ed. Davenport, Liverpool, 1949, p. 58.

[5] 'The First Anniversary of the Government under O.C.', ll. 351–6, *Poems and Letters*, ed. H. M. Margoliouth, 2nd ed., Oxford, 1952, i. 112.

[6] *Hudibras*, III, ii, 652–6, ed. A. R. Waller, Cambridge, 1905, p. 256.

land's hair-trigger edginess under the spur of the moment. The Juvenalian declamations of Oldham and the mock heroic vein of Marvell and Dryden favoured a statelier elaboration of a set topic. Still, they flourished a conceit of Cleveland's now and then, and Dryden's Eugenius (*Of Dram. Poesy*, i. 40) thought there could be salvaged from his poems a few heroic couplets: Dr. Johnson's favourite on Cain and the Scots, where the wit was 'independent of his words', or lines 39–40 of 'To P. Rupert', where the metaphor was 'so soft and gentle' that it did not shock. Grace and ingenuity did redeem Cleveland's wit often enough for Dryden to think of *The Character of a London-Diurnall* when he came to his famous definition of fine raillery: 'the fineness of a stroke that separates the head from the body, and leaves it standing in its place' ('A Discourse Concerning the Original and Progress of Satire, 1693', *Of Dram. Poesy. . .*, ii. 137). It is suggestive, perhaps, that what Dryden preserved as a memorable phrase for satirical deftness Cleveland treated as an impossibility, a sleight-of-hand comparable to the victories the Parliamentary press attributed to Sir William Waller.

In his non-political poems Cleveland is no longer required to exhort or discredit, and it is to these poems that Saintsbury's perceptive comment most aptly applies:

. . . I entertain a very serious doubt whether Cleveland *ever* wrote 'serious' poetry, in one sense—he was of course serious enough in his satires—at all.[1]

In his non-political poems Cleveland is writing light, coterie verse for amusement only, and the effective charge against him is his irresponsible carelessness and lack of art. In 'The Authours Mock-Song to Marke Anthony' he writes:

> When as the Night-raven sung Pluto's Mattins,
> And *Cerberus* cried three Amens at a houle;
> When night-wandring Witches put on their pattins,
> Midnight as darke as their faces are foule,
> > Then did the Furies doome
> > That my night-mare should come;
> > Such a mishapen gume
> > Puts downe *Su. Pomfret* cleane.   (1–8)

[1] Saintsbury, iii. 7.

This is careless writing, and Cleveland is very often guilty of it. It is the kind of writing which Hobbes attacked as 'the ambitious obscurity of expressing more then is perfectly conceived, or perfect conception in fewer words then it requires. Which Expressions, though they have had the honor to be called strong lines, are indeed no better then Riddles...'.[1] The lack of artistic responsibility which passages like this betray gives a fair indication of the degree of 'seriousness' to which Cleveland aspired.

Another of the qualities which may be held to vitiate Cleveland's integrity is his tendency towards burlesque. In several of the poems burlesque is the dominant tone, and in 'The Hecatomb to his Mistresse' the obvious intention is to produce an extravagant mockery of the 'Metaphysical' mode:

> From your own essence must I first untwine,
> Then twist again each Panegyrick line.
> Reach then a soaring Quill that I may write,
> As with a Jacobs staff to take her height.
> Suppose an Angel darting through the air,
> Should there encounter a religious prayer
> Mounting to Heaven, that Intelligence
> Should for a Sunday-suit thy breath condense
> Into a body. . . .   (15–23)

and so on it goes, from one folly to another. Cleveland's burlesque, unlike Butler's in *Hudibras*, is not vindicated by its forensic ingenuity. The attacks are all of one kind, exploiting the extravagance of the conceit but unaware of its profounder potentialities. Despite the detachment of the burlesque, and the element of self-mockery, there is, in poems like 'Upon a Miser', 'The Senses Festival', and 'Fuscara', a real sense of a style preying upon itself, of the exhaustion of a mode.

Cleveland's widespread use of the conceit illustrates the extent of this exhaustion. In his elegies on the Archbishop of Canterbury and on Edward King the convention is used not as an instrument of analysis but as a substitute for significant thought. Writing on the death of Edward King he says,

---

[1] 'Answer to Davenant', 1650. See *Critical Essays of the Seventeenth Century*, ed. Spingarn, ii. 63.

> I am no Poet here; my penne's the spout
> Where the rain-water of my eyes runs out
> In pitie of that name, whose fate we see
> Thus copi'd out in griefs Hydrographie.
>   ('Upon the death of M. King', 5–8)

The lines are an elaborate excuse for saying nothing, and the image suggests nothing beyond its own grotesque ingenuity. His love poems show the same tendency towards fragmentation:

> No Rosary this Votress needs,
> Her very syllables are beads.
> No sooner 'twixt those Rubies born,
> But Jewels are in Ear-rings worn.
>   ('To the State of Love', 57–60)

The immediate impression is of an elaborate, fantastic sleight of hand, and the effect is achieved by Cleveland's refusal to develop the lightly stated terms of the *discordia concors*. The poems are thick with these atomized conceits, each with its own kinetic possibilities, each thrown off unexplored and unexploited. What was in Donne a technique for the analysis of significant experience becomes in Cleveland's poems no more than a propulsive agent.

These qualities may be held to amount to Decadence, and if Decadence is in itself reprehensible then Cleveland stands condemned. Yet his poetry does exhibit the very qualities of his defects. In particular, the procession of undeveloped conceits produces an impression of boundless, effortless energy, and it is this which gives his lines their 'strength'. This marvellous fecundity of invention is Cleveland's dominant characteristic, and it is as significant in his love poems as it is in his satires. In 'The Mixt Assembly' it is a fanciful means of asserting the ridiculous. In 'Upon Sir Thomas Martin' it is the contemptuous bludgeon which leaves neither opportunity nor time for resistance. In 'The Antiplatonick', one of Cleveland's completely successful poems, the technique is deployed in the interests of high, fantastic fun:

> The souldier, that man of Iron,
> Whom Ribs of *Horror* all inviron,
> That's strung with Wire, in stead of Veins,

In whose imbraces you're in chains,
Let a Magnetick Girle appear,
Straight he turns *Cupids* Cuiraseer.

(33–38)

The ingenuity is wilful, often perverse, but it requires from the reader an imaginative attention, a quickness of wit, and a sophisticated response to allusion. The quality of the intellectual engagement is not the same here as it is in Donne. Donne's puzzles frequently demand the strenuous exercise of the reader's intelligence, Cleveland's require him to possess a store of abstruse knowledge. To this extent the charge of 'coterie poet' must be allowed, and the two poems, 'Square-Cap' and 'How the Commencement grows new', suggest that Cleveland was writing primarily for a University audience. Yet this 'coterie' demanded twenty-five separate editions of Cleveland's Poems before 1700, and the distinction between 'coterie poet' and 'popular poet' is in this instance not easy to draw.

His poise and sophistication as a satirist adumbrate Dryden rather than reflect Donne; as the celebrant of a defeated authority and order he has no competitors. His elegies and love poems lack offence because they make no pretensions to profundity. The game is to be enjoyed, and our interest is invited in a fantastic yet elegant eccentric. We can salute the intimations of Augustan satire as we admire the decadence, the last elegant flourish of a period rhetoric.

VI. THE PRESENT TEXT

The copy-text for the present edition is the first edition of 1647 (D1) for all the poems it contains. The copy used is Bodleian C. 10. 2. Linc., which has been collated against the British Museum copy, E. 375, and the copy in Dr. Williams's Library, PP. 3. 44. 6. No press variants have been discovered in these copies. Although the text of D1 is, for each poem, generally superior to that of any other witness, the agreement of CV and O in certain readings compels respect, and most departures from D1 are in favour of such readings. For the poems printed after D1, the first edition in which each appears has been taken as copy text, unless it had previously been separately published, and the agreement of CV and O is *a fortiori* respected.

Poems appearing only in manuscripts have been transcribed literally, except that scribal abbreviations have been expanded.

The text of the printed editions has been followed, with these exceptions: long 's' has been printed as 's', wrong-fount letters, turned letters, and irregular spacing have been silently corrected, disjunctive commas have been omitted, and where the question mark is clearly intended to serve as an exclamation mark it is printed as such.

The *apparatus criticus* includes all readings of equal stemmatic authority, and all substantive departures from copy-text. When a number of texts are listed as showing a particular variant there may be accidental differences between them; in every case the form recorded is that of the first text cited. It may be assumed throughout that P12 agrees with P11, and W with CV. A manuscript disagreeing with all others in any reading is recorded in brackets after a minus sign; e.g. '*MSS.(–H493)*' implies that H493 either has its own reading or agrees with the copy-text. The abbreviations 'a.c.' and 'b.c.' mean 'after correction' and 'before correction'.

Upon the death of *M.* King
drowned in the Irish Seas

I LIKE not tears in tune; nor will I prise
  His artificiall grief, that scannes his eyes:
Mine weep down pious beads: but why should I
Confine them to the Muses Rosarie?
I am no Poet here; my penne's the spout   5
Where the rain-water of my eyes runs out
In pitie of that name, whose fate we see
Thus copi'd out in griefs Hydrographie.
The Muses are not Mayr-maids; though upon
His death the Ocean might turn Helicon.   10
The sea's too rough for verse; who rhymes upon't,
With Xerxes strives to fetter th' Hellespont.
My tears will keep no channells, know no laws
To guide their streams; but like the waves, their cause,
Run with disturbance, till they swallow me   15
As a description of his miserie.
But can his spacious vertue find a grave
Within th' impostum'd bubble of a wave?
Whose learning if we sound, we must confesse
The sea but shallow, and him bottomlesse.   20
Could not the winds to countermand thy death,
With their whole card of lungs redeem thy breath?
Or some new Iland in thy rescue peep,
To heave thy resurrection from the deep?
That so the world might see thy safety wrought 25
With no lesse miracle then thy self was thought.
The famous Stagirite, who in his life
Had Nature as familiar as his wife,
Bequeath'd his widow to survive with thee
Queen Dowager of all Philosophie.   30

Upon the death of M. King *J. MSS.: RP142 H35 O* Title] *Upon the death of M.* King
drowned in the Irish Seas D5: no title *J*   6 runs *D5–P4 P11 CV:* run *J*
13 channells *D5:* chanell *J*

An ominous legacie, that did portend
Thy fate, and Predecessours second end !
Some have affirm'd, that what on earth we find,
The sea can parallel for shape and kind:
Books, arts, and tongues were wanting; but in thee   35
Neptune hath got an Universitie.
  We'll dive no more for pearls. The hope to see
Thy sacred reliques of mortalitie
Shall welcome storms, and make the sea-man prize
His shipwrack now more then his merchandise.   40
He shall embrace the waves, and to thy tombe
(As to a Royaller Exchange) shall come.
What can we now expect? Water and Fire
Both elements our ruine do conspire;
And that dissolves us, which doth us compound: 45
One Vatican was burnt, another drown'd.
We of the Gown our libraries must tosse,
To understand the greatnesse of our losse,
Be Pupills to our grief, and so much grow
In learning, as our sorrows overflow.   50
When we have fill'd the rundlets of our eyes,
We'll issue't forth, and vent such elegies,
As that our tears shall seem the Irish seas,
We floating Ilands, living Hebrides.

Upon the KINGS *return from* SCOTLAND

RETURN'D ? I'll ne'r believe't; First prove him hence;
 Kings travel by their beams and influence.
Who says the soul gives out her gests, or goes
A flitting progresse 'twixt the head and toes?
She rules by Omnipresence, and shall we   5
Denie a Prince the same ubiquitie?
Or grant he went, and 'cause the knot was slack,
Girt both the nations with his Zodiack:

Upon the Kings return from Scotland *IC. MSS.:* H35 O Title] *Upon the* KINGS
return from SCOTLAND *CR1-CR4 CV:* no title *IC*   7 the *CV MSS.:* their *IC*

Yet as the tree at once both upward shoots,
And just as much grows downward to the roots,　　　10
So at the same time that he posted thither
By counter-stages he rebounded hither.
Hither and hence at once; thus every sphere
Doth by a double motion enter-fere;
And when his native form inclines him East,　　　15
By the first mover he is ravisht West.
Have you not seen how the divided damme
Runs to the summons of her hungry lambe;
But when the twin cries halves, she quits the first?
Natures *Commendam* must be likewise nurst.　　　20
So were his journeys, like the spider's, spun
Out of his bowels of compassion.
Two realms, like Cacus, so his steps transpose,
His feet still contradict him as he goes.
Englands return'd, that was a banish'd soyl;　　　25
The bullet flying makes the gun recoyl.
Death's but a separation, though indors'd
With spade and javelin; we were thus divorc'd.
Our soul hath taken wing, while we expresse
The corps, returning to our principles.　　　30
But the Crab-Tropick must not now prevail;
Islands go back but when you're under sail.
So his retreat hath rectifi'd the wrong,
Backward is forward in the Hebrew tongue.
Now the Church-militant in plentie rests,　　　35
Nor fears like th' Amazon to lose her breasts.
Her means are safe, not squees'd untill the blood
Mix with the milk and choke the tender brood.
She, that hath been the floting Ark, is that
She that's now seated on Mount Ararat.　　　40
Quits Charles; Our souls did guard him northward thus,
Now He the Counterpane comes South to us.

*John Cleveland, Fellow of S*ᵗ *Johns Colledge*

20 *Commendam*] *Commendum IC*　　26 makes *CR1–CR4 CV*: made *IC*　　29 hath
CR1–CR4 CV: had *IC*　　34 forward *CR1–CR4 CV*: forwards *IC*

A Dialogue between two Zealots, upon the &c. in the Oath

SIR *Roger*, from a zealous piece of Freeze,
Rais'd to a Vicar of the Childrens threes;
Whose yearely Audit may, by strict accompt,
To twenty Nobles and his Vailes amount;
Fed on the Common of the femal charity,⠀⠀⠀⠀⠀5
Untill the Scots can bring about their parity;
So shotten, that his soule, like to himselfe,
Walks but in *Querpo*: This same Clergie Elfe,
Encount'ring with a Brother of the Cloth,
Fell presently to Cudgells with the Oath.⠀⠀⠀⠀10
The Quarrell was a strange mis-shapen Monster,
&c. (God blesse us) which they conster,
The Brand upon the buttock of the Beast,
The Dragons taile ti'd on a knot, a neast
Of young *Apocryphaes*, the fashion⠀⠀⠀⠀15
Of a new mentall Reservation.
⠀⠀While *Roger* thus divides the Text, the other
Winks and expounds, saying, My pious Brother,
Hearken with reverence; for the point is nice,
I never read on't, but I fasted twice,⠀⠀⠀⠀20
And so by Revelation know it better
Then all the learn'd Idolaters o' th' Letter.
With that he swell'd, and fell upon the Theame,
Like great *Goliah* with his Weavers beame:
I say to thee *&c.* thou li'st,⠀⠀⠀⠀25
Thou art the curled locke of Antichrist:
Rubbish of *Babell*, for who will not say
Tongues are confounded in *&c.* ?
Who sweares *&c.* sweares more oathes at once
Then *Cerberus* out of his Triple Sconce.⠀⠀⠀⠀30

A Dialogue between two Zealots *D1. MSS.: Ash36 RP26 S14 EG27 O R CT5 H18 RP117 A24 Douce E20*⠀⠀⠀2 Childrens] Chldrens *D1*⠀⠀⠀28 are *CV MSS.:* were *D1*

Who views it well, with the same eye beholds
The old halfe Serpent in his numerous foulds.
Accurst *&c.* thou, for now I scent
What the prodigious bloody Oysters meant.
Oh *Booker, Booker,* how cam'st thou to lack   35
This Fiend in thy Prophetick Almanack?
It's the darke Vault wherein th' infernall plot
Of powder 'gainst the State was first begot.
Peruse the Oath, and you shall soone descry it
By all the Father *Garnets* that stand by it.   40
'Gainst whom the Church, whereof I am a Member,
Shall keep another fifth day of November.
Yet here's not all, I cannot halfe untruss
&c. it's so abdominous.
The *Trojan* Nag was not so fully lin'd,   45
Unrip *&c.* and you shall find
Og the great Commissarie, and which is worse,
Th' Apparatour upon his skew-bald Horse.
Then (finally my Babe of Grace) forbeare,
&c. will be too farre to sweare: 50
For 'tis (to speake in a familliar stile)
A Yorkshire Wea-bit, longer then a mile.
     Here *Roger* was inspir'd, and by Gods-diggers,
Hee'l sweare in words at large, and not in figures.
Now by this drinke, which he takes off, as loth   55
To leave *&c.* in his liquid Oath.
His brother pledg'd him, and that bloody wine,
He swears shall seal the Synods *Cataline.*
So they drunk on, not offering to part
Til they had quite sworn out th' eleventh quart: 60
While all that saw and heard them joyntly pray,
They and their Tribe were all *&c.*

---

32 halfe] false *CV MSS.*   33 thou, for now] Now, now *CV MSS.*   34 the
CV MSS.: lately the *D1*   prodigious bloody *CV MSS.*: prodigious *D1*   36 Fiend
CV MSS. (*−Ash36*): signe *D1*   44 abdominous *CV MSS.*: abominous *D1*
53 Here *CV MSS.*: Then *D1*   54 large] length *CV MSS.*   55 Now] No
CV MSS.   60 quite] *Omit CV MSS.* (*−RP26*)

The Kings Disguise

AND why so coffin'd in this vile disguise,
Which who but sees blasphemes thee with his eyes?
My twins of light within their pent-house shrinke,
And hold it their Allegeance to winke.
Oh for a State-distinction to arraigne   5
Charles of high Treason 'gainst my Soveraigne.
What an usurper to his Prince is wont,
Cloyster and shave him, he himselfe hath don't.
His muffled fabrick speakes him a recluse,
His ruines prove it a religious house.   10
The Sun hath mew'd his beames from off his lamp,
And Majesty defac'd the Royall stamp.
Is't not enough thy Dignity's in thrall,
But thou'lt transcribe it in thy shape and all?
As if thy Blacks were of too faint a die,   15
Without the tincture of Tautologie.
Flay an Egyptian for his Cassock skin
Spun of his Countreys darknesse, line't within
With Presbyterian budge, that drowsie trance,
The Synods sable, foggy ignorance: 20
Nor bodily nor ghostly Negro could
Rough-cast thy figure in a sadder mould.
This Privie-chamber of thy shape would be
But the Close mourner to thy Royaltie.
Then breake the circle of thy Tailors spell,   25
A Pearle within a rugged Oysters shell.
Heaven, which the Minster of thy Person owns,
Will fine thee for Dilapidations.
Like to a martyr'd Abbeys courser doome,

The Kings Disguise *D1*. *MS.: O* (the citation *D4* implies the agreement of *D4–D6*:
K implies *K1* and *K2*)   1 so coffin'd *D4 CV O*: a Tenant *D1*   in *CV O*: to *D1*
4 Allegeance to *K D4 CV O*: Alleageance now to *D1*   9 fabrick *D4*: feature *D1*
10 it *D4 O*: him *D1*   14 transcribe *D4 CV O*: transmute *D1*   17 for] from *K*
20 ignorance:] ignorance. *D1*   21 Nor] No *K*   22 mould.] mould: *D1*
24 to *D4 CV O*: of *D1*   25 Then *D4 CV O*: 'Twill *D1*   Tailors *K2 D4 CV*
O: Jailors *D1*

Devoutly alter'd to a Pigeon roome: 30
Or like the Colledge by the changeling rabble,
Manchesters Elves, transform'd into a Stable.
Or if there be a prophanation higher,
Such is the Sacriledge of thine Attire.
By which th'art halfe depos'd, thou look'st like one   35
Whose looks are under Sequestration.
Whose Renegado form, at the first glance,
Shews like the self-denying Ordinance.
Angell of light, and darknesse too, I doubt,
Inspir'd within, and yet posses'd without.   40
Majestick twilight in the state of grace,
Yet with an excommunicated face.
Charles and his Maske are of a different mint,
A Psalme of mercy in a miscreant print.
The Sun wears Midnight, Day is Beetle-brow'd,   45
And Lightning is in Keldar of a cloud.
Oh the accurst Stenographie of fate !
The Princely Eagle shrunke into a Bat.
What charme, what Magick vapour can it be
That checkes his rayes to this Apostasie ?   50
It is no subtile filme of tiffany ayre,
No Cob-web vizard, such as Ladies weare,
When they are veyl'd on purpose to be seene,
Doubling their lustre by their vanquisht Skreene:
No, the false scabberd of a Prince is tough   55
And three-pil'd darknesse, like the smoaky slough
Of an imprisoned flame, 'tis *Faux* in graine,
Darke Lanthorn to our bright Meridian.
Hell belcht the damp, the *Warwick*-Castle-Vote
Rang *Britains* Curfeu, so our light went out.   60
The black offender, should he weare his sin
For penance, could not have a darker skin.

32 transform'd] reform'd *K*   45 Midnight] Nidnight *D1*   50 checkes
D4 CV O: shrinks *D1*   55 No, *K2 CV O*: Nor *D1*   Prince is *K2 CV O*:
Princes *D1*   56 And *K CV O*: Metall, and *D1*   like the smoaky *CV O*: like
unto the *K*: like the *D1*   58 bright *D4 CV O*: high *D1*   61–62 The . . .
skin. *D4 CV O*: *D1 and K do not print this couplet*

Thy visage is not legible, the letters,
Like a Lords name, writ in phantastick fetters:
Cloathes where a Switzer might be buried quicke,　　65
As overgrown as the Body Politique.
False beard enough, to fit a stages plot,
For that's the ambush of their wit, God wot.
Nay all his properties so strange appeare,
Y' are not i' th' presence, though the King be there.　　70
A Libell is his dresse, a garb uncouth,
Such as the *Hue* and *Cry* once purg'd at mouth.
Scribling Assasinate, thy lines attest
An eare-mark due; Cub of the Blatant Beast,
Whose breath before 'tis syllabled for worse,　　75
Is blasphemy unfledg'd, a callow curse.
The Laplanders when they would sell a wind
Wafting to hell, bag up thy phrase, and bind
It to the Barque, which at the voyage end
Shifts Poop, and breeds the Collick in the fiend.　　80
But I'le not dub thee with a glorious scar,
Nor sinke thy Skuller with a Man of War.
The black-mouth'd *Si quis* and this slandering suite,
Both doe alike in picture execute.
But since w' are all call'd Papists, why not date　　85
Devotion to the rags thus consecrate.
As Temples use to have their Porches wrought
With Sphynxes, creatures of an antick draught,
And puzling Pourtraitures, to shew that there
Riddles inhabited, the like is here.　　90
　　But pardon Sir, since I presume to be
Clarke of this Closet to Your Majestie;
Me thinks in this your dark mysterious dresse
I see the Gospell coucht in Parables.
The second view my pur-blind fancy wipes,　　95
And shewes Religion in its dusky types.

66 As overgrown as *D4*: Sure they would fit *D1*　　80 breeds *D4 P3–P17 CV*
O: brings *D1*　　85 Papists *K P1–P16 CV* O: Papist *D1*　　date *D4 P3 P6–P17*
CV O: date, *D1*　　95 The second *D4 CV* O: At my next *D1*　　view] view,
D1　　wipes *D4 CV* O: ripes *D1*

Such a Text Royall, so obscure a shade
Was *Solomon* in Proverbs all array'd.
  Now all ye brats of this expounding age,
To whom the spirit is in pupillage;   100
You that damne more then ever *Sampson* slew,
And with his engine, the same jaw-bone too:
How is't *Charles* 'scapes your Inquisition free,
Since bound up in the Bibles Liverie?
Hence Cabinet-Intruders, Pick-locks hence,   105
You that dim Jewells with your Bristoll-sense:
And Characters, like Witches, so torment,
Till they confesse a guilt, though innocent.
Keyes for this Cypher you can never get,
None but S. *Peter*'s op's this Cabinet.   110
This Cabinet, whose aspect would benight
Critick spectators with redundant light.
A Prince most seen, is least: What Scriptures call
The Revelation, is most mysticall.
  Mount then thou shadow royall, and with haste   115
Advance thy morning star, *Charles*'s overcast.
May thy strange journey contradictions twist,
And force faire weather from a Scottish mist.
Heavens Confessors are pos'd, those star-ey'd Sages,
To interpret an Ecclipse thus riding stages.   120
Thus *Israel*-like he travells with a cloud,
Both as a Conduct to him, and a shroud.
But oh! he goes to *Gibeon*, and renewes
A league with mouldy bread, and clouted shooes.

99 Now *D4 O*: Come *D1*   103 *Charles D4*: he *D1*   109 Cypher *D4*
CV O: Coffer *D1*   117 journey] journey, *D1*   119 Sages,] Sages *D1*
120 Ecclipse] Ecclipse, *D1*

Upon an Hermophrodite

SIR, or Madame, chuse you whether,
Nature twists you both together:
And makes thy soule two garbes confess,
Both peticoat and breeches-dress.
Thus we chastise the God of *Wine*   5
With water that is Feminine,
Untill the cooler Nymph abate
His wrath, and so concorporate.
Adam till his rib was lost,
Had both Sexes thus ingrost: 10
When providence our Sire did cleave,
And out of *Adam* carved *Eve*,
Then did man 'bout Wedlock treat
To make his body up compleat:
Thus Matrimony speakes but *Thee*   15
In a grave solemnity,
For man and wife make but one right
Canonicall *Hermophrodite*.
Ravell thy body, and I finde
In every limb a double kinde.   20
Who would not thinke that Head a paire,
That breeds such faction in the haire?
One halfe so churlish in the touch,
That rather then endure so much,
I would my tender limbes apparell   25
In *Regulus* his nailed barrell:
But the other halfe so small,
And so amorous withall,
That *Cupid* thinks each haire doth grow
A string for his invis'ble Bow.   30
When I looke babies in thine eyes,
Here *Venus*, there *Adonis* lyes.

Upon an Hermophrodite *D1. MSS.: O EG27 RP142*   2 twists *P11 CV O EG27*:
twist *RP142*: twist'd *D1*   10 both] the *CV MSS.*   16 solemnity,] solemnity.
D1   17 wife] wife, *D1*   26 In] With *CV MSS.*(*–RP142*)

And though thy beauty be high noone,
Thy Orbe contains both Sun and Moone.
How many melting kisses skip   35
'Twixt thy Male and Female lip?
'Twixt thy upper brush of haire
And thy nether beards dispaire.
When thou speak'st, I would not wrong
Thy sweetnesse with a double tongue: 40
But in every single sound
A perfect Dialogue is found.
Thy breasts distinguish one another,
This the sister, that the brother.
When thou joyn'st hands, my eare still fancies   45
The Nuptiall sound, I *Iohn* take *Frances*:
Feele but the difference, soft and rough,
This a Gantlet, that a Muffe:
Had sly *Ulysses*, at the sack
Of *Troy*, brought thee his Pedlers pack,   50
And weapons too to know *Achilles*
From King *Lycomedes' Phillis*,
His plot had fail'd; this hand would feele
The Needle, that the warlike steele.
When musick doth thy pace advance,   55
Thy right legge takes thy left to dance.
Nor is 't a Galliard danc't by one,
But a mixt dance, though alone.
Thus everie heteroclite part
Changes gender, but thy heart.   60
Nay those which modesty can meane,
And dare not speake, are Epicoene;
That Gamester needs must over-come,
That can play both Tib and Tom.
  Thus did natures mintage vary,   65
  Coyning thee a *Philip and Mary*.

39 speak'st, *D5–P17*: speak'st *D1*   wrong *D5–P17 CV MSS.*: wrong, *D1*
39–41 I . . . But] (I . . . But) *CV O*   52 *Lycomedes' CV O* (a.c.): *Nicomedes D1*
61 modesty *P2–P10 P13–P14 CV MSS.*: modestly *P11 P15–P17*: modest *D1*

The Authour to his Hermophrodite, *made after* M. Randolphs *death, yet inserted into his Poems*

PROBLEME of Sexes; must thou likewise bee
    As disputable in thy Pedigree?
Thou Twins-in-one, in whom Dame Nature tries
To throw lesse then Aumes-ace upon two dyes;
Wer't thou serv'd up two in one dish, the rather   5
To split thy Sire into a double father?
True, the worlds scales are even: what the maine
In one place gets, another quits againe.
Nature lost one by thee, and therefore must
Slice me in two, to keep her number just: 10
Plurality of livings is thy state,
And therefore mine must be impropriate.
For since the child is mine, and yet the claime
Is intercepted by anothers name,
Never did steeple carry double truer,   15
His is the Donative, and mine the Cure.
Then say my Muse (and without more dispute)
Who 'tis that fame doth superinstitute.
The *Theban* Wittoll when he once descries,
Jove is his rivall, falls to Sacrifice: 20
That name hath tipt his hornes: see on his knees
A health to Hans-en-Kelder *Hercules.*
Nay sublunary Cuckolds are content
To entertaine their Fate with complement;
And shall not he be proud whom *Randolph* daignes   25
To quarter with his Muse both armes and braines?
Gramercy Gossip ! I rejoyce to see
Shee'th got a leap of such a Barbarie.
Talke not of hornes, hornes are the Poets crest:
For since the Muses left their former nest,   30

The Authour to his Hermophrodite *D1. MSS.: O EG27 H17 RP142*   Title]
Authour to his CV O EG27: Authors D1

To found a Nunnerie in *Randolphs* quill,
Cuckold *Parnassus* is a forked hill.
   But stay I've wak't his dust, his Marble stirres,
And brings the wormes for his Compurgators.
Can Ghost have naturall Sons? say *Ogg*, is't meet   35
Pennance bear date after the winding sheet?
Were it a *Phoenix* (as the double kind
May seem to prove, being there's two combin'd)
I would disclaime my right: and that it were
The lawfull Issue of his ashes, sweare.   40
But was he dead? Did not his soule translate
Her selfe into a shop of lesser rate?
Or breake up house like an expensive Lord
That gives his purse a sob, and lives at board?
Let old *Pythagoras* but play the pimp,   45
And still there's hopes 'tmay prove his bastard imp.
But I'me prophane: For grant the world had one
With whom he might contract an union,
They two were one: yet like an Eagle spread,
I' th body joyn'd, but parted in the head.   50
   For you my brat that pose the porph'ry Chaire,
Pope *Iohn* or *Ioane*, or whatsoe're you are,
You are a Nephew. Grieve not at your state,
For all the world is illegitimate.
Man cannot get a man unlesse the sun   55
Club to the act of Generation;
The sun and man get man, thus *Tom* and I
Are the joynt-fathers of my Poetry.
For since (blest shade) thy Verse is Male, but mine
O' th' weaker Sex, a Fancy Fœminine;   60
Wee'l part the child, and yet commit no slaughter,
So shall it be thy Son, and yet my Daughter.

39 I *P11 CV MSS.* (–*RP142*): It *D1*   59 thy *CV MSS.*: this *D1*

Upon Phillis *walking in a morning before Sun-rising*

THE sluggish morne, as yet undrest,
  My *Phillis* brake from out her East;
As if shee'd made a match to runne
With *Venus* Usher to the sunne.
The trees like yeomen of her guard,   5
Serving more for pomp then ward,
Rank't on each side with loyall duty,
Weave branches to inclose her beauty.
The Plants whose luxurie was lopt,
Or age with crutches underpropt;   10
Whose wooden carkases were grown
To be but coffins of their owne;
Revive, and at her generall dole
Each receives his antient soule.
The winged Choristers began   15
To chirp their Matins: and the Fan
Of whistling winds like Organs plai'd,
Untill their Voluntaries made
The wakened earth in Odours rise
To be her morning Sacrifice.   20
The flowers call'd out of their beds,
Start, and raise up their drowsie heads:
And he that for their colour seekes,
May finde it vaulting in her cheekes,
Where roses mix: no Civill War   25
Betweeen her *Yorke* and *Lancaster*.
The Mary-gold whose Courtiers face
Eccho's the sunne, and doth unlace
Her at his rise, at his full stop
Packs and shuts up her gaudy shop,   30

Upon Phillis *D1. MSS.:* O *EG27*   5 her] the *CV EG27*   6 Serving more]
Serving her more *CV EG27*   8 Weave] Weav'd *CV MSS.*   11 were *CV MSS.:*
are *D1*   24 finde] see *CV MSS.*   in] to *CV O*

Mistakes her cue, and doth display.
Thus *Phillis* antidates the day.
  These miracles had cramp't the sunne,
Who thinking that his Kingdom's wonne,
Powders with light his frizled locks,   35
To see what Saint his lustre mocks.
The trembling leaves through which he plai'd,
Dapling the walke with light and shade,
Like Lattice-windowes, give the spye
Room but to peep with halfe an eye;   40
Least her full Orb his sight should dim,
And bid us all good-night in him,
Till she would spend a gentle ray
To force us a new fashion'd day.
But what religious Paulsie's this   45
Which makes the boughs divest their bliss?
And that they might her foot-steps strawe,
Drop their leaves with shivering awe.
Phillis perceiv'd, and (least her stay
Should wed October unto May;   50
And as her beauty caus'd a Spring,
Devotion might an Autumne bring)
With-drew her beames, yet made no night,
But left the Sun her Curate-light.

Upon a Miser *that made a great Feast,*
and the next day dyed for griefe

NOR 'scapes he so: our dinner was so good,
  My liquorish Muse cannot but chew the cood:
And what delight shee tooke i' th' invitation,
Strives to tast o're again in this relation.

---

34 thinking] fearing *CV MSS.*   42 bid *P13–P17 CV MSS.*: bids *D1*
43 would] should *CV EG27 O* (b.c.)   49 perceiv'd *CV MSS.*: perceives *D1*
Upon a Miser *D1. MSS.: O H18*

After a tedious Grace in *Hopkins* rithme,   5
Not for devotion, but to take up time,
March't the train'd-band of dishes usher'd there,
To shew their postures, and then *As they were.*
For he invites no teeth, perchance the eye
Hee will afford the Lovers gluttony;   10
Thus is the Feast a muster, not a fight;
Our weapons not for service, but for sight.
    But are we Tantaliz'd? is all this meat
Cook'd by a Limner for to view, not eat?
Th' Astrologers keep such *Houses* when they sup   15
On joynts of *Taurus*, or their heavenly Tup.
Whatever feasts he made are sum'd up here,
His table vyes not standing with his cheare.
His Churchings, Christ'nings, in this Meale are all,
And not transcrib'd, but i' th' Originall.   20
Christmas is no Feast movable: for loe
The self-same dinner was ten years agoe:
'Twill be immortall if it longer stay,
The Gods will eat it for *Ambrosia.*
    But stay a while; unlesse my whinyard faile,   25
Or is inchanted, I 'le cut of th' intaile.
Saint George for England then: have at the mutton,
When the first cut calls me bloud-thirsty glutton:
Stout *Ajax* with his anger-quodl'd braine
Killing a sheep thought *Agamemnon* slaine: 30
The fiction 's now prov'd true; wounding his roast,
I lamentably butcher up mine hoast.
Such sympathie is with his meat, my weapon
Makes him an Eunuch, when it carves his Capon.
Cut a Goose-legge, and the poore soule for moane   35
Turnes Creeple too, and after stands on one.
    Have you not heard th' abominable sport
A *Lancaster* grand Jurie will report?

The souldier with his Morglay watch't the Mill,
The Cats they came to feast, when lustie *Will*   40
Whips of great Pusses leg, which by some charme
Proves the next day such an old womans arme:
'Tis so with him whose karkase never 'scapes,
But still we slash him in a thousand shapes.
Our serving-men like Spaniels range, to spring   45
The fowle which he hath clock't under his wing.
Should he on Widgeon, or on Woodcock feed,
It were (*Thyestes*-like) on his owne breed.
To porke he pleads a superstition due,
But not a mouth is muzled by the Jew.   50
Sawces we should have none, had he his wish,
The Oranges i' th margent of the dish
He with such Huckster's care tells o'r and o'r,
Th' *Hesperian* Dragon never watcht them more.
   But being eaten now into dispaire,   55
Having nought else to doe, he falls to prayer:
As thou did'st once put on the forme of Bull,
And turn'st thy *Io* to a lovely Mull,
Defend my rump great *Iove*; grant this poor beefe
May live to comfort me in all this griefe.   60
But no *Amen* was said: See, see it comes,
Draw boyes, let Trumpets sound & strike up Drums.
See how his blood doth with the gravie swim,
And every trencher has a limb of him.
The Ven'son's now in view, our Hounds spend deeper, 65
Strange Deer, which in the Pasty hath a Keeper
Stricter then in the Park, making his guest
(As he had stoln't alive) to steale it drest:
The scent was hot; and we pursuing faster,
Then *Ovids* pack of dogs e're chas'd their Master, 70
A double prey at once we seize upon,
Actæon and his case of Venison:

46 hath] had *CV MSS.*   47 Widgeon, or on Woodcock] Woodcock, or on
Widgeon *CV MSS.*   53 He . . . o'r, *CV MSS.*: He Huckster-like so tells
them o're and o're, *P11*: He with such Hucsters tells them o're and o're, *D1*
54 watcht *D3 D5–P17 CV MSS.*: watch *D1*

Thus was he torne alive. To vex him worse,
Death serves him up now as a second coorse.
  Should we, like *Thracians*, our dead bodies eat,   75
  He would have liv'd only to save his meat.

A young Man to an old Woman Courting him

PEACE Beldam *Eve*: surcease thy suit,
  There's no temptation in such fruit.
No rotten Medlers, whil'st there be
Whole Orchards in Virginitie.
Thy stock is too much out of date   5
For tender plants t' inoculate.
A match with thee thy bridegroome fears
Would be thought Int'rest in his years,
Which when compar'd to thine, become
Odd money to thy Grandam summe.   10
Can Wedlock know so great a curse
As putting husbands out to Nurse?
How *Pond* and *Rivers* would mistake,
And cry new Almanacks for our sake!
Time sure hath wheel'd about his yeare,   15
December meeting *Ianivere*.
The Ægyptian Serpent figures time,
And stript, returnes unto his Prime:
If my affection thou would'st win,
First cast thy Hieroglyphick skin.   20
My moderne lips know not (alack)
The old Religion of thy smack.
I count that primitive embrace,
As out of fashion as thy face.
And yet so long 'tis since thy fall,   25
Thy Fornication's Classicall.

A young Man to an old Woman Courting him *D1. MSS.: O H17*   8 Int'rest]
Incest *CV MSS.*

Our sports will differ: thou must play
Leero, and I *Alphonso* way.
I'me no translator; have no veine
To turne a woman young againe: 30
Unlesse you'l grant the Tailors due,
To see the forebodies be new.
I love to weare cloathes that are flush,
Not prefacing old rags with plush:
Like Aldermen, or Monster Shreeves,   35
With Canvas Backs and Velvet Sleeves.
And just such discord there would be
Betwixt thy Skeleton and me.

   Goe study Salve and Treacle, ply
Your Tenants leg, or his sore eye;   40
Thus Matrons purchase credit, thank
Six penny-worth of Mountebank.
Or chew thy cood on some delight
Thou tastedst in thy *Eighty Eight*.
Or be but Bedrid once, and then   45
Thou'lt dream thy youthfull sinnes agen.
But if thou needs wilt be my Spouse,
First hearken, and attend my Vowes:
'When *Ætna's* fires shall undergo
'The penance of the *Alpes* in snow,   50
'When *Sol* at one blast of his horne
'Posts from the *Crab* to *Capricorne*,
'When th' heavens shuffle all in one,
'The Torrid with the Frozen *Zone*;
'When all these contradictions meet,   55
'Then (*Sybill*) thou and I will greet.
For all these similies do hold
In my young heat and thy dull cold;
Then if a Feaver be so good
A Pimp, as to inflame thy blood,   60

---

32 new.] new: *D1*   44 Thou tastedst in thy] That thou didst taste in *CV*
MSS. (–*H17*): Thou tookest in thy *P11*: Thou takest in thy *D1*   47 wilt *D2*
D5 P1–P17 CV O: will *D1*

Hymen shall twist thee and thy Page,
The distinct Tropicks of Mans age.
  Well (Madam Time) be ever bald,
I'le not thy Perywig be call'd:
I'le never be, 'stead of a Lover,   65
An aged Chronicles new Cover.

To M^{rs}. K. T. who askt him why hee was dumb

STAY, should I answer (Lady) then
  In vaine would be your question.
Should I be dumb, why then againe
Your asking me would be in vaine.
Silence nor speech (on neither hand)   5
Can satisfie this strange demand.
Yet since your will throwes me upon
This wished contradiction,
I'le tell you how I did become
So strangely (as you heare mee) dumb.   10
  Ask but the Chap-falne Puritan,
'Tis zeale that tongue-ties that good man:
For heat of Conscience, all men hold,
Is th' onely way to catch that cold.
How should loves zealot then forbear   15
To be your silenc'd Minister?
Nay your Religion which doth grant
A worship due to you my Saint,
Yet counts it that devotion wrong
That does it in the vulgar tongue.   20
My ruder words would give offence
To such an hallow'd excellence;
As th' English Dialect would vary
The goodnesse of an *Ave Mary.*

To M^{rs}. K. T. *D1. MSS.: O EG27 H18*

How can I speake, that twice am checkt   25
By this and that religious Sect?
Still dumb, and in your face I spie
Still cause, and still Divinitie.
As soone as blest with your salute,
My Manners taught mee to be mute: 30
For, least they cancell all the blisse
You sign'd with so divine a kisse,
The lips you seale must needs consent
Unto the tongues imprisonment.
My tongue in hold, my voice doth rise   35
(With a strange *E-la*) to my eyes;
Where it gets Baile, and in that sense
Begins a new-found Eloquence.
   Oh listen with attentive sight
To what my pratling eyes indite.   40
Or (Lady) since 'tis in your choice,
To give, or to suspend my voice,
With the same key set ope the doore
Wherewith you lockt it fast before;
Kisse once againe, and when you thus   45
Have doubly beene miraculous,
My Muse shall write with Handmaid duty
The Golden Legend of your Beauty.

He whom his dumbnesse now confines,
But meanes to speake the rest by signes.   50
               I. C.

47 Handmaid *CV MSS.:* Handmaids *D1*

A Faire Nimph scorning a Black Boy Courting her

Nymph.	Stand off, and let me take the aire,	
	Why should the smoak pursue the faire?	
Boy.	My face is smoak, thence may be guest	
	What flames within have scorch'd my brest.	
Nymph.	The flame of love I cannot view,	5
	For the dark Lanthorne of thy hue.	
Boy.	And yet this Lanthorne keeps loves Taper	
	Surer then yours, that's of white paper.	
	Whatever Midnight hath been here,	
	The Moon-shine of your face can cleare.	10
Nymph.	My Moon of an Ecclipse is 'fraid,	
	If thou should'st interpose thy shade.	
Boy.	Yet one thing (sweet-heart) I will ask,	
	Take me for a new fashion'd Mask.	
Nymph.	Done: but my bargaine shall be this,	15
	I'le throw my Maske off when I kiss.	
Boy.	Our curl'd embraces shall delight	
	To checquer limbs with black and white.	
Nymph.	Thy inke, my paper, make me guesse,	
	Our Nuptiall bed will prove a Presse;	20
	And in our sports, if any come,	
	They'l read a wanton Epigram.	
Boy.	Why should my Black thy love impaire?	
	Let the darke shop commend the ware:	
	Or if thy love from black forbeares,	25
	I'le strive to wash it of with teares.	

A Faire Nimph *D1. MSS.*: *O H35 EP25 H18 Firth EP50 A30*   5 The flame of] Thy flaming *CV MSS.* (–*EP50 A30*)   9 hath been] can be *CV MSS.*   10 face *P11 CV MSS.*: light *D1*   14 Take me for a new fashion'd Mask *CV MSS.*: Buy me for some new fashiond mask *P11*: Buy me for a new false Mask *D1*   15 Done *CV MSS.*: Yes *D1*   20 prove *P11 CV MSS.*: make *D1*   a] the *MSS.* 21 come *P11CV O*: came *D1*   24 the ware *P11 CV MSS.*: thy ware *D1*

Nymph. Spare fruitless teares, since thou must needs
       Still weare about thee mourning weeds:
       Teares can no more affection win,
       Then wash thy Æthiopian skin.   30

Smectymnuus, *or the Club-Divines*

SMECTYMNUUS? The Goblin makes me start:
I' th' Name of Rabbi *Abraham*, what art?
Syriac? or *Arabick?* or *Welsh?* what skilt?
Ap all the Bricklayers that *Babell* built.
Some Conjurer translate, and let me know it: 5
Till then 'tis fit for a West-Saxon Poet.
But doe the Brother-hood then play their prizes,
Like Mummers in Religion with disguises?
Out-brave us with a name in Rank and File,
A Name which if 'twere train'd would spread a mile?   10
The Saints Monopolie, the zealous Cluster,
Which like a Porcupine presents a Muster,
And shoots his quills at Bishops and their Sees,
A devout litter of young *Maccabees.*
Thus Jack-of-all-trades hath distinctly showne   15
The twelve Apostles in a Cherry-stone.
Thus Faction's All-a-Mode in Treasons fashion;
Now we have Heresie by Complication.
Like to *Don Quixots* Rosary of Slaves
Strung on a chaine; A Murnivall of Knaves   20
Packt in a Trick; like Gypsies when they ride,
Or like Colleagues which sit all of a side:
So the vaine Satyrists stand all a row,
As hollow teeth upon a Lute-string show.
Th' *Italian* Monster pregnant with his Brother,   25
Natures *Dyæresis*, halfe one another,

Smectymnuus, or the Club-Divines *D1. MSS.: H493 B50 O H35 RP142 HE70 EG27 H18*   15 Jack-of-all-trades] Jack-of-all-trades, *D1*   distinctly *CV MSS.:* devoutly *D1*   16 in *CV MSS.* (–*EG27*): on *D1*   22 Colleagues] the College *CV MSS.*   24 hollow] hallow *D1*

He, with his little Sides-man *Lazarus*,
Must both give way unto *Smectymnuus*.
Next *Sturbridge-Faire* is *Smec's*; for loe his side
Into a five fold *Lazar's* multipli'd.   30
Under each arme there's tuckt a double Gyssard,
Five faces lurke under one single vizzard.
The Whore of *Babylon* left these brats behind,
Heires of Confusion by *Gavell-kind*.
I think *Pythagoras's* soule is rambl'd hither,   35
With all her change of Rayment on together:
Smec is her generall Wardrobe, shee'l not dare
To thinke of him as of a thorough-fare;
He stops the Gossopping Dame; alone he is
The Purlew of a *Metempsuchosis*.   40
Like a Scotch Marke, where the more modest sense
Checks the loud phrase, & shrinks to thirteen pence:
Like to an *Ignis fatuus*, whose flame
Though sometimes tripartite, joynes in the same:
Like to nine Taylors, who if rightly spell'd   45
Into one man, are monosyllabled.
Short-handed zeale in one hath cramped many,
Like to the Decalogue in a single penny.
   See, see, how close the Curs hunt under a sheet,
As if they spent in Quire, and scan'd their feet;   50
One Cure and five Incumbents leap a Truss,
The title sure must be litigious.
The *Sadduces* would raise a question,
Who must be *Smec* at th' Resurrection.
Who cook'd them up together were to blame,   55
Had they but wyre-drawne and spun out their name,
'Twould make another Prentises Petition
Against the Bishops and their Superstition.
   Robson and *French* (that count from five to five,
As farre as nature fingers did contrive,   60

---

29 *Sturbridge D3–P17 CV MSS.*: Strubridge *D1*   36 her *CV MSS.*: the *D1*
45 spell'd] spell'd, *D1*   55 cook'd] coop'd *P5–P17 CV H18*   56 their]
the *CV MSS.* (–*H35*)

Shee saw they would be Sessers; that 's the cause
Shee cleft their hoof into so many clawes)
May tire their Carret-bunch, yet ne're agree
To rate *Smectymnuus* for Polemonie.

   Caligula, whose pride was Mankinds Baile,   65
As who disdain'd to murder by retaile,
Wishing the world had but one generall Neck,
His glutton blade might have found game in *Smec.*
No Eccho can improve the Authour more,
Whose lungs pay use on use to halfe a score.   70
No Fellon is more letter'd, though the brand
Both superscribes his shoulder and his hand.
Some Welch-man was his Godfather; for he
Weares in his name his Genealogie.

   The Banes are askt, would but the times give way,   75
Betwixt *Smectymnuus* and *Et cætera.*
The Guests invited by a friendly Summons,
Should be the Convocation and the Commons.
The Priest to tie the Foxes tailes together,
Moseley, or *Sancta Clara,* chuse you whether.   80
See, what an off-spring every one expects !
What strange Plurality of Men and Sects !
One sayes hee'l get a Vestery; another
Is for a Synod: Bet upon the Mother.
Faith cry *St. George,* let them go to 't, and stickle,   85
Whether a Conclave, or a Conventicle.
Thus might Religions caterwaule, and spight,
Which uses to divorce, might once unite.
But their crosse fortunes interdict their trade;
The Groome is Rampant, but the Bride is Spade.   90

   My task is done; all my hee-Goats are milkt;
So many Cards i' th stock, and yet be bilkt?
I could by Letters now untwist the rable;
Whip *Smec* from Constable to Constable.

70 pay *P3–P17 CV MSS.*: payes *D1*   82 Plurality *CV MSS.* (–*H493 H18*):
pluralities *D1*   83 another] but another *CV MSS.* (–*H35 RP142*)   84 Bet]
Bets *CV MSS.* (–*RP142*)   90 is Spade *CV H35*: is splaid *H493 B50 O EG27*: be
spade *H18*: displai'd *D1*

But there I leave you to another's dressing,   95
Onely kneel downe and take your Fathers blessing.
  May the *Queen-Mother* justifie your feares,
  And stretch her Patent to your leather-eares.

The Mixt Assembly

FLEABITTEN Synod: an Assembly brew'd
    Of Clerks and Elders *ana*, like the rude
Chaos of Presbyt'ry, where Lay-men guide
With the tame Woolpack Clergie by their side.
Who askt the Banes 'twixt these discolour'd Mates?   5
A strange *Grottesco* this, the Church and States
(Most divine tick-tack) in a pye-bald crew,
To serve as table-men of divers hue.
Shee that conceiv'd an *Æthiopian* heire
By picture, when the parents both were faire,   10
At sight of you had borne a dappl'd son,
You chequering her 'magination.
Had *Jacobs* flock but seen you sit, the dams
Had brought forth speckled and ringstreaked lambs.
Like an Impropriatours Motley kind,   15
Whose Scarlet Coat is with a Cassock lin'd.
Like the Lay-thiefe in a Canonick weed,
Sure of his Clergie e're he did the deed.
Like *Royston* Crowes, who are (as I may say)
Friers of both the Orders *Black* and *Gray*.   20
So mixt they are, one knowes not whether's thicker,
A Layre of Burgesse, or a Layre of Vicar.
  Have they usurp'd what Royall *Judah* had?
And now must *Levi* too part stakes with *Gad*?
The Scepter and the Crosier are the Crutches,   25
Which if not trusted in their pious Clutches,
Will faile the Criple State. And were't not pity
But both should serve the yardwand of the City?

95 another's *CV MSS.*: another *D1*

The Mixt Assembly *D1. MSS.: EG27 H18 H35 T465*   11 son,] son. *D1*

That *Isaac* might go stroke his beard, and sit
Judge of εἰς Ἅδου and *Elegerit*.   30
Oh that they were in chalk and charcole drawne !
The Misselany Satyr, and the Fawne,
And all th' Adulteries of twisted nature
But faintly represent this ridling feature,
Whose Members being not Tallies, they'l not own   35
Their fellowes at the Resurrection.
Strange Scarlet Doctors these, they'l passe in Story
For sinners halfe refin'd in Purgatory;
Or parboyl'd Lobsters, where there joyntly rules
The fading Sables and the coming Gules.   40
The flea that *Falstaffe* damn'd, thus lewdly shewes
Tormented in the flames of *Bardolphs* Nose.
Like him that wore the Dialogue of Cloaks,
This shoulder *Iohn a Styles*, that *Iohn a Noaks*.
Like Jewes and Christians in a ship together,   45
With an old Neck-verse to distinguish either.
Like their intended Discipline to boot,
Or Whatsoe're hath neither head nor foot:
Such may these strip't-stuffe hangings seem to be,
Sacriledge matcht with Codpeece-Symony;   50
Be sick and dream a little, you may then
Phansie these Linsie-Woolsie Vestry-men.
    Forbeare good *Pembroke*, be not over-daring,
Such Company may chance to spoile thy swearing:
And these Drum-Major oaths of Bulke unruly,   55
May dwindle to a feeble *By my truly*.
Hee that the Noble *Percyes* blood inherits,
Will he strike up a *Hotspur* of the spirits?
Hee'l fright the *Obadiahs* out of tune,
With his uncircumcised *Algernoon*.   60
A name so stubborne, 'tis not to be scan'd
By him in *Gath* with the six finger'd hand.
    See, they obey the Magick of my words.
Presto; they're gone. And now the House of Lords

29 might go *CV*: soe might *MSS.* (–*H35 T465*): might *D1*

Looks like the wither'd face of an old hagg,   65
But with three teeth, like to a triple gagg.
   A Jig, a Jig: And in this Antick dance
Fielding and doxy *Marshall* first advance.
Twiss blowes the Scotch pipes, and the loving brase
Puts on the traces, and treads Cinqu-a-pace.   70
Then *Say and Seale* must his old Hamstrings supple,
And he and rumpl'd *Palmer* make a couple.
Palmer's a fruitfull girle, if hee'l unfold her,
The Midwife may finde worke about her shoulder.
Kimbolton, that rebellious *Boanerges*,   75
Must be content to saddle Doctor *Burges*.
If *Burges* get a clap, 'tis ne're the worse,
But the fift time of his Compurgators.
Nol Bowles is coy; good sadnesse cannot dance
But in obedience to the Ordinance.   80
Her *Wharton* wheels about till *Mumping Lidy*,
Like the full Moone, hath made his Lordship giddy.
Pym and the *Members* must their giblets levy
T' incounter Madam *Smec*, that single Bevy.
If they two truck together, 'twill not be   85
A Childbirth, but a Gaole-Deliverie.
Thus every *Gibeline* hath got his *Guelph*,
But *Selden*, hee's a Galliard by himself,
And well may be; there's more Divines in him
Then in all this their Jewish *Sanhedrim*:   90
Whose Canons in the forge shall then bear date,
When Mules their Cosin-Germanes generate.
Thus *Moses* Law is violated now,
The Ox and Asse go yok'd in the same plough.
Resign thy Coach-box *Twisse; Brook's* Preacher, he   95
Would sort the beasts with more conformity.
   Water & earth make but one Globe, a Roundhead
Is Clergy-Lay *Party-per-pale* compounded.

---

80 Ordinance.] Ordinance, *D1*   81 Her] Here *CV MSS. (–H18 T465)*   85 'twill
D3 D5 D6 P6–P17 CV MSS. (–H35): 'will *D1*

The Rebell Scot

How? Providence? and yet a Scottish crew?
    Then Madam Nature wears black patches too:
What? shall our Nation be in bondage thus
Unto a Land that truckles under us?
Ring the bells backward; I am all on fire,   5
Not all the buckets in a Countrey Quire
Shall quench my rage. A Poet should be fear'd
When angry, like a Comets flaming beard.
And where's the Stoick can his wrath appease
To see his Countrey sicke of *Pym's* disease;   10
By Scotch Invasion to be made a prey
To such Pig-wiggin *Myrmidons* as they?
But that there's charm in verse, I would not quote
The name of *Scot*, without an Antidote;
Unlesse my head were red, that I might brew   15
Invention there that might be poyson too.
Were I a drowzie Judge, whose dismall Note
Disgorgeth halters, as a Juglers throat
Doth ribbands: could I (in Sir Emp'ricks tone)
Speak Pills in phrase, and quack destruction: 20
Or roare like *Marshall*, that *Genevah*-Bull,
Hell and damnation a pulpit full:
Yet to expresse a *Scot*, to play that prize,
Not all those mouth-Granadoes can suffice.
Before a *Scot* can properly be curst,   25
I must (like *Hocus*) swallow daggers first.
    Come keen *Iambicks*, with your Badgers feet,
And Badger-like, bite till your teeth do meet.
Help ye tart Satyrists, to imp my rage,
With all the Scorpions that should whip this age.   30
Scots are like Witches; do but whet your pen,
Scratch til the blood come; they'l not hurt you then.

The Rebell Scot *D1*. *MSS.:* *H18 T465 A3 EG27 O H35 R*   2 Madam Nature]
Madam, nature *D1*   9 Stoick *CV MSS.:* Stoick? *D1*   10 disease; *CV:*
disease *D1*   11 Invasion *CV:* invasion? *D1*

Now as the Martyrs were inforc'd to take
The shapes of beasts, like hypocrites, at stake,
I'le bait my *Scot* so; yet not cheat your eyes,   35
A *Scot* within a beast is no disguise.
   No more let *Ireland* brag, her harmlesse Nation
Fosters no Venome, since the Scots Plantation:
Nor can ours feign'd Antiquitie maintaine;
Since they came in, *England* hath Wolves againe.   40
The Scot that kept the Tower, might have showne
(Within the grate of his own brest alone)
The Leopard and the Panther; and ingrost
What all those wild Collegiats had cost
The honest High-shoes, in their Termly Fees,   45
First to the salvage Lawyer, next to these.
Nature her selfe doth Scotch-men beasts confesse,
Making their Countrey such a wildernesse:
A Land that brings in question and suspense
Gods omnipresence, but that CHARLES came thence: 50
But that *Montrose* and *Crawfords* loyall Band
Atton'd their sins, and christ'ned halfe the Land.
Nor is it all the Nation hath these spots;
There is a Church, as well as *Kirk* of Scots:
As in a picture, where the squinting paint   55
Shewes Fiend on this side, and on that side Saint.
He that saw Hell in's melancholie dreame,
And in the twilight of his Fancy's theame,
Scar'd from his sinnes, repented in a fright,
Had he view'd Scotland, had turn'd Proselite.   60
A Land where one may pray with curst intent,
O may they never suffer banishment !
Had *Cain* been *Scot*, God would have chang'd his doome,
Not forc'd him wander, but confin'd him home.
Like Jewes they spread, and as Infection flie,   65
As if the Divell had Ubiquitie.

---

39 maintaine] obtain *CV MSS.* (–*H35*)   49 Land] Land, *D1*   50 thence:]
thence. *D1*   52 sins] Sin *CV MSS.* (–*H35*)   Land.] Land: *D1*   61 Land]
Land, *D1*

Hence 'tis, they live at Rovers; and defie
This or that Place, Rags of Geographie.
They're Citizens o' th World; they're all in all,
Scotland's a Nation Epidemicall.   70
And yet they ramble not to learne the Mode
How to be drest, or how to lisp abroad,
To return knowing in the Spanish shrug,
Or which of the Dutch States a double Jug
Resembles most, in Belly, or in Beard: 75
(The Card by which the Mariners are stear'd.)
No; the *Scots-Errant* fight, and fight to eat;
Their Estrich-stomacks make their swords their meat:
Nature with Scots as Tooth-drawers hath dealt,
Who use to hang their Teeth upon their Belt.   80
Yet wonder not at this their happy choice;
The Serpent's fatall still to *Paradise.*
Sure *England* hath the Hemerods, and these
On the North Posterne of the patient seize,
Like Leeches: thus they physically thirst   85
After our blood, but in the cure shall burst.
Let them not think to make us run o' th' score,
To purchase Villanage, as once before,
When an Act past, to stroake them on the head,
Call them good Subjects, buy them Ginger-bread.   90
Nor gold, nor Acts of Grace; 'tis steel must tame
The stubborn *Scot*: A Prince that would reclaime
Rebells by yeelding, doth like him (or worse)
Who sadled his own back to shame his horse.

    Was it for this you left your leaner soyle,   95
Thus to lard Israel with Ægypts spoyle?
They are the Gospels Life-guard; but for them,
The Garrison of new Jerusalem,
What would the Brethren do? the Cause! the Cause!
Sack-possets, and the Fundamentall Lawes!   100

71 not *CV MSS.*: not, *D1*   76 Mariners] Travellers *D5 D6 MSS.* (–*H35*)
84 North Posterne *D5 D6 CV MSS.* (–*H35*): North-posture *D1*   87 o' th']
ot 'h' *D1*   93 him] him, *D1*   95 left *D5 D6 P4–P17 CV*: lost *P3*: quitt
MSS.: gave *D1*

Lord ! what a goodly thing is want of shirts !
How a Scotch-stomack, and no meat, converts !
They wanted food and raiment; so they took
Religion for their Seamstresse and their Cook.
Unmask them well; their honours and estate,   105
As well as conscience, are sophisticate.
Shrive but their Titles, and their money poize,
A Laird and Twenty pence pronounc'd with noise,
When construed, but for a plaine yeoman go,
And a good sober two-pence; and well so.   110
Hence then you proud Impostors, get you gone,
You Picts in Gentry and Devotion:
You scandall to the stock of Verse ! a race
Able to bring the Gibbet in disgrace.
Hyperbolus by suffering did traduce   115
The Ostracisme, and sham'd it out of use.
The Indian that heaven did forsweare,
Because he heard the Spaniards were there,
Had he but knowne what Scots in hell had been,
He would *Erasmus*-like have hung between.   120
My Muse hath done. A Voider for the nonce !
I wrong the Devill, should I picke the bones.
That dish is his: for when the Scots decease,
Hell like their Nation feeds on Barnacles.

　　A Scot, when from the Gallow-Tree got loose,   125
　　Drops into *Styx*, and turnes a Soland-Goose.

---

101 goodly] godly *D5 P11 CV H18 A3 H35: Omit R*   108 pence *D5 D6 CV MSS.*
(*–H35*): pound *D1*   113 scandall *P1–P17 CV MSS.* (*–H35*): scandalls *D1*
race] race ! *D1*

To P. Rupert

O THAT I could but vote my selfe a Poet !
  Or had the Legislative knacke to do it !
Or, like the Doctors Militant, could get
Dub'd at adventures Verser Banneret !
Or had I *Cacus* tricke to make my Rimes   5
Their owne Antipodes, and track the times:
Faces about, saies the *Remonstrant* Spirit;
Allegeance is Malignant, Treason Merit:
Huntington-colt, that pos'd the Sage Recorder,
Might be a Sturgeon now, and passe by Order: 10
Had I but *Elsing's* guift (that splay-mouth'd Brother)
That declares one way, and yet meanes another:
Could I but write a-squint; then (Sir) long since
You had been sung, *A Great and Glorious Prince.*
I had observ'd the Language of the dayes;   15
Blasphem'd you; and then Periwigg'd the'Phrase
With Humble Service, and such other Fustian,
Bels which ring backward in this great Combustion.
I had revil'd you; and without offence,
The Literall and *Equitable Sence*   20
Would make it good: when all failes, that will do't:
Sure that distinction cleft the Devill's Foot.
This were my Dialect, would your Highnesse please
To read mee but with Hebrew Spectacles;
Interpret Counter, what is Crosse rehears'd: 25
Libells are commendations, when revers'd.
Just as an Optique Glasse contracts the sight
At one end, but when turn'd doth multiply't.
But you're enchanted, Sir; you're doubly free
From the great Guns and squibbing Poetrie: 30
Whom neither Bilbo nor Invention pierces,
Proofe even 'gainst th' Artillerie of Verses.

To P. Rupert *D1. MSS.: H35 H18 EG27 O*   28 multiply't *D2–P17 CV MSS.:*
multip'y't *D1*

Strange! that the Muses cannot wound your Maile;
If not their Art, yet let their Sex prevaile.
At that knowne Leaguer, where the *Bonny Besses*   35
Supplyed the Bow-strings with their twisted tresses,
Your spells could ne're have fenc'd you: every arrow
Had launc'd your noble breast and drunk the marrow:
For beauty, like white powder makes no noise;
And yet the silent Hypocrite destroyes.   40
Then use the Nuns of *Helicon* with pity,
Lest *Wharton* tell his Gossops of the City
That you kill women too; nay maids, and such
Their *Generall* wants *Militia* to touch.
Impotent *Essex*! is it not a shame   45
Our Commonwealth, like to a *Turkish Dame*,
Should have an *Eunuch*-Guardian? may she bee
Ravish'd by *Charles*, rather then sav'd by thee.
But why, my Muse, like a Green-sicknesse-Girle,
Feed'st thou on coales and dirt? a Gelding-Earle   50
Gives no more relish to thy Female Palat,
Then to that Asse did once the Thistle-Sallat.
Then quit the barren Theme; and all at once
Thou and thy sisters like bright *Amazons*,
Give *RUPERT* an alarum, *RUPERT!* one   55
Whose name is wit's Superfœtation,
Makes fancy, like eternitie's round wombe,
Unite all Valour; present, past, to come.
He, who the old Philosophie controules,
That voted downe plurality of soules,   60
He breaths a grand Committee; all that were
The wonders of their Age, constellate here.
And as the elder sisters, growth and sence
(Soules Paramount themselves) in man commence
But faculties of reasons Queen; no more   65
Are they to him, who was compleat before,

38 breast] breast: *D1*   42 City] City, *D1*   56 Superfœtation,] Superfœtation. *D1*   60 soules,] soules. *D1*   66 was *CV EG27 O*: were *D1*   before,]
before. *D1*

Ingredients of his vertue. Thread the Beads
Of *Cæsar's* Acts, great *Pompey's* and the Sweds:
And 'tis a bracelet fit for *Rupert's* hand,
By which that vast *Triumvirate* is spann'd.　　　70
Here, here is Palmestry; here you may read
How long the world shall live, and when't shal bleed.
Whatever man winds up, that RUPERT hath:
For nature rais'd him on the *Publike Faith*,
Pandora's Brother, to make up whose store,　　　75
The Gods were faine to run upon the score.
Such was the Painters Brieve for *Venus* face;
Item an eye from *Jane*, a lip from *Grace*.
Let *Isaac* and his Cit'z. flea off the plate
That tips their Antlets for the Calfe of State;　　　80
Let the zeale-twanging Nose, that wants a ridge,
Snuffling devoutly, drop his silver bridge:
Yes, and the Gossips spoon augment the summe,
Although poore *Caleb* lose his Christendome:
Rupert out-weighs that in his Sterling-selfe,　　　85
Which their self-want payes in commuting pelfe.
Pardon, great Sir; for that ignoble crew
Gaines, when made bankrupt, in the scales with you.
As he, who in his character of light
Stil'd it *Gods shadow*, made it farre more bright　　　90
By an Eclipse so glorious; (light is dim,
And a black nothing, when compar'd to him)
So 'tis illustrious to be *Ruperts* Foile,
And a just Trophee to be made his spoile.
I'le pin my faith on the *Diurnalls* sleeve　　　95
Hereafter, and the *Guild-Hall* Creed beleeve;
The conquests, which the Common-Councell hears
With their wide-list'ning mouths from the great Peers
That ran away in triumph: such a Foe
Can make them victors in their overthrow.　　　100

67 vertue. Thread *P9 P13–P17*: Virtues. Thread *CV*: vertue thread *D1*　　　74 on
CV MSS. (–*H18*): of *D1*　　　79 plate *P9 P11 P13–P17 CV MSS.*: Place *D1*
80 State *D6 P9 P11 P13–P17 CV MSS.*: Stace *D1*　　　86 self-want *P15–P17 CV*
MSS. (–*EG27*): selfe-wants *D1*

Where providence and valour meet in one,
Courage so poiz'd with circumspection,
That he revives the quarrell once againe
Of the Soules throne, whether in heart or braine;
And leaves it a drawn match: whose fervour can   105
Hatch him, whom Nature poach'd but Half a Man.
His Trumpet, like the Angell's at the last,
Makes the soul rise by a miraculous blast.
'Twas the Mount *Athos* carv'd in shape of man
(As't was desin'd by th' *Macedonian*)   110
Whose right hand should a populous Land containe,
The left should be a Channell to the maine:
His spirit might informe th' Amphibious figure;
Yet straight-lac'd sweats for a Dominion bigger:
The terrour of whose name can out of seven,   115
(Like *Falstaffe*'s Buckram-men) make fly eleven.
Thus some grow rich by breaking; Vipers thus
By being slaine, are made more numerous.
No wonder they'l confesse no losse of men;
For *Rupert* knocks 'em, till they gigg agen.   120
They feare the Giblets of his traine; they fear
Even his Dog, that four-legg'd *Cavalier*:
He that devoures the scraps, which *Lundsford* makes,
Whose picture feeds upon a child in stakes:
Who name but *Charles*, hee comes aloft for him,   125
But holds up his Malignant leg at *Pym*.
'Gainst whom they've severall Articles in souse;
First, that he barks against the sense o'th House:
Resolv'd Delinquent, to the Tower straight;
Either to th' Lions, or the Bishops Grate.   130
Next, for his ceremonious wag o'th taile:
But there the Sisterhood will be his Baile,
At least the Countesse will, *Lust*'s *Amsterdam*,
That lets in all religious of the game.

---

119 confesse *D3–P17 CV MSS.*: confesse, *D1*   120 'em] them *P16–P17 MSS.*
128 House:] House. *D1*   134 religious] Religions *D3 P9 P11–P17 CV MSS.*
(–*EG27*)

Thirdly, he smells Intelligence, that's better, 135
And cheaper too, then *Pym*'s from his owne Letter:
Who's doubly pai'd (fortune or we the blinder?)
For making plots, and then for Fox the Finder.
Lastly, he is a Devill without doubt:
For when he would lie downe, he wheels about, 140
Makes circles, and is couchant in a ring;
And therefore score up one for conjuring.
What canst thou say, thou wretch? O Quarter, quarter!
I'me but an Instrument, a meer Sir *Arthur*.
If I must hang, ô let not our fates varie, 145
Whose office 'tis alike to fetch and carry.
No hopes of a reprieve, the mutinous stir
That strung the Jesuite, will dispatch a cur.
Were I a Devill as the Rabble feares,
I see the House would try me by my Peeres. 150
There *Jowler*, there! ah *Jowler*! st! 'tis nought
Whate're the Accusers cry, they're at a fault;
And *Glyn* and *Maynard* have no more to say,
Then when the glorious *Strafford* stood at Bay.

Thus Labells but annex'd to him we see, 155
Enjoy a copyhold of Victorie.
S. *Peters* shadow heal'd; *Ruperts* is such,
'Twould find S. *Peters* worke, yet wound as much.
He gags their guns, defeats their dire intent,
The Cannons doe but lisp and complement. 160
Sure *Iove* descended in a leaden shower
To get this *Perseus*: hence the fatall power
Of shot is strangled: bullets thus allied,
Feare to commit an act of Parricide.
Go on brave Prince, and make the world confesse 165
Thou art the greater world, and that the lesse.
Scatter th' accumulative King; untruss
That five-fold fiend, the States *SMECTYMNUUS*;

139 doubt:] doubt; *D1*   140 about,] about; *D1*   144 Sir *CV MSS.*: S. *D1*
149 Rabble *CV MSS.* (–*H35*): Rebell *D1*   152 Whate're] Which *MSS.*
165 confesse] confesse, *D1*

Who place Religion in their Velam-ears;
As in their Phylacters the Jewes did theirs.   170
England's a Paradise, (and a modest Word)
Since guarded by a Cherub's flaming Sword.
Your name can scare an Athiest to his prayers;
And cure the Chin-cough better then the bears.
Old *Sybill* charmes the Tooth-ach with you: Nurse   175
Makes you still children; nay and the pond'rous curse
The Clownes salute with, is deriv'd from you;
(*Now* RUPERT *take thee, Rogue; how dost thou do?*)
In fine, the name of *Rupert* thunders so,
Kimbolton's but a rumbling Wheel-barrow.   180

On the Archbishop of Canterbury

I NEED no Muse to give my passion vent,
He brews his teares that studies to lament.
Verse chymically weeps; that pious raine
Distill'd with Art, is but the sweat o'th' braine.
Who ever sob'd in numbers? can a groane   5
Be quaver'd out by soft division?
Tis true, for common formall Elegies,
Not *Bushells* Wells can match a Poets eyes
In wanton water-works: hee'l tune his teares
From a *Geneva* Jig up to the Spheares.   10
But then he mournes at distance, weeps aloof,
Now that the Conduit head is our owne roof,
Now that the fate is publique, (we may call
It *Britaines* Vespers, *Englands* Funerall)
Who hath a Pensill to expresse the Saint,   15
But he hath eyes too, washing off the paint?
There is no learning but what teares surround
Like to *Seths* Pillars in the Deluge drown'd.

On the Archbishop of Canterbury *D1. MSS.: EG27 O*   6 by] in *CV MSS.*
11 then *CV MSS.*: when *D1*   13–14 (we . . . Funeral) *CV*: we . . . Funerall. *D1*

There is no Church, Religion is growne
From much of late, that shee's encreast to none;   20
Like an Hydropick body full of Rhewmes,
First swells into a bubble, then consumes.
The Law is dead, or cast into a trance,
And by a Law dough-bak't, an Ordinance.
The *Lyturgie*, whose doome was voted next,   25
Died as a Comment upon him the Text.
There's nothing lives, life is since he is gone,
But a Nocturnall Lucubration.
Thus you have seen deaths inventory read
In the sum totall—*Canterburie's dead.*   30
A sight would make a Pagan to baptize
Himselfe a Convert in his bleeding eyes:
Would thaw the rable, that fierce beast of ours,
(That which *Hyena*-like weeps and devoures)
Tears that flow brackish from their soules within,   35
Not to repent, but pickle up their sin.
Meane time no squallid griefe his looke defiles,
He guilds his sadder fate with noble smiles.
Thus the worlds eye with reconciled streames
Shines in his showers as if he wept his beames.   40
How could successe such villanies applaud?
The state in *Strafford* fell, the Church in *Laud*:
The twins of publike rage adjudg'd to dye,
For Treasons they should act, by Prophecy.
The facts were done before the Lawes were made,   45
The trump turn'd up after the game was plai'd.
Be dull great spirits and forbeare to climbe,
For worth is sin and eminence a crime.
     No Church-man can be innocent and high,
     'Tis height makes *Grantham* steeple stand awry.   50

32 eyes:] eyes. *D1*   33 rable,] rable *D1*   34 *Hyena*-like *D5 D6 P5–P10*
P12–P17 CV MSS.: Agena-like *D1*

A Song of Marke Anthony

WHEN as the Nightingall chanted her Vesper,
    And the wild Forrester coutch'd on the ground,
Venus invited me in th' Evening whisper,
Unto a fragrant field with Roses crown'd:
    Where she before had sent   5
    My wishes complement,
    Who to my soules content
    Plaid with me on the Green.
        Never Marke Anthony
        Dallied more wantonly   10
    With the faire Egyptian Queen.

First on her cherry cheekes I mine eyes feasted,
Thence feare of surfetting made me retire
Unto her warmer lips, which, when I tasted,
My spirits dull were made active as fire.   15
    This heate againe to calme
    Her moyst hand yeilded balme,
    While we join'd palme to palme
    As if they one had beene.
        Never Marke, &c.   20

Then in her golden hayre I my armes twined,
Shee her hands in my locks twisted againe,
As if our hayre had been fetters assigned,
Great litle Cupids loose captives to chaine.

A Song of Marke Anthony *D1A*. *MSS.*: *Ash 47 A27 EP25 RP147 H35 Ash 38*
1 Vesper *MSS.* (*–Ash 38*): Vespers *D1A*   3 whisper *MSS.* (*–Ash 38*): whispers
D1A   6 complement,] complement *D1A*   7 Who to *MSS.*: Unto *D1A*
soules *Ash 47 A27 EP25 RP147*: hearts *D1A*   content *MSS.*: content, *D1A*
13 Thence *P3–P17 CV MSS.* (*–A27 H35*): Then *D1A*   retire] retire: *D1A*
14 Unto *MSS.* (*–A27*): Next on *D1A*   warmer *P6–P10 P13–P17 CV MSS.* (*–Ash
47 A27*): warme *D1A*   lips] lip *Ash 47 EP25 RP147*   15 spirits dull *Ash 47
EP25*: duller spirits *D1A*   were made *MSS.* (*–H35*): made *D1A*   (16–24 copy-
text *EP25*)   19 they] wee *Ash 47 A27*   beene.] beene *EP25*   21 hayre *Ash
47 A27 RP147*: lockes *EP25*   twined,] twined *EP25*   22 hands *Ash 47 A27*:
hande *EP25*   locks *Ash 47 A27 RP147*: hayre *EP25*   23 our] her *Ash 47 A27*
been *Ash 47 A27*: been for *EP25*   24 Great] Sweete *Ash 47 A27*   chaine.]
chaine, *EP25*

Then we did often dart 25
Each at the others heart,
Arrowes that knew no smart;
Sweet lookes and smiles between.
  Never Marke, &c.

Wanting a glasse to pleat those amber trasses, 30
Which like a bracelet deckt richly mine arme;
Gawdier than *Juno* weares, when as she blesses
Jove with embraces more stately than warme,
  Then did she peepe in mine
  Eyes humour Chrystaline; 35
  And by reflexive shine
  I in her eye was seene.
    Never Marke, &c.

Mysticall Grammer of amorous glances,
Feeling of pulses, the Phisicke of Love, 40
Rhetoricall courtings, and Musicall Dances;
Numbring of kisses Arithmeticke prove.
  Eyes like Astronomy,
  Streight limbs Geometry,
  In her arts ingeny 45
  Our wits were sharpe and keene.
    Never Marke, &c.

25 did often *EP25 RP147*: begin to *D1A*   26 the others *EP25*: anothers *D1A*
28 lookes *Ash 47 A27 EP25 RP147*: lips *D1A*   30 those *Ash 47 A27 EP25*
RP147: her *D1A*   31 deckt richly *MSS.*: rich decked *D1A*   32 blesses
Ash 47 EP25 RP147: graces *D1A*   36 And by reflexive shine *EP25 RP147*:
I in her eyes was seen, *D1A*   37 I in her eye was seene *EP25 RP147*: As if we
one had been. *D1A*   40 pulses,] pulses *D1A*   44 limbs *Ash 47 A27*
RP147: limbe *D1A*   Geometry,] Geometry: *D1A*   45 arts *CV MSS.* (–*A27*):
hearts *D1A*   46 were *CV MSS.*: are *D1A*

The Authours Mock-Song to Marke Anthony

WHEN as the Night-raven sung Pluto's Mattins,
  And *Cerberus* cried three Amens at a houle;
When night-wandring Witches put on their pattins,
Midnight as darke as their faces are foule,
  Then did the Furies doome   5
  That my night-mare should come;
  Such a mishapen gume
  Puts downe *Su. Pomfret* cleane.
    Never did Incubus
    Touch such a filthy Sus,   10
    As was this foule Gipsie Queane.

First on her gooseberry cheekes I mine eyes blasted;
Thence feare of vomiting made me retire
Unto her blewer lips, which when I tasted,
My spirits were duller than Dun in the mire.   15
  But then her breath tooke place,
  Which went an ushers pace,
  And made way for her face;
  You may guesse what I meane.
    Never did, &c.   20

Like Snakes engendring were platted her tresses,
Or like the slimy streakes of ropy Ale;
Uglier than Envy weares, when she confesses
Her head is perewigg'd with Adders taile.

The Authours Mock-Song to Marke Anthony *D1A. MSS.: EP25 O* Title] *D5–P17:* no
title *D1A*   2 houle *D5–P8 P10 P12 MSS.:* howl *P9 P11 P13–P17 CV:* hole *D1A*
4 foule,] foule. *D1A*   6 my *MSS.:* the *D1A*   should *MSS.:* was *D1A*
7 gume *EP25:* Groom *D1A*   11 was this *MSS.:* this *D1A*   12 on]
one *D1A*   cheekes] cheek *MSS.*   14 lips] lip *MSS.*   16 then her breath
tooke] her breath did take *MSS.*   19 guesse] smell *MSS.*   21 were] are
her *MSS.*   platted *D5–P17 CV MSS.:* placed *D1A*   her] Omit *MSS.*   22 of]
in *MSS.*   24 Adders] serpents *MSS.*

But as soone as she spake,   25
I heard a harsh Mandrake:
Laugh not at my mistake,
Her head is Epicæne.
    Never did, &c.

Mysticall Magicke of conjuring wrinckles,   30
Feeling of pulses, the Palmestry of Haggs,
Scolding out belches for Rhetoricke twinckles,
With three teeth in her head like to three gaggs;
    Rainebowes about her eyes,
    And her nose weatherwise;   35
From them their Almanacke lies
Frost, Pond, and Rivers gleane.
    Never did, &c.

Square-Cap

COME hither *Apollo's* bouncing Girle,
    And in a whole *Hippocrene* of Sherry
Let's drink a round till our braines do whirle,
Tuning our pipes to make our selves merry:
A Cambridge-Lasse, *Venus*-like, borne of the froth   5
Of an old half-fill'd Jug of Barley broth,
    She, she is my Mistris, her Suiters are many,
    But shee'l have a *Square-cap* if ere she have any.

And first for the Plush-sake the *Monmouth-cap* coms,
Shaking his head like an empty bottle;   10
With his new-fangled Oath, *By Iupiters thumbs*,
That to her health hee'l begin a pottle:

28 head] face *MSS.*   32 out] foorth *MSS.*   twinckles,] twinckles; *D1A*
33 With] And *MSS.*   gaggs;] gaggs, *D1A*   36 their *O*: th' *D1A*   lies]
lies, *D1A*   37 gleane *MSS.*: cleane *D1A*

Square-Cap *D5. MSS.*: *H18 Firth*   2 whole] full *MSS.*   3 a round till] untill
MSS.   5 A] Your *MSS.*   6 an old] a *MSS.*   9 for the Plush-sake] of all
MSS.   12 to] unto *MSS.*   hee'l] hee'd *MSS.*

He tells her that after the death of his Grannam
He shall have—God knowes what *per annum*:
But still she replied, good Sir La-bee,   15
If ever I have a man, *Square-cap* for mee.

Then Calot-*Leather-cap* strongly pleads,
And faine would derive the pedigree of fashion:
The *Antipodes* weare their shoes on their heads,
And why may not he in their imitation?   20
Oh, how this foot-ball noddle would please,
If it were but well tost on *St. Thomas* his Lees.
But still she replied, &c.

Next comes the Puritan in a *wrought-Cap*,
With a long-wasted conscience towards a Sister,   25
And making a Chappell of Ease of her lap,
First he said grace, and then he kist her.
Beloved, quoth he, thou art my Text,
Then falls he to Use and Application next:
But then she replied, your Text (Sir) I'le be,   30
For then I'm sure you'l ne'r handle me.

But see where *Sattin-Cap* scouts about,
And faine would this wench and his fellowship marry,
He told her how such a man was not put out,
Because his wedding he closely did carry.   35
Hee'l purchase Induction by Simonie,
And offers her money her Incumbent to be.
But still she replied, good Sir La-bee,
If ever I have a man *Square-cap* for me.

13 Grannam] Grannam, *D5*   15 replied *P6–P10 P13–P17 CV MSS.*: replies
D5   good Sir La-bee] I pray let me bee *MSS.*   18 of] oth' *MSS.*   20 he
MSS.: we *D5*   22 St. *MSS.*: S. *D5*   23 *complete chorus CV MSS.*   24 Next]
Then *MSS.*   comes] came *MSS.*   25 a Sister] his sister *MSS.*   26 And]
he *MSS.*   making] made *MSS.*   27 First] and first *MSS.*   28 thou art] you
shall be *MSS.*   29 and weell fall to the use of application next; *MSS.*
30 Kind Sir quoth she your text I will bee *MSS.*   31 I'm] I am *MSS.*
32 scouts about] Sattin cap scouts *MSS.*   33 and *MSS.*: in *D5*   37 offers]
would giue *MSS.*   38 good *D6–P17 CV MSS.*: god *D5*

The Lawyer's a Sophister by his *round-cap*, 40
Nor in their fallacies are they divided,
The one milks the pocket, the other the tap;
And yet this wench he faine would have brided.
Come leave these thred-bare Schollers, quoth he,
And give me livery and season of thee: 45
    But peace *Iohn-a-Nokes*, and leave your Oration,
    For I never will be your Impropriation.
    I pray you therefore good Sir La-bee;
    For if ever I have a man *Square-cap* for me.

THE HUE AND CRY AFTER
S^{ir} JOHN PRESBYTER

WITH Hair in Characters, and Lugs in text;
  With a splay mouth, & a nose circumflext;
With a set Ruff of Musket bore, that wears
Like Cartrages or linen Bandileers,
Exhausted of their sulpherous Contents 5
In Pulpit fire-works, which that Bomball vents;
The *Negative* and *Covenanting* Oath,
Like two Mustachoes issuing from his mouth;
The Bush upon his chin (like a carv'd story,
In a Box knot) cut by the *Directory*: 10
Madams Confession hanging at his eare,
Wiredrawn through all the questions, *How* & *Where*,
Each circumstance so in the hearing Felt
That when his ears are cropt hee'le count them gelt;
The sweeping Cassock scar'd into a Jump, 15
A signe the *Presbyter's* worne to the stump;
The *Presbyter*, though charm'd against mischance
With the *Divine right* of an *Ordinance:*

41 divided,] divided; *D5*   42 tap;] tap, *D5*   43 yet] to *MSS.*   have] be *MSS.*

The Hue and Cry after Sir John Presbyter *H1. MS.: L22*

If you meet any that doe thus attire 'em,
Stop them, they are the tribe of Adoniram.   20
What zealous Frenzie did the *Senate* seize,
That tare the *Rotchet* to such Rags as these?
Episcopacy minc't, Reforming *Tweed*
Hath sent us *Runts*, even of Her Churches breed;
Lay-interlining *Clergie*, a Device   25
That 's nick-name to the stuff call'd *Lops* and *Lice*.
The Beast at wrong end branded, you may trace
The Devils foot-steps in his cloven Face.
A Face of severall Parishes and sorts,
Like to a Sergeant shav'd at Inns of Courts.   30
    What mean the *Elders* else, those Kirk *Dragoons*,
Made up of *Ears* and *Ruffs*, like *Duckatoons*?
That *Hierarchie* of *Handicrafts* begun?
Those new *Exchange-men* of *Religion*?
Sure they're the *Antick heads*, which plac'd without   35
The *Church* do gape and disembogue a spout;
Like them above the *Commons House*, have bin
So long *without*, now both are gotten *in*.
    Then what Imperious in the Bishop sounds,
The same the *Scotch* Executor rebounds;   40
This stating *Prelacy*, the *Classick* Rout,
That spake it often, ere it spake it out.
    So by an Abbyes Scheleton of late,
    I heard an Eccho supererogate
    Through imperfection, and the voice restore   45
    As if she had the hicop or'e and or'e.
Since they our mixt Diocesans combine
Thus to ride double in their Discipline,
That Paul's shall to the Consistory *call*
A Deane *and* Chapter *out of* Weavers-Hall,   50
Each at the Ordinance for to assist
With the five thumbs *of his* groat-changing *Fist.*

Downe Dagon Synod *with thy motley ware*,
Whilst we doe swagger for the Common-Prayer;
That Dove-like Embassie, that wings our sence   55
To Heavens gate in shape of innocence.
Pray for the Miter'd Authors, and Defie
These Demicasters *of Divinitie.*
   For where S^r. John *with* Jack *of all Trades joynes*
   His Finger's thicker then the Prelat's *Loyns.*   60

TO THE
STATE of LOVE,
OR,
The Senses Festival

I SAW a Vision yesternight
   Enough to sate a *Seekers* sight:
I wisht my self a *Shaker* there,
And her quick Pants my trembling sphear.
It was a She so glittering bright   5
You'd think her soul an *Adamite*;
A person of so rare a frame,
Her bodie might be lin'd with th' same.
Beauties chiefest Maid of Honour,
You may break Lent with looking on her.   10
   Not the fair Abbess of the skies,
   With all her Nunnery of eyes,
   Can shew me such a glorious prize.

---

60 *Loyns*] *Loyn's H1*

To the State of Love *P1. MSS.: H18 T306 L22*   2 sate *CV*: feast *MSS.*: tempt *P1*
4 Pants *CV MSS. (–L22):* pulse *P1*   8 th' same *CV MSS.*: 'same *P1*   10 You
may break *P11 CV MSS. (–H18):* You'd break a *P1*

And yet, because 'tis more renown
To make a shadow shine, she's brown;   15
A brown for which Heaven would disband
The Gallaxye, and stars be tann'd;
Brown by reflection, as her eye
Deals out the Summers livery.
Old dormant windows must confesse   20
Her beams; their glimmering spectacles,
Struck with the splendour of her face,
Do th' office of a burning-glass.
   Now where such radiant lights have shown,
   No wonder if her cheeks be grown   25
   Sun-burnt with lustre of her own.

My sight took pay, but (thank my charms)
I now empale her in mine arms,
(Loves Compasses) confining you,
Good Angels, to a Circle too.   30
Is not the Universe strait-lac't,
When I can clasp it in the Waste?
My amorous foulds about thee hurl'd,
With *Drake* I girdle in the world.
I hoop the Firmament, and make   35
This my Embrace the Zodiack.
   How would thy Center take my Sense
   When Admiration doth commense
   At the extream Circumference?

Now to the melting kiss that sips   40
The jelly'd Philtre of her lips;
So sweet, there is no tongue can phras't,
Till transubstantiate with a taste.
Inspir'd like *Mahomet* from above,
By th' billing of my heav'nly Dove,   45

19 Deals out *CV MSS.*: Dazels *P1*   30 Circle *P11 CV MSS.*: Compass *P1*
34 girdle *CV MSS.*: compass *P1*   42 phras't] prais't *P5–P10 P13–P17 CV H18*

Love prints his Signets in her smacks,
Those Ruddy drops of squeezing wax,
Which, wheresoever she imparts,
They're Privie Seals to take up hearts.
 Our Mouthes encountering at the sport,   50
 My slippery soul had quit the fort,
 But that she stopt the Salley-port.

Next to those sweets, her lips dispence
(As Twin-conserves of Eloquence)
The sweet perfume her breath affords,   55
Incorporating with her words.
No Rosary this Votress needs,
Her very syllables are beads.
No sooner 'twixt those Rubies born,
But Jewels are in Ear-rings worn.   60
With what delight her speech doth enter;
It is a kiss oth' second venter.
 And I dissolve at what I hear,
 As if another *Rosomond* were
 Couch'd in the Labyrinth of my Ear.   65

Yet that's but a preludious bliss;
Two souls pickearing in a kiss.
Embraces do but draw the Line,
'Tis storming that must take her in.
When Bodies joyn, and victory hovers   70
'Twixt the equal fluttering Lovers,
This is the game; make stakes my Dear,
Hark how the sprightly *Chanticlere*,
That Baron *Tell-clock* of the night,
Sounds *Boot-esel* to *Cupids* knight.   75
 Then have at all, the pass is got,
 For coming off, oh name it not:
 Who would not die upon the spot?

46 his *CV MSS.*: her *P1*   70 joyn *CV MSS.*: twine *P11*: whine *P1*

THE HECATOMB TO HIS MISTRESSE

BE dumb ye beggers of the rhiming trade,
Geld your loose wits, and let your Muse be splaid.
Charge not the parish with your bastard phrase
Of Balm, Elixar, both the Indias,
Of shrine, saint, sacriledge, and such as these   5
Expressions, common as your Mistresses.
Hence ye fantastick Postillers in song,
My text defeats your art, ties natures tongue,
Scorns all her tinsil'd metaphors of pelf,
Illustrated by nothing but her self.   10
As Spiders travel by their bowels spun
Into a thread, and when the race is run,
Wind up their journey in a living clew,
So is it with my Poetry and you.
From your own essence must I first untwine,   15
Then twist again each Panegyrick line.
Reach then a soaring Quill that I may write,
As with a Jacobs staff to take her height.
Suppose an Angel darting through the air,
Should there encounter a religious prayer   20
Mounting to Heaven, that Intelligence
Should for a Sunday-suit thy breath condense
Into a body. Let me crack a string
In ventring higher; were the note I sing
Above heavens *Ela*, should I then decline,   25
And with a deep-mouth'd *Gammut* sound the Line
From pole to pole, I could not reach her worth,
Nor find an Epithet to set it forth.
Mettals may blazon common beauties, she
Makes pearls and planets humble herauldy.   30

The Hecatomb to his Mistresse *P1. MSS.: L22 H18 O*   2 your ... your *CV MSS.*:
the ... the *P1*   3 with your *CV MSS.*: with the *P1*   5 sacriledge] Sacrifice
CV MSS.   6 your *CV MSS.*: their *P1*   9 her *CV MSS.*: its *P11*: his *P1*
10 her *P11 CV MSS.*: his *P1*   18 her *CV MSS.*: the *P1*   24 In ventring]
And venture *CV MSS.*   25 then decline *CV MSS.*: undecline *P1*   26 the
Line *CV*: a myne *MSS.*: agen *P1*   28 set it] shadow't *P11 CV MSS.*
30 pearls *P16–P17 CV MSS.*: pearl *P1*

As then a purer substance is defin'd
But by an heap of Negatives combin'd;
Ask what a spirit is, you'l hear them crie
It hath no matter, no mortalitie:
So can I not define how sweet, how fair,   35
Onely I say she's not as others are.
For what perfections we to others grant,
It is her sole perfection to want.
All other forms seem in respect of thee
The Almanacks mishap'd Anatomie,   40
Where *Aries* head and face, *Bull* neck and throat,
The *Scorpion* gives the secrets, knees the *Goat*:
A brief of limbs foul as those beasts, or are
Their name-sake signs in their strange character.
As the Philosophers to every Sence   45
Marry its object, yet with some dispence,
And grant them a polygamie withal,
And these their *common Sensibles* they call:
So is't with her who, stinted unto none,
Unites all Sences in each action.   50
The same beam heats and lights; to see her well
Is both to hear and feel, to taste and smell.
For can you want a palate in your eyes,
When each of hers contains a double prize,
Venus's apple? can your eyes want nose,   55
When from each cheek buds forth a fragrant Rose?
Or can your sight be deaf to such a quick
And well-tun'd face, such moving Rhetorick?
Doth not each look a flash of light'ning feel
Which spares the bodies sheath, yet melts the steel? 60
Thy soul must needs confess, or grant thy sence
Corrupted with the objects excellence.

35 define] describe *CV MSS.*   44 name-sake *CV MSS.*: name-sak'd *P1*
45 the] your *CV MSS.*   52 to taste] and taste *CV MSS.*   54 hers *P11*
P15–P17 CV MSS. (including *L22*): his *P1*   a double] the beauteous *CV MSS.*
55 *Venus*'s *CV*: *Venus* his *P1*   your *CV MSS.*: th' *P1*   56 When from] Seeing
CV MSS.   57 your *CV MSS.*: the *P1*   to such a quick *CV MSS.*: if she but
speak, *P1*   58 And *CV MSS.*: A *P1*   60 spares *P4–P17 CV MSS.* (including *L22*): spare *P1*   yet *CV MSS.*: and *P1*

Sweet Magick, which can make five sences lye
Conjur'd within the circle of an eye.
In whom, since all the Five are intermixt,   65
Oh now that *Scaliger* would prove his sixt.
Thou man of mouth, that canst not name a She
Unless all nature pay a Subsidie,
Whose language is a Tax, whose Musk-cat verse
Voids nought but flowers, for thy Muses herse   70
Fitter than *Celia's* looks, who in a trice
Canst state the long disputed Paradice,
And (what Divines hunt with so cold a sent)
Canst in her bosom find it resident.
Now come aloft, come, come and breath a vein,   75
And give some vent unto thy daring strain.
Say the Astrologer, who spells the Stars,
In that fair Alphabet reads Peace and Wars,
Mistakes his Globe, and in her brighter eye
Interprets Heavens phisiognomy.   80
Call her the Metaphysicks of her Sex,
And say she tortures wits, as *Quartans* vex
Physitians; call her the *Square Circle*, say
She is the very rule of *Algebra*.
What ere thou understand'st not, say't of her,   85
For that's the way to write her Character.
Say this and more, and when thou hop'st to raise
Thy fansie so as to inclose her praise,
Alas poor *Gotham* with thy Cookko hedge,
Hyperboles are here but sacriledge.   90
Then roll up Muse, what thou hast ravel'd out,
Some comments clear not, but increase the doubt.
She that affords poor mortals not a glance
Of knowledge, but is known by ignorance,
She that commits a rape on every sence,   95
Whose breath can countermaund a pestilence,

73 what *P11 CV MSS.* (including *L22* a.c.): with *P1*   75 come, come] come
now, *CV MSS.*   83 *Square*] squar'd *CV MSS.*   85 thou understand'st
CV MSS.: you undertake *P1*   91 roll *P11 CV MSS.*: rouse *P1* ravel'd *P11 CV*
MSS.: reveal'd *P1*

She that can strike the best invention dead,
Till bafled Poetry hangs down her head,
She, she it is that doth contain all bliss,
And makes the world but her Periphrasis.   100

Upon Sir Thomas Martin,

Who subscribed a Warrant thus: *We the Knights and Gentlemen of the Committee,* &c. when there was no Knight but himself

Hang out a flag, and gather pence! A piece
Which *Africke* never bred, nor swelling *Greece*
With stories timpany, a beast so rare
No *Lecturers* wrought cap, nor *Bartlemew* Fare
Can match him; Natures whimsey, one that out-vyes   5
Tredeskin and his ark of Novelties.
The *Gog* and *Magog* of prodigious sights,
With reverence to your eyes, Sir *Thomas Knights*.
But is this bigamy of titles due?
Are you Sir *Thomas* and Sir *Martin* too?   10
Issachar Couchant 'twixt a brace of Sirs,
Thou Knighthood in a pair of Panniers:
Thou that look'st, wrapt up in thy Warlike leather,
Like *Valentine* and *Orson* bound together.
Spurs representative! thou that art able   15
To be a *Voider* to King *Arthurs* Table;
Who in this sacrilegious mass of all,
It seems hast swallowed *Windsors* Hospital;
Pair-royal headed *Cerberus* his Cozen,
Hercules labours were a Bakers dozen,   20

Had he but trumpt on thee, whose forked neck
Might well have answered at the Font for *Smeck*.
But can a Knighthood on a Knighthood lie?
Mettal on Mettal is ill Armorie;
And yet the known *Godfrey* of *Bulloin*'s coat   25
Shines in exception to the Heraulds vote.
Great spirits move not by pedantick laws;
Their actions, though eccentrick, state the cause,
And *Priscan* bleeds with honour; *Cæsar* thus
Subscrib'd two Consuls with one *Julius*.   30
And soe this blazond Solecisme unites
Single soled Thomas to a yoake of Knights.
Tom, never oaded Squire, scarce Yeoman high,
Is *Tom* twice dipt, Knight of a double dy!
Fond man! whose fate is in his name betray'd,   35
It is the setting Sun doubles his shade.
But its no matter, for *Amphibious* he
May have a Knight hang'd, yet Sir *Tom* go free.

The Antiplatonick

FOR shame, thou everlasting Woer,
Still saying Grace and ne're fall to her!
Love that's in Contemplation plac't,
Is *Venus* drawn but to the Wast.
Unlesse your Flame confesse its Gender,   5
And your Parley cause surrender,
Y'are Salamanders of a cold desire,
That live untouch't amid the hottest fire.

31–32 And . . . Knights. *H18: Omit P1*

The Antiplatonick *P1A. MSS.: RP116 H18 RP147 L22 RP173*   2 ne're fall
P11 CV MSS.: never falling *P1A*   6 surrender,] surrender; *P1A*   8 amid]
amidst *CV MSS.*

What though she be a Dame of stone,
The Widow of *Pigmalion*; 10
As hard and un-relenting She,
As the new-crusted *Niobe*;
Or what doth more of Statue carry
A Nunne of the Platonick Quarrey?
Love melts the rigor which the rocks have bred, 15
A Flint will break upon a Feather-bed.

For shame you pretty Female Elves,
Cease for to Candy up your selves;
No more, you Sectaries of the Game,
No more of your calcining flame. 20
Women Commence by *Cupids* Dart,
As a Kings Hunting dubs a Hart.
Loves Votaries inthrall each others soul,
Till both of them live but upon Paroll.

Vertue's no more in Woman-kind 25
But the green-sicknesse of the mind.
Philosophy, their new delight,
A kind of Charcoal Appetite.
There is no Sophistry prevails,
Where all-convincing Love assails, 30
But the disputing Petticoat will Warp,
As skilfull Gamesters are to seek at Sharp.

The souldier, that man of Iron,
Whom Ribs of *Horror* all inviron,
That's strung with Wire, in stead of Veins, 35
In whose imbraces you 're in chains,
Let a Magnetick Girle appear,
Straight he turns *Cupids* Cuiraseer.
Love storms his lips, and takes the Fortresse in,
For all the Brisled Turn-pikes of his chin. 40

18 selves;] selves: *P1A* 21 Dart,] Dart; *P1A* 25 Woman-kind *P2–P17*
CV RP147 L22 RP173: Women-kind *P1A* 29 There is *P11–P17 CV MSS.*:
There's *P1A* 30 assails,] assails: *P1A* 34 inviron,] inviron; *P1A*

Since Loves Artillery then checks
The Breast-works of the firmest Sex,
Come let us in Affections Riot,
Th' are sickly pleasures keep a Diet.
Give me a Lover bold and free,   45
Not Eunuch't with Formality;
Like an Embassador that beds a Queen,
With the Nice Caution of a sword between.

How the COMMENCEMENT grows new

IT is no *Curranto*-news I undertake,
New teacher of the town I mean not to make,
No New England voyage my muse does intend,
No new fleet, no bold fleet, nor bonny fleet send:
But if you'l be pleas'd to hear out this ditty   5
Ile tell you some news as true and as Witty;
    And how the Commencement grows new.

See how the Symony-Doctours abound,
All crowding to throw away forty pound.
They'l now in their wives stammel-petticoats vaper,   10
Without any need of an Argument draper.
Beholding to none, he neither beseeches
This friend for ven'son, nor tother for Speeches.
    And so the Commencement grows new.

Every twice a day teaching Gaffer   15
Brings up his Easter book to Chaffer;
Nay some take degrees who never had steeple,
Whose means, like degrees, comes from placets of people.
They come to the fair, & at the first pluck
The Toll-man *Barnaby* strikes 'um good luck.   20
    And so the Commencement grows new.

43 let us *CV MSS.*: let's *P1A*

How the Commencement grows new *P2. MSS.: H18 O T465 RP147 C42*   5 out
CV: but *P2*   20 'um] them *MSS.*

The Country Parsons come not up
On Tuesday night in their old Colledge to sup;
Their bellyes and table books equally full,
The next Lecture dinner their notes forth to pull;   25
How bravely the *Margaret* Professor disputed,
The Homylies urg'd, and the school-men confuted.
    And so the Commencement grows new.

The Inceptor brings not his father, the clown,
To look with his mouth at his Grogoram gown;   30
With like admiration to eat roasted beef,
Which invention pos'd his beyond-Trent-beleif;
Who should he but hear our Organs once sound,
Could scarce keep his hoof from Sallingers round.
    And so the Commencement grows new.   35

The Gentleman comes not to shew us his sattin,
To look with some Judgment at him that speaks lattin,
To be angry with him that markes not his cloaths,
To Answer O Lord Sir and talke play-book oaths,
And at the next Bear-bayting (full of his sack)   40
To tell his Comrades our disciplin's slack.
    And so the Commencement grows new.

We have no Prevaricators wit,
Ay marry Sir, when have we had any yet?
Besides no serious Oxford man comes,   45
To cry down the use of Jesting and Hums.
Our ballad, beleive't, is no stranger than true,
Mun Salter is sober, and *Jack Martin* too.
    And so the Commencement grows new.

                            J. C.

---

31 roasted] Rost *MSS.*   34 hoof] hoofs *MSS.*   38 markes *T465 RP147*:
make *H18*: makes *P2*   39 play-book *P7–P17 CV MSS.*: play books *P2*
45 man *P9 P11–P17 CV T465 RP147*: men *P2*

Fuscara; or The Bee Errant

Natures Confectioner, the *Bee*,
  Whose suckets are moyst *Alchimie*,
The Still of his refining mould
Minting the Garden into Gold,
Having rifled all the fields   5
Of what dainties *Flora* yields,
Ambitious now to take Excise
Of a more fragrant Paradise,
At my *Fuscara*'s sleeve ariv'd,
Where all delicious sweets are hiv'd.   10
The ayrie Free-booter distreins
First on the Violets of her Veins,
Whose tinckture, could it be more pure,
His ravenous Kiss had made it bluer.
Here did he sit, and Essence quaff,   15
Till her coy Pulse had beat him off;
That Pulse which he that feels may know
Whether the World's long-liv'd or no.
The next he preys on is her Palm,
That Alm'ner of transpiring balm;   20
So soft, 'tis ayr but once remov'd,
Tender as 'twere a Jellie glov'd.
Here, while his canting drone-pipe scan'd
The mystick figures of her hand,
He tipples Palmestry and dines   25
On all her fortune telling lines.
He bathes in bliss, and finds no odds
Betwixt her Nectar and the Gods.
He perches now upon her wrist,
A Proper hawk for such a fist,   30
Making that flesh his bill of fare
Which hungry Canibals would spare;

Fuscara; or The Bee Errant *P2. MSS.: RP116 O*   25 dines *P11 CV MSS.:* dives *P2*
26 lines *P11 CV MSS.:* lives *P2*   28 her] this *CV O*

Where Lillyes in a lovely brown
Inoculate Carnation.
He *Argent* skin with *or* so stream'd   35
As if the milky way were cream'd.
From hence he to the wood-bine bends
That quivers at her fingers ends,
That runs division on the tree
Like a thick branching pedegree.   40
So 'tis not her the Bee devours,
It is a pretty maze of flowers;
It is the rose that bleeds when he
Nibbles his nice Phlebotomy.
About her finger he doth cling   45
I' th' fashion of a wedding ring,
And bids his Comrades of the swarm
Crawl as a brace-let 'bout her arm.
Thus when the hovering Publican
Had suck'd the Toll of all her span,   50
Tuning his draughts with drowsy hums,
As Danes carowse by Kettle-drums,
It was decreed, that posy glean'd,
The small familiar should be wean'd.
At this the Errants Courage quails,   55
Yet ayded by his native sayls
The bold *Columbus* still designes
To find her undiscovered mynes.
To th' *Indies* of her arm he flyes,
Fraught both with East and Western prize;   60
Which when he had in vain assayd,
Arm'd like a dapper Lance-presade
With *Spanish* pike, he broacht a pore,
And so both made and heal'd the sore:
For as in Gummy trees there's found   65
A salve to issue at the wound,
Of this her breach the like was true,
Hence trickled out a balsom too.

35 He] Her *P9 P11–P17 CV MSS.*   48 as] like *CV O*

But oh ! what waspe was 't that could prove
Ravilliack to my *Queen of Love*?   70
The King of Bees now 's jealous grown
Lest her beams should melt his throne;
And finding that his Tribute slacks,
His Burgesses and state of wax
Turn'd to an Hospital, the Combes   75
Built rank and file, like Beads-mens rooms,
And what they bleed but tart and sowre
Matcht with my *Danaes* golden showre,
Live-Hony all, the Envyous Elfe
Stung her, cause sweeter than himself.   80
    Sweetness and she are so ally'd
    The *Bee* committed parricide.

To JULIA to expedite her promise

SINCE 'tis my Doom, Love's under-Shreive,
        Why this Repreive?
Why doth my She-Advowson flie
        Incumbency?
Panting Expectance makes us prove   5
The Anticks of benighted Love,
And withered Mates when wedlock joynes,
Th' are *Hymens* Monkeys which he ties by th' loynes,
To play (alas !) but at Rebated Foynes.

To sell thy self dost thou intend   10
        By Candle end?
And hold the contract thus in doubt,
        Life's Taper out?
Think but how soon the market failes;
Your Sex lives faster than the males;   15

70 *Ravilliack P11 CV*: Ratillias *P2*   71 now's] now *P15–P17 CV*   78 *Danaes*]
'*Danaes P2*

To Julia to expedite her promise *P6. MSS.:* RP84 *O*   1 under-Shreive,] under-
Shreive *P6*   15 males;] males, *P6*

As if to measure Age's span
The Sober *Julian* were th' Account of Man,
Whil'st You live by the fleet *Gregorian*.

Now since you bear a Date so short
 Live double for't.   20
How can thy Fortresse ever stand
 If't be not man'd?
The Seige so gaines upon the Place,
Thou'lt find the Trenches in thy Face.
Pitty thy self then, if not me, 25
And hold not out, least (like *Ostend*) thou be
Nothing but Rubbish at Deliverie.

The Candidates of *Peter*'s chair
 Must plead gray hair,
And use the Simony of a cough 30
 To help them off;
But when I woe thus old and spent,
I'le wed by Will and Testament.
No, let us love while crisp'd and curl'd,
The greatest Honours on the aged hurl'd 35
Are but gay Furlowes for another world.

Tomorrow what thou tender'st me
 Is Legacie;
Not one of all those rav'nous houres
 But thee devoures. 40
And though thou still recruited be,
Like *Pelops*, with soft Ivorie,
Though thou consume but to renew,
Yet Love, as Lord, doth claim a Herriot due.
That's the best quick thing I can find of you. 45

29 Must] must *P6* 42 Ivorie,] Ivorie; *P6*

I feel thou art consenting ripe
           By that soft gripe,
And those regealing christal spheares.
           I hold thy teares
Pledges of more distilling sweets,   50
The Bath that ushers in the sheets.
Else pious *Julia* (Angel-wise)
Moves the *Bethesda* of her trickling eyes
To cure the spittle-world of maladies.

On *Princess Elizabeth* born the Night before *New-Years Day*

Astrologers say *Venus*, the same starr,
  Is both our Hesperus and Lucifer;
The Antitype, this Venus, makes it true,
Shee shutts the old yeare and begins the new.
Her Brother with a star at noone was born,   5
Shee, like a star both of the Eve and Morne.
Count ore the stars (*Faire Queen*) in Babes, & vie
With every year a new Epiphanie.

Parting with a Freind upon the Rode

I'ME rent in 'twayne, your horses turning thus
  Transcribing mee the torne *Hippoletus.*
No Traytor suffers a more Quarterd fat
When doomed to stride from Lud to Bishopsgate.
Hither & hence at once, thy euery Sphere   5
Doth by a double Motion Enterfere,
And when his native forme inclines him East
By his first mouer hee is ravisht west.
Peace fond Philosopher thy Problems donne
No rest ith' poynt of my Reflection: 10
My Tropick whirles mee to a distant soyle
The Bullet flying makes the Gun recoyle.
Death's but a Separation though endorst
With Spade & Jauelin, wee are thus diuorst.
My soule hath taken wing, & I expresse   15
The Corps returning to my Principles.
But Death's not all, Reluctance tags the Curse
With black Despayre, aske but the aged Nurse
Shee proues salvation from a death thats mild
Hee went away iust like a Chrysome child   20
But Loue like Cacus makes mee trauell so
My feet still contradict mee as I goe.
In proofe wherof see how this foundered Rhyme
Hunts counter & Rebounds into thy Clyme.
My splay-foot Journey is both right & wrong   25
Backwards is forwards in the Hebrew tongue.
Then since my soule bends Northward thus with thee
Let thine the Counterpane goe South with mee.

Parting with a Freind *O. P11 RP84 L22*   Title] upon the Rode] on the way *P11*
1 The horses at their suddain turning, thus *P11*   2 Transcribing mee]
Transcribe my self *P11*   *Hippoletus P11*: Suffetius *O*   5 hence] thither *P11*
thy] Thus *P11*   6 Doth] Does *P11*   7 his ... him] my ... mee *P11*
8 his ... hee is] my ... I am *P11*   11 mee] mee, *O*   15 wing] Wings *P11*
I expresse] now I feele *P11*   16 The] My *P11*   my Principles] its Principle *P11*
17 tags] tugs *P11*   24 thy] your *P11*

Epitaphium *Thomae Spell* Coll.
Divi *Johannis Præsidis*

Hɪc jacet Quantillum Quanti,
    Ille, quatenus potuit mori
    Thomas Spellus:
Fuit nomen, erit Epitheton.
Posthumus sibi perennabit, idem   5
    Olim & olim.
Ille qui sibi futurus Posteri,
Ut esse poterat Majores sui,
Honestis quicquid debuit Natalibus
Mactus in sese; disputandus utrum   10
Sui magis, an ex Patrum traduce;
Quem vitae Drama Mitionem dedit;
Qui verba protulit, ut Alcedo pullos
    Omine pacis;
Quocum sepulta jacet Urbanitas,   15
Et Malaci mores tanquam Soldurii
    Commoriuntur.
Pauperum *Scipio*, & amor omnium.
Collegii Coagulum, Honorum Climax,
Scholaris, Socius, Senior, Præses,   20
In sacra Theologia Baccalaureus
Et Pastor gregis in cruce providus.
Oculos à flendo non moror amplius.
    Vixit.

Epitaphium Thomae Spell *CV.MS.:O*   Title] *Omit O*   6 &] ut *O*
21 this line is found only in *O*   22 cruce] rare *O*

POEMS PROBABLY BY CLEVELAND

FROM PRINTED TEXTS

Elegy on Edward King

WHILES Phebus shines within our Hemisphere,
There are no starres, or at least none appear.
Did not the sunne go hence, we should not know
Whether there were a night and starres, or no.
Till thou ly'dst down upon thy western bed,   5
Not one Poetick starre durst shew his head;
Athenian owls fear'd to come forth in verse,
Untill thy fall darkned the Universe.
Thy death makes Poets; Mine eyes flow for thee,
And every tear speaks a dumbe elegie.   10
Now the proud sea, grown richer then the land,
Doth strive for place, and claim the upper hand;
And yet an equall losse the sea sustains,
If it lose alwayes so much as it gains.
Yet we who had the happinesse to know   15
Thee what thou wast, (oh were it with us so !)
Enjoy thee still, and use thy precious name
As a perfume to sweeten our own fame.
And lest thy body should corrupt by death,
To Thetis we our brinish tears bequeath.   20
As night, close-mourner for the setting sunne,
Bedews her cheeks with tears when he is gone

Elegy on Edward King *J*. Title] *Elegy on Edward King*] *Another to the Memory of Mr.*
Edward King, Drown'd in the Irish Seas. P11: no title *J*   1 Whiles] Whilst *P11*
4 were] where *P11*   and] or *P11*   5 ly'dst] laydst *P11*   6 his]
its *P11*   14 so much as it] but as much as 't *P11*   17 Enjoy] T' enjoy *P11*
19–20 *Omit P11*   21 As] The *P11*

To th' other world, so we lament and weep
Thy sad untimely fall, who by the deep
Didst climbe to th' highest heav'ns; Where being crown'd 25
A King, in after-times 'twill scarce be found
Whether (thy life and death being without taint)
Thou wert Edward the Confessour, or Saint.

Epitaph on the Earl of Strafford

HERE lies Wise and Valiant Dust,
  Huddled up 'twixt Fit and Just:
STRAFFORD, who was hurried hence
'Twixt Treason and Convenience.
He spent his Time here in a Mist;   5
A *Papist*, yet a *Calvinist*.
His Prince's nearest Joy, and Grief.
He had, yet wanted all Reliefe.
The Prop and Ruine of the State;
The People's violent Love, and Hate: 10
One in extreames lov'd and abhor'd.
Riddles lie here; or in a word,
Here lies Blood; and let it lie
Speechlesse still, and never crie.

23 world] Word *P11*   25 crown'd] crown *P11*   28 Saint *P11*: the Saint *J*

Epitaph on the Earl of Strafford *D1. MSS.: EG24 EP50 H35 A2 H493 Douce RD10
EG27 H18 RP71 SP16 A37 Don HE70 RP26 R*   6 yet] and *MSS.*

The Scots Apostasie

IST come to this? what? shal the cheeks of Fame,
Stretcht with the breath of learned *Lowdons* name,
Be flag'd again? and that great piece of Sence,
As rich in Loyalty, as Eloquence,
Brought to the Test, be found a trick of State?   5
Like Chymists tinctures, prov'd adulterate?
The Devill sure such language did atchieve,
To cheat our un-fore-warned Grandam *Eve*,
As this Impostor found out, to besot
Th' experienc'd *English*, to believe a *Scot*.   10
Who reconcil'd the Covenants doubtfull Sence?
The Commons Argument, or the Cities Pence?
Or did you doubt, Persistance in one good
Would spoile the fabrick of your Brotherhood,
Projected first in such a forge of sin,   15
Was fit for the grand Devils hammering?
Or was't ambition, that this damned fact
Should tell the world you know the sins you act?
The infamie this super-treason brings,
Blasts more then murders of *Your sixty Kings*.   20
A crime so black, as being advis'dly done,
Those hold with this no competition.
Kings onely suffer'd then, in this doth lie
Th' Assasination of *Monarchie*.
Beyond this sin no one step can be trod,   25
If not t' attempt deposing of your *God*.
Oh were you so ingag'd, that we might see
Heavens angry lightning 'bout your eares to flee,
Till you were shrivel'd to dust; and your cold Land
Parcht to a drought, beyond the *Lybian* sand!   30
But 'tis reserv'd; and till heaven plague you worse,
Be Objects of an Epidemick curse.

The Scots Apostasie *D5*   20 Blasts] Blast's *S*   29 to] into *S*

First, may your *Brethren*, to whose viler ends
Your pow'r hath bawded, cease to count you friends;
And prompted by the dictate of their reason,   35
Reproach the Traytors, though they hug the treason.
And may their Jealousies increase and breed,
Till they confine your steps beyond the *Tweed*.
In forraigne Nations may your loath'd name be
A stigmatizing brand of Infamie;   40
Till forc'd by generall hate, you cease to rome
The world, and for a plague go live at home:
Till you resume your poverty, and be
Reduc'd to beg, where none can be so free
To grant; and may your scabbie Land be all   45
Translated to a generall Hospitall.
Let not the Sun afford one gentle Ray,
To give you comfort of a Summers day.
But, as a Guerdon for your traiterous War,
Live cherisht onely by the Northern Star.   50
No Stranger deign to visit your rude Coast,
And be to all, but banisht Men, as lost.
And *such*, in height'ning of th'infliction due,
Let provok'd Princes send them all to you.
Your State a Chaos be, where not the Law,   55
But Power, your Lives and Liberties may awe.
No Subject 'mongst you keep a quiet brest,
But each man strive through blood to be the best;
Till, for those miseries on us you've brought,
By your own sword our just revenge be wrought.   60
To summe up all——let your *Religion* be,
As your *Allegiance*, mask'd hypocrisie:
Untill, when CHARLES shall be compos'd in dust,
Perfum'd with Epithetes of GOOD and *JUST*;
HE sav'd; incensed Heaven may have forgot   65
T'afford one act of mercy to a *Scot*;
 Unlesse that *Scot* deny himselfe, and do
 (What's easier farre) renounce his *Nation* too.

67-68 *Omit* S

The General Eclipse

LADIES that guild the glittering Noon,
 And by Reflection mend his Ray,
Whose Beauty makes the sprightly Sun
To dance, as upon Easter-day;
  What are you now the Queen's away?   5

Courageous Eagles, who have whet
Your Eyes upon Majestick Light,
And thence deriv'd such Martial heat,
That still your Looks maintain the Fight;
  What are you since the King's Goodnight?   10

Cavalier-buds, whom Nature teems,
As a Reserve for *England*'s Throne,
Spirits whose double edge redeems
The last Age, and adorns your own;
  What are you now the Prince is gone?   15

As an obstructed Fountain's head
Cuts the Intail off from the Streams,
And Brooks are disinherited;
Honour and Beauty are mere Dreams,
  Since *Charles* and *Mary* lost their Beams.   20

Criminal Valors! who commit
Your Gallantry, whose *Pæan* brings
A Psalm of Mercy after it;
In this sad Solstice of the King's,
  Your Victory hath mew'd her wings.   25

See how your Souldier wears his Cage
Of Iron, like the Captive Turk,
And as the Guerdon of his Rage!
See how your glimmering Peers do lurk,
  Or at the best work Journey-work!   30

The General Eclipse *CV. AD and MS. Ash 78*   3 Beauty] lustre *AD Ash 78*
19 mere] but *AD Ash 78*

Thus 'tis a General Eclipse,
And the whole World is al-a-mort;
Only the House of Commons trips
The Stage in a Triumphant sort,
    Now e'n *John Lilburn* take 'em for't.   35

FROM MANUSCRIPTS

Mr Cleauelands reply from Belvoir to the 3 Newarke Poets

ALL haile to the Poeticke Gleeke,
   Bob, and Bob, and Steeuen eke.
The Puny-demy-riming Terse,
The dwarfes, the Elues, Tom Thumbs in verse;
The very Jeoffryes of the times   5
Both for reasons, and for rimes:
Who write but buttermilke and whey,
And yet for Sacke and Clarret pray.
You that are Poets of the Dale
Must take the finger first in Ale,   10
And leaue the Sacke and Clarretteeres,
To us the Belvoir-Mountaineeres.
Wee are high Comers, Birds of fame,
You are but Tonies of the game.
I will noe more Invention brew,   15
But cut the rope, and bid adieu.
For wee loose time to play at Wasters,
With 3 such greivous Poetasters.
                    J. Cleauland

Mr Cleauelands reply *EG27*.

A Translation of Lovelace's "Song"

PERJURUM caput me appellas
   Ex quo me tuum vovi
Abegit iam Aurora stellas
   Per quas jurabam quam te fovi
Quod fieri non posse novi.   5

Amavi te diu & multum
   bis tædio sex horarum
Quot formosarum damnem vultum
   Quo fructu fraudem te formarum
Os mihi tuum si sit tam charum.   10

In nitidis q[ua]mvis capillis
   multum est delicjarum
est t[ame]n pulcher & nigellus
   decorq[ue] amor, ut gazarum
multum est visceribus terrarum.   15

Per omnes formas sic vagatus
   si firmam te expectabo
Aliarum spolijs oneratus
   ovans ad te tum remeabo
Amore satur variato.   20

To his Mistress

FETCH me an Occulist for the Sunne
   And bid some Posthume blow the Moone,
For since my M^rs eyes appear'd
Those illustrious twins are blear'd.
The Chrystall Orbe that Rowls aboue   5
Doubles its heaven in my love;

A Translation of Lovelace's 'Song' *RP147*.
To his Mistress *Fol*. Title] To his Mistress] no title *Fol*.

Where each reflexion that 's espy'd
Returnes the body glorifyed.
How poore is Jove, whoe Nectar sipps,
While I drinke healthes vpon her lippes;   10
Those Ruddy grapes which, plump with blisse,
Bleede at the wine-presse of a Kisse.
Heere Virgins of the Vestall Quire
Her lip Enshrine; the immortall fire,
The lovely warmth that it bequeathes,   15
Kindling the incense which shee breathes.
To which then shall I first apply?
Hot service both in lip and eye.
And if her lookes can scortch a suter,
Tis ordiall tryall to salute her.   20

                              J: Cleveland

On the Pouder Plot

I NEEDE not call thee from thy miterd Hill
Apollo, anger will inspire my quill.
If nature should deny, rage would infuse
Virtue as mutch as could supply a muse.
Satyres run best when Classhing tearms do meet,   5
And Indignation makes them knock their feet.
To bee methodicall in Verse, & rhime
In sutch inuectiues is the highest crime.
Who Euer saw a firy passion breake
But in abruptnes? thus my pen must speak   10
Make at Each word a period, which may show
As Cornes of pouder, & then fire the row
With sharp artic'late blasts, which breathing on
Those lines, may 'nflame each hot expression.
This Annuall subiect (which now cals the nine)   15
Must be shot through with quils of porcupine.

On the Pouder Plot *L22.*

What soul is that, which thinkes hee doth but see
Laws in the graue, & bleeding maiesty,
Purple redy'd in Blood, the miter Croune
And all inferiour Eminence cast downe?   20
But he will truly sweare that dire intent
Is both deuoyd of name & president.
Poore infant Roome thought parricide a crime
Beyond Commission, but succeeding Time
(Made conuert by Experience) wisely tyd   25
The Viper with his fellow Parricide.
That sin (though highest & prodigious) is
A Veniall mischiefe if compard to this,
A sin accumulate, where you may see
All other sins not in Epitome   30
But in full Volume, not claspt up in one
But the sum totall in expansion.
The auncient Stagarite that did Controule
The transmigration of a flitting soul,
Had he now breathd would haue reuers'd his pen,   35
And sworn Cethegus & those hayr-braynd men
Had here reuiud, & in this romish trayne
Came to react their former selues agayn.
And had success applauded the designe,
We might in blood haue pledgd thee, Cateline.   40
Diuinity (that cannot yet search out
Hels proper ubi, leuing all in doubt
Whether in ayre, fire, or earth cannot tell)
Might in their vault haue found the locall Hell.
There might one Blast (had fortune giuen way)   45
Outvy'd Joues cannon & turnd night to day.
White, had become Pluto's black hall, the Throne
His footstoole, Thames had turnd to Phlegethon,
The boats to Charons vessels, which had bin
Too few for Soules then to haue Sayled in.   50
But neerer prouidence, & higher powers
Surround a King, whose Soul though cloathd like ours

In robes of mortall clay, yet doth it ly
Beyond the sphere of strongest Villany
If then heauens King of Kings doth send from thence   55
At birth a tutelar Intelligence
Unto ignobler persons, sure for him
He hath assign'd an Angell for each limb.
Then
Let not succes of smaller crimes egg on   60
The daringst spirit to attempt a Throne.
This high wrought plot untreasond, may cast down
The proudest hopes of striking at a Crowne.

Εἰς τὸ δεῖν πίνειν—Anacreon

THE fruitfull earth carouses, and
The Trees pledge her at secondhand,
The Sea drinkes of the aire, the maine
Is suckd up by the Sun againe.
The Sun is tipled by the Moone   5
And if all these bee so boone
Tell mee my noble fellow-Skinkers
Why may not wee & all turne drinkers.

News news News

NEWS news News is come from the North;
Tis chopping News & new come.
The cheife intent wherefore it was sent
To shew how the Scots do rooke 'em.

Newcastle is now fetcht over the coles;   5
The whole Town is a sacking.
The greatest medler is Lesley the Pedler
Who hath sent their goods a packing.

Εἰς τὸ δεῖν πίνειν—Anacreon *O. EG27*   8 may] should *EG27*
News news News *O.*

The organs may go whistle now;
They 'r silencd by the Rabbyes.   10
The Scots have the Pigs that play the holy Jiggs
And say they are Sow-Babyes.

The Bishoprick is cut & slasht
  in Sippets & in slices.
The men of Durham are fayn to bestir 'em   15
To hinder these Devises.

The zealous now have told al in;
Each Scot looks like a Sexton.
They would not beleeue him that wrote on his sleeue
Good Brother I am John Blakston.   20

The Sisters of the mother are cur'd
And passe this Holy Sentence:
Those men must bee sau'd, that have so behaud
Themselues on the stoole of Repentance.

No Hubbub surnamd Hue & cry

No Hubbub surnamd Hue & cry
   Wide-mouthd o yes or curious Spy
(Whether Menippus in the moone
Or Cynicks Candle-Light at Noone
Lithgow with never a Word of Creed   5
or Tom: of Odcombe for a need)
No Colledge Siquis can discover
A Gentleman such as my Lover.
Whose Gentility if 't bee scann'd
Is not deriued from his Land   10
As the Plow-men sprang your God
Triptolemus beneath a clod;

No Hubbub surnamd Hue & cry *0*.

Who practises no comely Grace
How to forget his freinds known Face,
nor after hee hath us'd his Paper   15
scornes his Declamation Draper;
eccho 's no empty courtling sound
And complements not by rebound;
Can button up that Lust of talke
Your Gallants use it'h Dialect of their Hawke;   20
Commits no Rape on his Freinds Eare
With New-Yeares Gifts names hee giues his Deare—
A Buck, a Sow, a Sorrel, a pricket;
Bets not on White Rose nor on Crickett,
Nor takes the Glasse and 's sure to nick it;   25
Can argue upon better ground
Then his Quotation—lay ten pound;
Sweares not by 's Wine because hee 's loth
To leaue a Drop of all his oath;
Rides no set stage of wordes; one story   30
Is not his Language Inventory,
Set al at once— Wit, Learning, Skill—
As if hee meant to make his will;
Nor like a superstitious Nunne
Talkes o're his Beads, ere hee hath done;   35
Nor that he may haue prase enough
Commas each sentence with a puffe,
Taking Tobacco least forsooth
The Goose of non plus come in 's mouth.

On an Alderman who married a very young wife

LET's charme some Poet from his grave
    That many Ages hath beene dead
A nuptiall ode this night must have
    To bring the Bridegroome to his bed.
        So ould so wondrous old   5
        That his chin felt the weight
        Of an Aldermans beard
        Before eighty-eight.

His thin mustachoe still decayes
    Like winters snow chilld into cares.   10
But cause hee's rich weele change our phrase
    And call his graynesse silver hayres.
        So ould &c.

A Hayre or 2 is all the tithe
    That from his bald pate you can gather   15
Give him an houre glasse or a sithe
    You'le stile him time or else Times father.
        So ould &c.

His brinish Spittle from his Jawes
    Hangs dingle dangle to his Coate   20
Like *Hocus* Pocus when hee draws
    Some yards of riband through his throat.
        So ould.

In summer time to cause a sweate
    Hee layes on 30 foulds of clothes   25
Yet all this will not get him heate
    But pus a dropping at the nose
        (So ould &c

On an Alderman who married a very young wife O.

And when hee coughs to hold his back
  A man would thinke that hee was gone.   30
His gutts within him they do crack
  Like eele-skinns dryed in the Sun
      so ould &c

But let not this his bride offend
  Ould men are twice children rightly stild   35
If hee be able to ascend
  Tis ten to one shee bears a child
      So ould so wond &c

Vpon Lee & Owens Fencing,
a Dr Roan & a Jeffray

THE Tables spread & they begin.
  The Beefe & Pheasant enter in.
The Banes are askt & thus youl know 'em:
I great Lee take thee Owen;
In a Familiar stile to say,   5
I Godfray take thee Jeffray.
Thus the Riddle weele untrusse,
The Scotch Hobby & Bucephalus.
How Davids pibble twists the Theam
And crusht Goliahs lusty Beame.   10
Thus they are shuffeled & packt,
An ordinance foyling and an Act.
How Crumwells handful prunes & blotts
Whole Legions & Herds of Scots.
The Italian monster was outvy'd   15
By the little Brother in his side
Thus 'tis prophesyed by the Wizard,
A goodly Capon & his Gizard.

Vpon Lee & Owens Fencing, a Dr Roan & a Jeffray *0.*

COMMENTARY

Upon the death of M. King (*page 1*)

J, D5–W. The transmission is uncertain. J presents a good text, and all but two of the variants in D5 (see *apparatus criticus*) can confidently be rejected. D5 probably derives independently from the archetype; P1 is a conflated text, printed from D5 but corrected against a MS. (though not one of the surviving ones). Since CV was probably set up from a printed text, an editor's choice of readings lies between J, D5, and the reconstructed hyparchetype of the MSS. As J and the MSS. nearly always agree against D5, J has been taken as copy-text. Selections from the poem, probably written from memory, are in British Museum Add. MS. 47111, pp. 25–26.

Edward King, admitted to Christ's College on the 9th of June 1626 at the age of 14, obtained a Fellowship at Christ's in 1630 and was drowned on the 10th of August 1637 while crossing to Ireland from Chester Bay. His vessel was not far from shore when it struck a rock and foundered almost immediately. Although the day was clear, and the water calm, very few escaped, and King's body was never recovered. A full account of King's life and work is in *DNB*. For discussion of this and the other elegies in J see Ruth Wallerstein, *Studies in Seventeenth Century Poetic*, Wisconsin, 1950, chap. iv, and George Williamson, *Seventeenth Century Contexts*, 1960, chap. vi.

l. 10. *Helicon.* See note on 'To P. Rupert', 41. Cleveland seems to be confusing the mountain with the fountains upon it, though he has used 'Hippocrene' correctly in 'Square-Cap', 2. This conceit is quoted in Joshua Poole's *English Parnassus*, 1657, p. 272.

l. 12. *With Xerxes* etc. See Herodotus, viii. 35, and cf. Juvenal, *Satire* x, 198 ff. and Robert Wild's *Iter Boreale*, 394–5 in *Poems on Affairs of State*, ed. George de Forest Lord, New Haven, 1963, i. 18.

l. 18. *impostum'd.* Swollen, affected with a purulent swelling or cyst in any part of the body.

l. 22. *card of lungs.* Many of the maps of this period are adorned with pictures of the four winds blowing from the four corners.

l. 27. *The famous Stagirite.* Aristotle, from his birth-place, Stagira in Macedonia.

l. 32. *Predecessours second end.* For the story that Aristotle drowned himself in Euripus because he couldn't find a reason for its 'ebb and flow seven times a day', see Browne, *Pseudodoxia Epidemica*, vii. 13 (Sayle, iii. 42–49).

ll. 33–34. *Some have affirm'd . . . and kind*. See Browne, *Pseudodoxia Epidemica*, iii. 24 (Sayle, ii. 73):

> That all Animals of the Land, are in their kind in the Sea, although received as a principle, is a tenent very questionable, and will admit of restraint.

l. 46. *One Vatican was burnt* etc. Since there is no record of the burning of the Vatican, Berdan (p. 214) assumes that it is used here as a synonym for 'Library' and conjectures that Cleveland confused the Vatican Library with the Library of Alexandria, burnt by Caesar. Perhaps Cleveland had in mind the burning of the Lateran in 1308 and 1360 and simply confused the names of the papal residences, although the Papal Library is the principal point of the allusion and there is no evidence to show that this was ever destroyed by fire. Matthew Poole borrowed this conceit for his verses on the death of Cleveland's old tutor, Richard Vines, on 7 Feb. 1656:

> You brood of *Munster*, whose prodigious Ire
> Destines all Libraries unto the Fire;
> Surcease your barbarous Rage, within one Span
> Here lies the ashes of the *Vatican*.
>
> —*Cambridge in the Seventeenth Century*, ed. J. E. B. Mayor, Cambridge, 1856, II. iii. 32.

l. 47. *tosse*. To turn over and over, as the leaves of a book.

l. 51. *rundlets*. Casks or vessels of varying capacity, little barrels.

l. 54. *floating Ilands*. Originally Delos, the mysterious and magical birthplace of Apollo. For an account of the legend see W. A. Laidlaw, *A History of Delos*, Oxford, 1933, pp. 1–5. Cf. also Strode's play, *The Floating Island* (*Complete Works*, ed. Dobell, 1907, pp. 137–240), first acted at Oxford in 1636.

Upon the Kings return from Scotland (*page 2*)

IC, CR1–4, CV, W. IC, the copy-text, has been repunctuated. Ten lines of the poem appear in RP142.

This poem marks one of the two occasions on which Cleveland contributed to the University miscellanies. IC contains poems in Latin, Greek, Hebrew, English, and Anglo-Saxon, commemorating the King's return to London after several months in Scotland. The visit accomplished very little, but the return on 25 November 1641, in Clarendon's words, 'was received with the greatest acclamations of joy that had been known upon any occasion'. To see how Cleveland could rework his material, compare the conceits here with the similar ones in the earlier poem or sketch for a poem, 'Parting with a Freind', p. 63.

l. 3. *gests*. The various stages of a journey, especially of a royal progress. Cf. Browne, *Pseudodoxia Epidemica*, ii. 2 (Sayle, i. 218):

... it takes not away this vertue of the Earth, but more distinctly sets down the gests and progress thereof, and are conceits of eminent use to salve Magnetical Phenomena's.

l. 4. *A flitting progresse* etc. Cf. 'To P. Rupert', 103–5 and note.

l. 8. *Girt both the nations with his Zodiack*. The King, the Sun of the State, has encircled the whole kingdom in the Zodiack of his 'influence'.

l. 12. *counter-stages*. Stages are the several portions into which a road is divided for coaching purposes, and the nonce-word 'counter-stages' is probably formed on analogy with 'counter-weights': the King's 'stages' in one direction are balanced by his 'counter-stages' in the other.

ll. 13–16. *thus every sphere . . . ravisht West*. The natural motion of the spheres was from west to east, but the Primum Mobile, by its own movement, moved them every day from east to west. Cf. Donne, 'Goodfriday, 1613. Riding Westward', 1–10 (*The Divine Poems*, ed. Helen Gardner, Oxford, 1952, p. 30). 'Enter-fere' means 'come into collision, or opposition, so as to affect the course of something'.

l. 19. *cries halves*. Claims a half-share in what is found by another.

l. 20. *Commendam*. A benefice or office held in the absence of a regular incumbent. When the King is in England, Scotland is 'Natures *Commendam*', and vice versa.

ll. 21–22. *So were . . . of compassion*. Cf. 'The Hecatomb to his Mistresse', 11–14.

ll. 23–30. *Two realms . . . principles*. Since Charles is the soul of England (ll. 3, 25) and Scotland, these two realms transpose his steps as Cacus did when he concealed the real movement of Hercules' cattle by dragging them into his cave by their tails. When Charles goes to Scotland, his feet seem to leave England, but he *is* England and cannot leave it; only the 'soyl' is 'banisht' from him, as a gun recoils from its bullet or a body is divorced from its soul.

l. 31. *Crab-Tropick*. The northern tropic, Cancer, standing here for Scotland.

l. 34. *Backward is forward* etc. Cf. 'To P. Rupert', 24 and note.

ll. 35–38. *Now . . . brood*. In his speech on entering the City (25 November) the King said that he had come back with a hearty affection to his people and would govern them according to the laws, maintaining the Protestant religion as it had been established in the times of Elizabeth and his father. 'This', he added, 'I will do, if need be, to the hazard of my life and all that is

l. 16. *mentall Reservation*. A qualification tacitly introduced in making a state-ment or taking an oath, when it is thought inexpedient or unnecessary to speak or dissent openly. Cf. Randolph, 'An Apologie for his false Prediction that his Aunt Lane would be deliver'd of a Sonne', 111–12 (*Poems*, ed. G. Thorn-Drury, 1929, p. 70):

> What ere I said by simple Affirmation,
> I meant the right by mentall reservation.

l. 24. *Goliab*. This spelling of Goliath, which *OED* describes as 'incorrect', is in all the editions. The 'Weavers beame' was Goliath's spear (1 Samuel xvii. 7).

l. 26. *curled locke*. One mark of the Cavalier.

l. 32. *The old halfe Serpent*. See Saintsbury, p. 44:

> 'False' is very feeble; 'Half' refers picturesquely to the delineation of the Serpent tempting Eve with a human head, being coiled below like the curves of the *&c.*

'Half' is certainly the better reading, and a confusion is easily possible between the two words in manuscript.

l. 34. *the prodigious bloody Oysters*. Two contemporary allusions to this portent support this reading of DD, CV, and the MSS.:

> I beleeue you haue hard, that my lord of Arundell eateing of oyesters, the oyesters were bluddy, and afterwards thought he sawe a man runeing at him with a drawne sword; but none ells could see what he thought he sawe.—Lady Brilliana Harley, 'To my deare Sonne Mʳ Edward Harley . . ., Pheb. [Feb.] this first, 1638 [1639]', *Letters of the Lady Brilliana Harley*, ed. Thomas Taylor Lewis, Camden Soc., lviii, 1854, pp. 25–26.

In T306, MS. Don. d. 158, EG27, and a MS. leaf in Thomason Tract E. 205. (3) (from which we quote), 'A Satyre upon the state of things this Parliament. About Decemb: 1640' also associates the vision with the reported madness of 'our greate Marshal':

> He has bene observed of late to be muddie
> He is sicke of his Oisters that whilome were bloudie.

Howard, second Earl of Arundel, was Earl Marshal of England and general of Charles's army against the Scots in 1638. At the end of 1639 Northumberland became general because of Arundel's frequent 'indispositions'. [*Calendar of State Papers, Domestic* (1639–40), ccccxxxvi. 193–4.]

l. 35. *Booker*. John Booker, an astrologer, one of the almanack-makers of the period, who predicted the deaths of Gustavus Adolphus and the Elector Palatine as the effects of a solar eclipse.

l. 36. *Fiend*. Ash36's 'friend' must be a misreading of 'fiend', which is certainly a more energetic reading than the 'signe' of D1. It is also more apt in the context, which is concerned with 'prodigious Oysters', 'halfe Serpents', and 'Cerberus'.

l. 40. *Father Garnets*. Henry Garnet, the superior of the Jesuits in England, found guilty of high treason for his complicity in the Gunpowder Plot and hanged in St. Paul's Churchyard on the 3rd of May 1606. See E. L. Taunton, *The History of the Jesuits in England, 1580–1773*, 1901. His nephew, Father Thomas Garnet, was also hanged at Tyburn on the 23rd of June 1608, for refusing the Oath of Allegiance. But the real sting of the line lies in the tail, which, as Saintsbury points out (p. 44), refers to the 'archbishops, bishops, deans and archdeacons' immediately preceding the '&c.' in the Oath; these are stigmatized as Jesuits and traitors to Church and State by the 'zealot'.

l. 44. *abdominous*. 'Untruss' in l. 43, and 'The *Trojan* Nag' in l. 45, all lose their point if we prefer the reading of D1, 'abominous'. 'Abominous' is, in any case, a rare word; *OED* does not record it at all.

l. 47. *Og the great Commissarie*. See 'The Authour to his Hermophrodite', 35. A Commissary was an officer exercising spiritual or ecclesiastical jurisdiction as the representative of the bishop in parts of his diocese.

l. 48. *Apparatour*. The Apparitor was an officer of a civil or an ecclesiastical court. Both 'Commissary' and 'Apparitor' in Cleveland's time could inspire hatred and fear.

skew-bald. A word often applied to horses, meaning 'irregularly marked with white and brown or red'; very often confused with 'piebald' meaning 'marked with black and white'. It is not certain which of these is Cleveland's meaning here.

l. 49. *Babe of Grace*. A term used by the Puritans of themselves, emphasizing that they were the children of God by the gift of Divine Grace, and used by their opponents with less reverence. Cf. 'The Character of a London-Diurnall', D1 (sig. B1ᵛ):

The greatest wonder is at *Fairefax*, how he comes to be a Babe of Grace ? . . . regenerated *ab extra*, by the zeale of the House he sate in, as Chickins are hatcht at *Grand Cairo*, by the adoption of an Oven.

l. 52. *A Yorkshire Wea-bit*. A short distance which turns out to be far longer than expected. See J. Ray, *Collection of English Proverbs*, 4th ed., 1768, p. 263.

l. 53. *Gods-diggers*. God's nails or fingers: a common oath of the period, though (Saintsbury, p. 45) more common in the corrupted form 'Ods niggers'.

l. 54. *at large*. 'Figures' in this line can mean both 'abbreviations' and 'rhetorical patterns'. The ambiguity is anticipated by a similar double meaning in 'at large', which may mean both 'at liberty' and 'in full'. The reading of CV and the MSS.—'at length'—lacks this wit and is probably a corruption, but cf. *Hudibras*, III. iii. 419–22.

l. 58. *the Synods Cataline*. Berdan is probably right (p. 220) that 'Cataline' here is the use of the particular for the general, signifying not the Roman traitor, but a general destruction.

l. 62. *&c*. The comic surprise here is quite lost in those editions which extend the ampersand to 'et caetera'.

The Kings Disguise (*page 6*)

K, D1–W. Reprinted in *The Rump*, 1662. The transmission is complicated by what are probably authorial revisions in some of the witnesses, and by conflation in the text of D4. The pamphlet K1 was published on or by 21 January 1647 (*Catalogue of the Thomason Tracts*) and had been corrected in the course of printing so that it exists in two states, represented by the British Museum copy (E. 372 (2) uncorrected) and the Harvard copy (EC 65. C5993. 647k corrected) and distinguished as K1 and K2. The British Museum copy contains corrections in manuscript which show that it was either collated against another manuscript or against both K2 and D1. D1 was published by 13 February 1647 and was not printed from K1 or K2; it must derive independently from the archetype. The archetype was later revised, and from this revised state derives the hyparchetypal ancestor of CV and O. A further stage of revision took place before this manuscript or a descendant served to check the text in D4 set up from a copy of D1. The present text is set up from D1, but incorporates the reconstructed readings of the second state of revision.

On the 27th of April 1646 the King, realizing that his cause was lost, left Oxford in secret. After wandering for eight days he gave himself up to the Scots of Southwell, near Newark, on the 5th of May. See Clarendon, *The History of the Rebellion* (Macray, iv. 192). CV's 'A Short Account of the Author's Life' says that in this poem Cleveland was a 'Vates' indeed, for

. . . upon some private Intelligence, three dayes before the King reached them [at Newark], he [Cleveland] foresaw the Pieces of Silver paying upon the Banks of *Tweed*, and that they were the price of his Sovereign's blood, and predicted the Tragical Events.

This dating cannot be true since O, which omits the couplet on the Warwick-Castle-Vote, does not represent an original version of the poem. Nevertheless, Vaughan's poem, 'The King Disguis'd Written about the same time that Mr. John Cleveland wrote his' (*Works*, ed. Martin, 2nd ed., Oxford, 1957, pp. 625–6) helps us to see why Cleveland's poem was associated in the minds of his admirers with prophecy. Vaughan's 'Thou Royal Riddle, . . . | The true white Prince, our Hieroglyphic King' (ll. 39–40), like much of Cleveland's poem, is an ironic comment on the stir caused by *The Prophecie of a White King of Brittaine Taken Out of the Library of Sir Robert Cotton . . .*, published in the spring of 1643. As interpreted in a succession of pamphlets before and after 'The Kings Disguise', it predicted the ravages of a Civil War or curfew in England when 'Ovens shall be made like Kirkes'—i.e., according to William Lilly, when churches would be turned into stables under a White King influenced by the Papists. In defeat, this King for a time would wander lost to the view of his people, after which 'it shall bee said by Brittaine (King is King,) King is no King'; he would die, but not on the battlefield. Christofer Sym's interpretation was for the 'pur-blind *Timothies* [bishops] who cannot discern Antichrist' (*The Swords Apology . . . With a further explanation of the prophecy of the White King . . .*, 1644, p. 4 with the MS. date 'Sept 19' on the Thomason copy); Lilly's was confirmation of his own inquiries 'into the Cabbinet of Heaven' (*A Prophecy of the White King: And Dreadfull Dead-man Explaned . . .*, 1644, sig. A1ᵛ with 'August 8th' in MS. on the Thomason copy) and (*A Collection of Ancient and Moderne Prophecies*, 1645) of that 'Art [astrology] knowne to few men, which doth so illustrate the faithfull and pure minde of man, that he may on a sudden be brought out of the foggs of ignorance to the light of wisedome and learning, &c.' (sig. A3ʳ). While Lilly did not profess to understand all the prophecy in 1645, he pointed out that, on the advice of Laud, Charles had spurned the purple robes customary for coronation in favour of white satin (*A Collection*, sig. E1). Cleveland's references to light and darkness, the 'wiping' of his 'purblind fancy' to see into the riddles, cyphers, Cabinets, and eclipses that puzzle 'star-ey'd Sages', are rejoinders to the fakirs who cannot see the doom inevitable in removing Charles from his Archbishop to the circle of his 'Tailors spell', who do not understand the true inner meaning of white or what it means to keep 'A Pearle within a rugged Oysters shell'.

l. 1. *so coffin'd in.* D4's reading 'so coffin'd to' suggests an incomplete revision, since the sense requires 'in'. It may be that the printers of D4 were here referring to a MS. in which 'a Tenant to' had not been properly deleted before the revision was written in.

l. 3. *pent-house.* Eyelid. Cf. *Macbeth*, I. iii. 19–20:

> Sleep shall, neither night nor day
> Hang upon his pent-house lid. . . .

l. 4. *Allegeance to winke.* D1's 'Allegeance now to winke' is probably an attempt to correct what was felt to be a metrically defective line.

l. 7. *What an usurper* etc. An elliptic construction: 'What an usurper might well do to the Prince he has deposed, i.e. put him in a cloister, and shave his beard, this Prince has done to himself.'

l. 9. *fabrick*. The word could mean either 'building' or 'person, body', and both meanings are active in this context. It appears only in D4, and is probably part of the second revision.

l. 10. *His ruines prove* etc. Cf. R. Fletcher, 'A Hue and Cry after the Reformation', 1–2 (*Ex Otio Negotium*, 1656, P13–P17, and W):

> When Temples lye like batter'd Quarrs
> Rich in their ruin'd Sepulchers. . . .

Reference to the 'dissolved' monasteries had an extra sting at a time when churches were being regularly despoiled by the Roundheads. Cf. ll. 29–32.

l. 11. *mew'd*. A term used of a hawk, when it moulted or shed its feathers; also used more generally in the sense of 'shed' or 'changed'. Cf. 'The General Eclipse', 25 and Dryden's 'Nine times the Moon had mew'd her Hornes' in his translation of Ovid's *Met.* x.

l. 14. *transcribe*. The two forms 'transmute' and 'transcribe' might be confused in manuscript, but it is more likely that 'transcribe' is a revision to make the 'ink and paper' image clearer. For further discussion of these lines see p. lxii.

ll. 17–22. *Flay . . . mould*. These lines represent a single, developing thought. The allusion in l. 18 is to the ninth of the Ten Plagues of Egypt. See Exodus x. 21–23, and cf. *Twelfth Night*, IV. ii. 44 ff.:

> Madman, thou errest: I say, there is no darkness but ignorance, in which thou art more puzzled than the Egyptians in their fog.

See also the quotation from Lilly in the headnote.

'Budge' is a kind of fur, consisting of lamb's skin, with the wool dressed outwards. Cf. Milton, *Comus*, 707; 'To those budge doctors of the Stoick Furr'.

In l. 21 the 'bodily' and the 'ghostly' Negroes refer respectively to the 'Egyptian' of l. 17, and the 'Presbyterian' whose presence is implied in l. 19.

l. 24. *Close mourner*. A near relative of the deceased. Cf. 'Elegy on Edward King', 21.

l. 25. *Tailors*. Probably the reading of the archetype, misread by the compositors of both K1 (Gaolers) and D1 (Jailors). The error is corrected in K2 and D4.

l. 26. *a rugged Oysters shell*. OED quotes (s.v. Rugged, *a*¹, 2) '1681 GREW *Musæum* I. VI. ii. 146 The Rugged-Oyster . . . is of a dull ash-colour'.

l. 29. *courser*. The regular spelling of 'coarser' in the seventeenth century.

ll. 31–32. *Or like . . . Stable*. As Berdan says, 'The case unfortunately was too common to admit of precise identification'. Edward Montagu, who became the second Earl of Manchester in 1642 (see note to 'The Mixt Assembly', 75), was ordered on the 22nd of January 1644 to 'purify' the University of Cambridge, which he did with great thoroughness. See S. R. Gardiner, *History of the Great Civil War*, 1893, i. 302. His 'Elves', the Parliamentary troops, are 'changeling', not only in the common fairy-tale sense but also in the sense of 'turncoat' or 'renegade'.

l. 38. *the self-denying Ordinance.* Passed, after a great deal of trouble, by the Commons on the 19th of December 1644 and by the Lords on 3 April 1645, this Ordinance marked the victory of Cromwell in his struggle with Manchester, who was often reluctant to prosecute the war with real ruthlessness. The Ordinance established that no one should hold a command in the army and a seat in either House at the same time.

ll. 39–42. *Angell . . . face.* The King is presented as both celestial and fallen Angel, divinely inspired in himself by the one, and yet (in his disguise) 'devil-possessed' by the other. The 'twilight' of his majesty (for his defeat was imminent and obvious) is still a state of grace, but his 'face', or outward appearance, is a denial of his divine right.

l. 44. *A Psalme of mercy.* That sung or recited on the scaffold before an execution. Cf. 'The General Eclipse', 22–23.

l. 46. *Keldar.* The womb, from the Dutch *Kelder*, a cellar. Cf. note to 'The Authour to his Hermophrodite', 22.

l. 47. *Stenographie.* Shorthand. *OED*, s.v. Stenography, 2, quotes this line as its earliest example of the figurative use.

l. 50. *That checkes his rayes.* The dominant image is that of the darkened Sun in l. 45. The Sun and the Eagle are types of the King, and in ll. 49–50 the poet asks, 'What is the magical quality of this disguise that can block the rays of light which shine forth from the person of the King, until he appears something less than himself?' 'Checkes' is probably a revision of D1's 'shrinks' because of the proximity of 'shrunke' in l. 48.

l. 51. *It is no subtile filme of tiffany ayre.* No cloud. Tiffany was a thin, transparent silk or muslin.

ll. 55–56. *No . . . slough.* This seems to be a case of corruption and correction rather than revision. The archetype probably read:

> Noe the false scabberd of a Princes tough
> And three-pil'd darknesse, like the slough. . . .

'Noe', easily misread as 'Nor', and 'Princes' survived into K1 and D1, which made independent additions to l. 56. K2 corrected l. 55 and accepted l. 56.

Both lines were corrected in the first revision, and the true readings are pre-served in CV and O, but, for some reason, the compositor of D4 followed D1 at this point.

l. 57. *Faux*. Guy Fawkes, of the Gunpowder Plot, always shown in old prints and drawings carrying a dark lantern as he enters Parliament House.

l. 59. *Hell belcht the damp* etc. The damp is the 'choke-damp', the 'slough' of l. 56, which puts out a light. The 'Warwick-Castle-Vote', passed by the Commons on 6 May 1646, unanimously rejected by the Lords on 8 May, and reaffirmed by the Commons on 11 May, was a positive command that the person of the King should be sent forthwith to Warwick Castle. For various reasons this command was not heeded by the Scots. See Clarendon, *The History of the Rebellion* (Macray, iv. 209).

ll. 61–62. *The black . . . skin*. 'If Satan should repent, and come forth in his true colours, his skin could not be blacker.'

l. 64. *Like a Lords name, writ in phantastick fetters*. The allusion is to the practice of embellishing one's signature with elaborate scroll-work, so that the letters can hardly be distinguished from the decoration.

l. 65. *Switzer*. Probably a member of the Swiss Guard. Large, imposing, Swiss mercenaries were used as special bodyguards by European kings and are still used at the Vatican. Cf. Marston, Satyre vii. *Scourge of Villainye*, 116–19, and *Hudibras*, II. iii. 1133–4:

> . . . a *Monster*, with huge *Whiskers*,
> More formidable than a *Switzer's* . . . .

l. 66. *As overgrown as*. D4 only; and probably part of the second revision.

l. 69. *properties*. A nicely balanced pun, using 'properties' in the senses of 'personal attributes' and 'articles of stage furniture or costume'.

l. 72. *the Hue and Cry*. D1 has the marginal note 'Britanicus'. A Hue and Cry after the King was issued in *Mercurius Britanicus*, no. 92, 28 July–4 August 1645. The editor and licenser, Thomas Audley, was imprisoned and his co-editor Marchamont Nedham forced to apologize. See also *Mercurius Anti-Britanicus*, 1645, the second part of which gives the facts about Audley's imprisonment in the Gate-House and soundly chastises 'Britanicus' over the whole affair; and Joseph Frank, *The Beginnings of the English Newspaper*, Cambridge, Mass., 1961, p. 99.

l. 74. *Cub of the Blatant Beast*. Spenser, *The Faerie Queene*, vi.

l. 76. *callow*. Blount's *Glossographia*, 1656, gives the meaning 'lewd or wicked' and Berdan suggests that this is the sense here. But the usual 'unfledged, without feathers' is plentifully attested by *OED*, which quotes this line under Callow, A, 3, in the figurative sense of 'inexperienced, raw'.

l. 77. *The Laplanders* etc. The myth of Lapland witches, who sold winds to sailors, was widespread and long-lasting. Cf. *Hudibras*, II. ii. 343–4 and other examples in Grey's note for these lines.

l. 80. *Shifts Poop*. 'Which' in l. 79 must refer to 'thy phrase' in l. 78. 'Shifts Poop' looks like a piece of nautical jargon for 'changes berths'; *Britanicus*'s words, when they have wafted a ship to Hell, would migrate into Satan himself and give him a belly-ache. D4's 'breeds', slightly stronger than D1's 'brings', is probably a revision.

l. 83. *The black-mouth'd Si quis*. 'Black-mouth'd' was a common expression meaning 'slanderous, calumnious'. A *Si quis* is properly a proclamation posted on the door of the parish church, asking 'if anyone' knows cause or impediment why such-and-such a candidate should not be admitted to holy orders. More generally the Latin described any notice beginning in this way. Cf. Joseph Hall, *Virgidemiarum*, II. v. 1–2 (*Collected Poems*, ed. A. Davenport, Liverpool, 1949, p. 28):

> Saw'st thou euer *Siquis* patch'd on *Pauls* Church dore,
> To seeke some vacant Vicarage before ?

Cleveland's couplet seems to mean that both the *Si quis*, which invites slander, and the *Hue and Cry*, which is a slander, condemn at one remove from the subject. 'This slandering suite' may also be referring to the disguise.

l. 88. *With Sphynxes* etc. In Greek art these usually took the form of a female head on a winged body. Cf. Henry Reynolds, 'Mythomystes', *Critical Essays of the Seventeenth Century*, ed. Spingarn, Oxford, 1908, i. 156, and Philemon Holland's translation of Plutarch's *Moralia*, 1603, 1290: 'Setting up ordinarily before the porches and gates of their temples, certaine Sphinges: meaning thereby, that all their Theologie containeth under aenigmaticall and covert words, the secrets of wisdome.' 'Draught', commonly applied to painting and drawing, was also used to mean 'representation in sculpture' and often pronounced to rhyme with 'wrought'.

l. 92. *Clarke of this Closet*. Priest in private attendance upon a monarch, a Royal Confessor.

l. 95. *The second view* etc. The revision was probably made to increase the clarity of the image. A 'pur-blind' fancy can hardly 'ripen', and the metaphor is changed to one in which a mist is cleared from before the eyes.

l. 98. *Solomon in Proverbs*. Solomon, one of the 'dusky types' or prefigurations of Christ, is seen here as a prefiguration of King Charles as well. The King is obscured by his disguise, just as Solomon was arrayed in all his Proverbs. But the word 'array'd' suggests the contrast between the state of Charles and that of 'Solomon in all his glory' (Matthew vi. 29).

ll. 101–2. *You . . . too.* Judges xv. 15.

l. 105. *Cabinet-Intruders.* See the quotation from Lilly in the headnote. A pamphlet-skirmish began on the 14th of June 1645, with the publication of Henry Parker's *The Kings Cabinet opened: or certain packets of secret Letters and Papers written in the Kings own hand and taken in his Cabinet at Nasby-Field.* This brought forth in August a number of replies: *A Satyr, Occasioned by the Author's Survey of a Scandalous Pamphlet Intituled, The King's Cabanet Opened, Mercurius Anti-Britannicus; or, Part of the King's Cabinet vindicated . . .,* and *A Key to the Kings Cabinet. A Vindication of King Charles . . . from those Aspersions in a Libell entituled The Kings Cabinet Opened* was published as late as November 1647. In the *Satyr . . .,* originally published at Oxford and reprinted in *The Rump,* i. 169–78, 'Intruders' figure prominently:

> What bold *Intruders* then are who assaile,
> To cut their Princes *Hedge* and break His *Pale!*
> . . . [*several lines omitted*] . . .
> But see a *stay'd, demure, grave Preface too:*
> Which seems to show they would not thus intrude,
> Nor presse so farre but for the Publike Good.

l. 106. *Bristoll-sense.* The 'Bristol-diamond' is a transparent rock-crystal found in the Clifton limestone near Bristol, resembling a diamond in brilliance. Thus the 'Bristoll-sense' is the suspicious nature which thinks every jewel a fake. Cf. Christopher Wase, 'Divination', *Poems on Affairs of State,* 1963, i. 58:

> Thus when two gems their emulous light display,
> That in a true, this in a glist'ring ray,
> Vulgar spectators with distracted eyes
> Gaze, or more highly the false jewel prize,
> Till, to a skilful lapidary shown
> He parts the diamond from the Bristol stone.

ll. 109–10. *Keyes . . . Cabinet.* The readings of D1 (Coffer) and D4, CV, and O (Cypher) present two quite different interpretations. Cleveland has revised 'Coffer' to 'Cypher' for the sake of witty obfuscation. The King in disguise is a 'Cypher' or hieroglyph, incomprehensible without a key. The 'brats of this expounding age' will never find such a key, despite their skill as 'Picklocks'. The 'Cabinet' of the King's disguise will yield only to the keys of St. Peter.

l. 113. *A Prince most seen is least.* Cf. *1 Henry IV,* III. ii. 46–47.

l. 116. *Advance thy morning star.* Rev. ii. 27–28.

l. 119. *Heavens Confessors are pos'd.* 'Confessors', accented on the first syllable, was the word in the early Church for those who had suffered for their faith short of martyrdom, and later for those declared by the Pope to be markedly holy men. In the Roman litany 'Omnes sancti Pontifices et Confessores' followed by 'Omnes sancti Doctores' are asked to pray for us; Confessors had not been in the Anglican litany since the time of Cranmer. Cf. Donne, *A Litanie*, xi; (*Divine Poems*, ed. Gardner, pp. 20, 83 n.). 'Pos'd' means 'puzzled'.

l. 120. *To interpret an Ecclipse* etc. The Eclipse is the disguised King, who is 'riding stages', or moving in leaps and bounds. The 'stages' are the several portions into which a road is divided for coaching or posting purposes.

l. 121. *Israel-like*. Exodus xiii. 21–22.

l. 123. *he goes to Gibeon*. See Joshua ix. 3–15. The whole story is apposite to the King's action, but see especially verse 5: 'And old shoes and clouted upon their feet, and old garments upon them; and all the bread of their provision was dry and mouldy.'

Upon an Hermophrodite (*page 12*)

D1–W. Randolph's *Poems*, 1640; Beaumont's *Poems*, 1653; *Deliciae Poeticae*, 1706; *Athenian Sport*, 1707; nine lines are quoted in Joshua Poole's *The English Parnassus*, apparently from the version in Randolph's *Poems*.

Title. OED cites examples of this spelling from 1593 to 1711, but Cleveland's Greek should have told him that the term was a compound of 'Hermes' and 'Aphrodite'.

l. 6. *water that is Feminine*. Latin *aqua*, as opposed to *Bacchus*, masculine. Cf. Sandys, *Ovid's Metamorphosis Englished*, revised edition, Oxford, 1632, pp. 102–3: '... the malignity of wine should be allayed with water. So of old they qualified the fury of *Bacchus* with the sober Nymphs.'

l. 10. *ingrost*. Included. In the seventeenth century 'engrossers' were merchants who monopolized or 'made a corner in' a commodity. Adam, the original and perfect hermaphrodite, had a monopoly of both the sexes. See Browne, *Pseudodoxia Epidemica* (Sayle, ii. 10 and iii. 5–8).

l. 26. *In Regulus his nailed barrell*. The earliest reference to this probably untrue version of Regulus' death by torture at the hands of the Carthaginians is found in Seneca, *De Prov.*, 3. See also *Whitney's 'Choice of Emblemes'*, ed. Henry Green, 1866, p. 114, and 'Regulus's Death by Carthage two Ways', in *Poems on Affairs of State*, ii, 1703, p. 265.

l. 31. *When I looke babies in thine eyes*. This phrase, common in seventeenth-century poetry, refers to the reflection of himself that the lover sees in the eyes of his lady, and may come from a pun on the Latin *pupilla*, which can mean either 'the pupil of the eye' or 'a little girl'.

l. 34. *Orbe.* Sphere or region of action or activity.

l. 40. *double tongue.* Deceitful, from the erroneous idea that the serpent's forked tongue was his stinging organ.

l. 52. *Lycomedes' Phillis.* To escape service at the siege of Troy, where he was fated to be killed, Achilles was sent, disguised as a maiden, to Lycomedes, King of Scyros. When Ulysses offered swords and needles for sale, he chose the sword. See Apollodorus, III. xiii. 8. 'Phillis' is simply a conventional name; the daughter of Lycomedes with whom Achilles was concerned was called Deidameia.

l. 59. *heteroclite.* A grammatical term meaning 'irregularly inflected', frequently applied to people and things in the sense of 'abnormal, anomalous'. Note the uncommon, but not unprecedented, accent on the third syllable.

l. 62. *Epicoene.* A grammatical term referring to nouns which, without changing their grammatical gender, may denote either sex. Here it means 'having the characteristics of both the sexes'.

l. 63. *over-come.* 'Win the game' and 'conquer in the sexual fight'.

l. 64. *Tib and Tom.* Tib, formerly a common name for a woman of the lower classes, made this phrase roughly equivalent to 'Jack and Jill'. But Tib is also the ace and Tom the knave of trumps in the game of gleek.

l. 66. *Philip and Mary.* The Philip and Mary shilling (1554–5) has the two profiles close together and facing one another. Cf. Butler, *Hudibras*, III. i. 686–8:

> Still *Amorous, and fond, and Billing,*
> *Like* Philip *and* Mary *on a shilling.*

The Authour to his Hermophrodite (*page 13*)

D1–W. Beaumont's *Poems*, 1653.

Title. The relationship of this poem to the previous one is explained on p. xxv.

l. 4. *Aumes-ace.* Both aces, the lowest possible throw at dice.

ll. 7–8. *True, the worlds scales are even* etc. The allusion is to the process of tidal erosion, and Cleveland may have in mind Artegall's dispute with the giant about the 'balance' between sea and land in Spenser's *Faerie Queene* v. ii. 32. See also Burton's *Anatomy of Melancholy*, Part. 2, Sec. 2, Mem. 3.

l. 16. *His is the Donative, and mine the Cure.* The 'Donative' is the right of the patron of a living to bestow it at will, and the 'Cure' is the actual occupation, the 'cure of souls'. The conceit is completed in l. 18 where to 'superinstitute' is to institute one person to a benefice over the head of another.

l. 19. *The Theban Wittoll*. Amphytrion, husband of Alcmene, the mother of Hercules by Zeus. Amphytrion's sacrifice is mentioned by Plautus (*Amphytrion*, 1124 ff.).

l. 21. *tipt*. Gilded at the tip, i.e. made the disgrace of cuckoldry easier to bear.

l. 22. *Hans-en-Kelder*. A common Dutch phrase for an unborn child, popular in England during the seventeenth century, especially as a toast. Cf. Robert Dixon, *Canidia*, 1683, The Third Part, p. 120, and Lovelace, 'To Ellinda', 21–24 (*Poems*, ed. Wilkinson, Oxford, 1930, pp. 80 and 287).

ll. 25–26. *And shall not he be proud* etc. 'Quarter' here means 'to lodge (body and soul)', but 'Armes' is probably suggested by the subservient, heraldic meaning of 'quarter'.

l. 35. *Ogg*. The original Og was King of Bashan (Deuteronomy iii. 1–13) and in Rabbinical mythology an antediluvian giant who survived the flood by climbing on the roof of the ark. The name also occurs in l. 47 of 'A Dialogue between two Zealots', for which RP26 (f. 94) has the marginal note 'Roan'. Simpson and Thorn-Drury identify him as William Roan, one of the doctors in Laud's ecclesiastical courts (Saintsbury, p. 31), and quote from *Foure fugitives meeting or, The Discourse amongst my Lord Finch, Sir Francis Windebank, Sir John Sucklin, and Doctor Roane . . .*, 1641, where Windebank says of Roane:

... they have given him a great Addition, they stile him, Og the great Commissary, they say he was as briske in discharging the new Canons as he that made them.

Roane proceeded Doctor of Civil Law at Cambridge in 1637 (Venn and Venn, *Alumni Cantabrigienses*, I. iii. 464), when Cleveland was Rhetoric Reader. RP142 records, on f. 79^v, a scrap entitled 'Cleaueland in ye schools to great Dr Roan comencing D^r of ye Civill Law':

nec imerito te [in] Corpus Juris Civilis ducere possum, nec miror q[uod] alma te iam diu in utero gesserit cum tandem aliq.[uando] tam p[ro]digios[um] elephantem parturiverit.

l. 44. *sob*. The act, on the part of a horse, of recovering its wind after exertion; hence, a respite.

l. 51. *the porph'ry Chaire*. A chair of porphyry marble in the Cloister of St. John Lateran at Rome. The allusion is to the story that after the 'Pope Joan' scandal (see below) the Papal throne was arranged so that the youngest cardinal deacon could ceremonially test the masculinity of the Pope. Cf. Butler, *Hudibras*, I. iii. 1249–50. 'Pose' here means 'puzzle, put to it a question which it cannot answer'.

l. 52. *Pope . . . Ioane*. It was widely believed in the Middle Ages that in 855 or *c.* 1100 a woman, disguised as a man, succeeded to the Papacy, reigned for more than two years, and died immediately after giving birth to a child during a procession to the Lateran. See Alexander Cooke, *Pope Joan: A Dialogue between a Protestant and a Papist . . .*, 1625 (*Harleian Miscellany*, iv. 9–109).

l. 53. *Nephew*. Euphemism for the child of a Pope.

ll. 55–56. *Man cannot get a man* etc. See Aristotle, *Physics*, 194, b, 13; and cf. Lord Herbert of Cherbury, 'A Description', 7–8 (*Poems*, ed. G. C. Moore Smith, Oxford, 1923, p. 3). John Collop stole this couplet for his verses 'Of the blood', *Poesis Rediviva* (*Poems*, ed. C. Hilberry, Madison, Wis., 1962, p. 90, ll. 15–16).

l. 61. *Wee'l part the child*. Cf. the judgement of Solomon (1 Kings iii. 16–28) and the parting of the hermaphrodites in Aristophanes' myth in Plato's *Symposium*.

Upon Phillis (*page 14*)

D1–W. The subject was popular in the seventeenth century. See *Seventeenth Century Lyrics*, ed. Ault, revised edition, 1950, pp. 245, 265, 285.

l. 10. *Or age with crutches underpropt*. Or whose age was propped up with crutches.

l. 14. *Each receives his antient soule*. Cf. Frazer, *The Golden Bough*, abridged edition, 1950, pp. 112–17.

l. 16. *Fan*. The motion of air caused by or as by a fan.

ll. 27–31. *The Mary-gold . . . display*. The passage from 'whose' in l. 27 to 'shop' in l. 30 is a parenthesis. 'Her', in l. 29, is reflexive, referring to the marigold.

l. 47. *strawe*. A variant of 'strew'.

Upon a Miser (*page 15*)

DI–W. The feast, a stock situation for satire, appears in Lucian, Lucilius, Petronius, Horace, Juvenal, and Martial. The meagre meal is found in the Renaissance satire of Berni Capitolo, Requier, Boileau, and Joseph Hall. See also Rochester's 'Satyr LVI'.

l. 5. *Hopkins*. John Hopkins and Thomas Sternhold compiled *The Whole Booke of Psalmes*, the metrical version first published in 1562. The verse form was usually a simple ballad metre, which later generations found vulgar and monotonous. Cf. Cleveland, 'The Character of a London-Diurnall' (sig. A3ᵛ in D1):

> Thus they kill a man over and over, as *Hopkins* and *Sternhold* murder the Psalmes, with another to the same.

l. 5. *rithme*. Rhymed verse; pronounced to rhyme with 'time'.

l. 18. *His table vyes not standing with his cheare*. His table cannot compete in durability with the food he places on it. The feast, like the table, was a 'standing' one.

l. 26. *intaile*. Cf. 'The General Eclipse', 16–18.

ll. 29–30. *Stout Ajax . . . slaine*. This story, not in the *Iliad*, is a later accretion, best known from Sophocles, *Ajax*, 51–73.

l. 38. *A Lancaster grand Jurie*. Lancashire was famous for its witches. The great witch trials of 1613 (see *Pott's Discovery of Witches* &c., ed. Crossley, Chetham Society, Old Series, vi, 1845) were followed by a second report of witchcraft in the Pendle Forest area in 1634 (see T. D. Whitaker, *An History of the Original Parish of Whalley*, 1818, pp. 213–17).

ll. 39–42. *The souldier . . . arme*. The incident occurs in *The Late Lancashire Witches*, by Thomas Heywood and Richard Brome, 1634 (*The Poetry of Witchcraft*, ed. J. O. Halliwell-Phillips, 1853).

l. 46. *clock't*. A possible spelling for either 'cloaked' or 'clucked'. Saintsbury preferred the former (p. 38, note), *OED* the latter. CV's 'cluck'd' is apter in the context.

l. 48. *Thyestes-like*. See Seneca, *Thyestes*, 885 ff.

l. 50. *But not a mouth is muzled by the Jew*. The variant reading of CV, H18, and O (a.c.), 'But we subscribe neither to *Scot*, nor *Jew*', refers to the fact that, in Cleveland's time, very little pork was eaten in Scotland. See *The Rump*, 1662, i. 337:

> The Jewish *Scots* that scorns to eat
> The flesh of Swine. . . .

l. 54. *Th' Hesperian Dragon*. See Apollodorus, II. v. 11.

l. 57. *the forme of Bull*. Ovid, *Met*. ii. 846 ff.

l. 58. *Io*. Ovid, *Met*. i. 601 ff.

l. 65. *spend*. A hunting term, meaning to bark or give tongue on finding the game. Cf. 'Smectymnuus', 50.

ll. 69–72. *The scent . . . Venison*. Ovid, *Met*. iii. 155 ff.

l. 75. *like Thracians.* The Thracians usually cremated or buried their dead (see *Cambridge Ancient History*, viii. 547 ff.). Cleveland, with Ovid in mind, is probably generalizing from the experience of Tereus, King of Thrace (called 'Threicus Tereus' and 'rex Odrysius' in *Met.* vi), whose son was served up to him in a banquet by his wife Procne to avenge his rape of her sister.

A young Man to an old Woman Courting him (*page 18*)

D1–W. The marriage or courtship of youth and age, a popular subject for poets in this period, appears in Henry King's 'Paradox, That it is best for a Young Maid to marry an Old Man', Flatman's 'Advice to an Old Man of sixty-three about to Marry a Girl of sixteen' (both in Saintsbury, iii) and R. Fletcher's 'An Old Man Courting a Young Girl' in *Ex Otio Negotium*, 1656. See also Conrad Hilberry's 'The Deformed Mistress: A Genre', in *Poems of John Collop*, pp. 19–26. A very stupid parody of Cleveland is in *Poetical Recreations*, 1688, p. 174.

l. 1. *Beldam.* An aged woman.

l. 3. *Medlers.* Fruit resembling small, brown-skinned apples, edible when they have decayed to a soft, pulpy state.

l. 6. *inoculate.* To engraft or implant one stock upon another. Cf. 'Fuscara', 33–34.

ll. 13–14. *How Pond . . . our sake.* Edward Pond and Peregrine Rivers, two of the many almanack-makers of the period, published at Cambridge—Pond from 1601 to 1709 and Rivers from 1627. Cf. 'The Authours Mock-Song to Marke Anthony', 36–37.

ll. 17–20. *The Ægyptian Serpent* etc. The snake with its tail in its mouth, a common symbol of Time or Eternity, is described here as 'Egyptian' because of the contemporary interest in it as an Egyptian hieroglyph. See Browne, *Pseudodoxia Epidemica*, v. 20 (Sayle, ii. 258 ff.). See also Valeriano, *Hieroglyphica sive De Sacris Ægyptiorum*, XIV. iv (1631, p. 168), and Cesare Ripa, *Della Novissima Iconologia*, Parte Prima, Eternita, Section 4 (Padua, 1625, p. 216), who quotes Claudian, *De Consulatu Stilichonis*, ii. 424 ff. 'Figures' in l. 17 means 'stands for, acts as a type or symbol of'. Line 18 alludes to the snake's characteristic of sloughing its skin, taken here to signify a renewal of youth.

l. 28. *Leero, and I Alphonso way.* 'Leero' may be some game, and to play 'Alphonso way' would mean 'to play like Alphonso', i.e. like a typical Spaniard. But if the comma is disjunctive Leero and Alphonso must be two people, perhaps two characters in one of the popular Italian *novelle* or many plays of Calderón or Lope de Vega. If the line is corrupt, a possible emendation would be 'Leeno' or 'Leno' for 'Leero'. The reference might be to the Latin 'leno', a pimp, but the Italian word 'Lena', meaning 'a Bawd, or pander' (see Florio, *Queen Anna's New World of Words*, 1611, p. 280), did appear as a cant word in English. See Chettle, *Kind-Harts Dreame*, 1592 (*The Bodley Head Quartos*, iv. 1923, pp. 40–41):

the venerian virgins . . . are faine to leaue their sutes for offerings to the olde *Lenos* that are shrine-keepers, and themselues (when they begin to break) are faine to seeke harbour in an Hospitall.

ll. 29–38. *I'me no . . . and me.* 'I cannot give a woman back her youth (unless you count dressing up her outward appearance, just as a Tailor puts new fronts on old garments). But I prefer clothes to fit. I have no use for a plush garment with a lining of old rags, the kind of thing you see on civic dignitaries, velvet in front, but canvas behind.'

l. 39. *Salve and Treacle.* Salve was a general name for a healing ointment, and a Treacle a medicinal compound used as an antidote to venomous bites, poisons, and malignant diseases.

l. 42. *Mountebank.* An itinerant quack. The old Woman can make herself indispensable to men by the simple purchase of six-pennyworth of any Mountebank's remedies.

l. 44. *Thou tastedst in thy Eighty Eight.* 'Cood' (l. 43) is Cleveland's usual spelling of 'Cud': cf. 'Upon a Miser', 2. 'Eighty Eight', the year of the Armada, was often taken as a standard of remoteness within living memory.

l. 61. *Hymen shall twist* etc. 'Twist' here means 'to unite'. Misunderstanding oₗ this word probably led to confused punctuation in later reprints and to the form 'Tropick' for 'Tropicks' in l. 62. Dɪ's punctuation is obviously correct, and both Cancer and Capricorn are required in the final appositive phrase.

To Mrs. K. T. who askt him why hee was dumb (*page 20*)

Dɪ–W. Lines 17–20 indicate that 'Mrs. K. T.' was Catholic; O, in its title for the poem, explains that she was 'Mrs. Katharine Thorold'. The Revd. A. R. Maddison says, 'The Thorold pedigree has never been satisfactorily worked up' (*Lincolnshire Pedigrees*, 1902, Pubs. of the Harleian Soc., iii. 985), but Katharine could be the cousin of one Edmund (Venn and Venn, *Alumni Cantabrigienses*) or Edward (*Lincs. Peds.*, p. 980) Thorold whose career at Christ's and St. John's coincides with Cleveland's; if so, she was the daughter of Alexander Thorold of Hough-on-the-Hill who 'mar. . . . Speed' (*Lincs. Peds.*, p. 979). One of her nieces became Abbess of Pontoise in France in 1661 and another married John Thimbleby or Thimelby, an equally distinguished Catholic name.

CV adds to the title 'written calente Calamo'. Saintsbury points out (p. 41) that the more common phrase is 'currente calamo', and that the statement may have been made to excuse the bad opening rhyme.

l. 11. *Chap-falne Puritan.* 'Dejected' or 'crestfallen'. Cf. Vaughan, 'The Charnel House', 44 ff. (*Works*, ed. Martin, p. 42).

l. 15. *loves zealot.* The rigorous enthusiast, the fanatic sectary of love. 'Zealots' (cf. 'A Dialogue between two Zealots') was a name attached (often pejoratively and in Cleveland with cheerful contempt) to the Puritans. See *Memoirs of the Life of Colonel Hutchinson*, Everyman's Library, 1908, p. 56:

> Upon the great revolution which took place at the accession of Queen Elizabeth to the crown, the nation became divided into three great factions, the papists, the state protestants, and the more religious zealots, who afterwards were branded with the name of Puritans.

l. 16. *silenc'd Minister.* By the time Cleveland wrote, some Puritans had been ejected from their livings (hence 'silenc'd') for their opinions, though the great 'silencing' came during and after the Civil War.

l. 36. *E-la.* The highest note in the gamut: the E which is the fourth space in the treble clef, often used figuratively as a type of something high-flown. Cf. Randolph, 'Upon a deformed Gentlewoman, but of a voice incomparably sweet', 19–20 (*Poems*, ed. Thorn-Drury, p. 115).

l. 40. *pratling eyes.* Cf. Vaughan's 'In Amicum fœneratorem', 43–44 (*Works*, ed. Martin, p. 44):

> Then peep for babies, a new Puppet-play,
> And riddle what their *pratling Eyes* would say.

l. 48. *The Golden Legend.* The original *Legenda Aurea*, also known as the *Lombardica Historia*, drawn up by Jacob of Voragine, consisted mainly of lives of the saints and commentaries on the Church services. In England it was published by Caxton in or soon after 1483 and reprinted many times. In the sixteenth century the *Legend* was condemned by some scholars as historically inaccurate, and Bacon reflects the contemporary distrust in the opening words of his essay 'Of Atheisme':

> I had rather beleeue all the Fables in the *Legend*, and the *Talmud*, and the *Alcoran*, then that this vniuersall Frame, is without a Minde.

l. 50. *But meanes* etc. All the editions from P8–W omit the initials 'I. C.' after the last line, but without them the last couplet (in the form printed from D1–P17) is nonsense.

A Faire Nimph (*page 22*)

D1–W. Other poems on the marriage or courtship of the fair and black are
'On a Black Gentlewoman' in *Parnassus Biceps*, ed. Thorn-Drury, 1927, p. 75;
'On a faire Gentlewoman married to a blackman' and 'One the same', in *The
Poetical Works of Robert Herrick*, ed. Martin, Oxford, 1956, pp. 436–8; also 'A
Blackmoor Maid wooing a fair Boy: sent to the Author by Mr. Hen. Rainolds'
and 'The Boy's Answer to the Blackmoor' in Henry King's *Poems* (ed.
Margaret Crum, Oxford, 1965—see especially p. 226). Saintsbury (p. 171)
is probably right in identifying Mr. Hen. Rainolds with Drayton's friend,
the translator of Tasso's *Aminta* and author of *Mythomystes*, though his
inference that 'A Blackmoor Maid' predates 'A Faire Nimph' cannot be
substantiated. Lines 5–10 and 17–18 of the 'Nimph' do suggest that Cleveland is elaborating brief analogies in 'The Boy's Answer' rather than that
King is epitomizing Cleveland's linked conceit. See also *Eldred Revett: Selected
Poems*, ed. Donald M. Friedman, Liverpool University Press, 1966, pp. xviii ff.

l. 2. *Why should the smoak pursue the faire?* See Browne, *Pseudodoxia Epidemica*,
v. 22 (Sayle, ii. 267):

That smoak doth follow the fairest, is an usual saying with us, and in many parts
of *Europe*; whereof although there seem no natural ground, yet it is the continuation
of a very ancient opinion, as *Petrus Victorius* and *Causabon* have observed from a passage in *Athenaeus*: wherein a *Parasite* thus describeth himself:

> To every Table first I come,
> Whence Porridge I am cal'd by some:
> A Capaneus at Stares I am,
> To enter any Room a Ram;
> Like whips and thongs to all I ply,
> Like smoake unto the Fair I fly.

See also Tilley, p. 613.

l. 5. *The flame of love.* There is nothing to commend 'Thy flaming Love', the
reading of CV and four of the six MSS. It would destroy the rhetorical pattern-
ing created by the repetition of 'flame' and 'Lanthorne', where each speaker
picks up the key word of the last, and turns its application around.

ll. 9–10. *Whatever . . . cleare.* D1's reading 'hath been' in l. 9 must be preferred,
since the repetition of 'can be' and 'can cleare' in consecutive lines would be
intolerably harsh. The choice between 'light' and 'face' in l. 10 is less straightforward, but 'light' introduces an unnecessary tautology, while 'face' makes
the image clear.

l. 14. *Take me for a new fashion'd Mask.* The reading of D1, 'false Mask', is
again tautologous and weak, and 'But me', although it anticipates the image
contained in 'bargaine' in the following line, vitiates the Boy's appeal. He
is offering himself without hope of reward, in true courtly fashion, and the

reading 'Take me' allows the offer to be asserted correctly. With the word 'Done' the Nymph turns the offer neatly into a sale, and turns the conceit inside out by the terms of her 'bargaine'.

l. 20. *prove*. 'Make', the reading of D1, is almost certainly an eye-slip from the previous line.

l. 21. *come*. Despite the fact that only P11, CV, and O preserve this reading, the future tenses in ll. 20 and 22 require 'come' rather than 'came'. The rhyme is bad in either case.

l. 24. *the ware*. Again, D1's 'thy ware' may well be an eye-slip from the previous line. The general statement, as recorded by P11, CV, and the MSS., is much to be preferred.

Smectymnuus (*page 23*)

D1–W. *The Rump*, 1662; *Poems on Affairs of State*, iii. 1704. For the misattribution to 'Mr. Cresswell' see p. xxv.

This satire must be seen as part of the pamphlet war over Church reform provoked by the Long Parliament's consideration of the Root and Branch Petition of December 1640, and by Bishop Joseph Hall's *An Humble Remonstrance to the High Court of Parliament* a few weeks later. On 20 March 1641 five Puritan divines—Stephen Marshall, Edmund Calamy, Thomas Young, Matthew Newcomen, and William Spurstow—gave their initials to the most famous Presbyterian *Answer to . . . An Humble Remonstrance*. Some time after Hall's reply on 12 April Milton published *Of Reformation Touching Church Discipline in England* and *Of Prelatical Episcopacy*; later, probably in July, he defended 'Smectymnuus' in *Animadversions upon the Remonstrants Defense*, and, in the following spring, himself, in *An Apology against a pamphlet calld A Modest Confutation of the Animadversions*.

The reference in l. 57 of Cleveland's poem dates it later than December 1641, when the 'Prentises Petition' was submitted.

l. 3. *what skilt?* What does it matter?

l. 4. *Ap*. The Welsh 'Ap', meaning 'son of' in pedigrees and surnames, survives in modern surnames like Price (Ap Rhys) and Bevan (Ap Evan). Cf. 'The Character of a London-Diurnall' (D1, sig. A2):

It would tire a Welch pedigree, to reckon how many aps 'tis remov'd from an Annall:

l. 6. *a West-Saxon Poet*. Abraham Wheloc held together at Cambridge the lectureship in Anglo-Saxon founded by Spelman in 1623 and a lectureship in Arabic founded by Thomas Adams some ten years later. His contribution to the University miscellany *Irenodia Cantabrigiensis . . . 1641* was a sixteen-line Hebrew poem with an Old English translation on the facing page. See Henry Bosley Woolf, 'John Cleveland's "West Saxon Poet"', *PQ*, xxx, October 1951, pp. 443–7.

l. 7. *play their prizes.* Probably used in the sense 'play their parts'. Cf. 'The Rebell Scot', 23.

l. 9. *Rank and File.* Both 'the lower orders in a military command' and 'a mysterious, acrostic formation'. The two functions of the phrase are taken up by 'train'd' in the following line, which not only completes the military 'trained-band' image, but also means 'drawn out at length, extended'.

l. 14. *Maccabees.* Cleveland's reference to the celebrated Jewish family is ironic, since their revolt against the tyranny of Syria, begun in 168 B.C. by Mattathias and carried on by his five sons (types here for the five authors in 'Smectymnuus'), was usually considered an heroic assertion of Judaea's liberty.

l. 17. *All-a-Mode.* Fashionable in dress, from French *à la mode*. Adopted into English in the seventeenth century, it was often written as if it contained the English word 'all'. Cf. 'Al-a-mort' in 'The General Eclipse', 32.

l. 19. *Don Quixots Rosary of Slaves.* For the chain of slaves freed by Don Quixote in the First Part of *The Historie of Don Quixote*, III. viii, see Thomas Shelton's translation, made in 1612 and 1620, and reprinted in *The Tudor Translations*, ed. W. E. Henley, xiii, 1896. See also Edwin B. Knowles, Jr., 'Allusions to "Don Quixote" before 1660', *PQ*, xx, October 1941, pp. 573–86. Cleveland, one of the very few before 1660 to allude to any incident except the tilt at the windmills, refers to that, too, in 'The Character of a London-Diurnall' (D1, sig. A3):

Thus the Quixotes of this Age fight with the Wind-mils of their owne heads; quell Monsters of their owne creation, make plots, and then discover them;

l. 20. *A Murnivall of Knaves.* A set of four knaves in one hand, especially in the game of gleek.

l. 22. *Or like Colleagues which sit all of a side.* CV and most of the MSS. prefer 'the College' to 'Colleagues', but D1's reading may be preferable as an echo of the following argument in Smectymnuus's *An Answer to . . . an Humble Remonstrance*, 1641, p. 36:

First, for *Ordination, Cyprian* in his exile writing to his charge, certifies then, that *Aurelius was ordained by him and his Colleagues, who were present with him*; who were these Colleagues, but his Presbyters ? as he himselfe expounds it, writing to *Lucius* in his owne name and the name of his Clergie and people, *Ego & Collegae & fraternitas omnis*, &c. I and my Colleagues, and my whole people send you these Letters to you, &c. So that it is cleare in *Cyprians* time, *Presbyters* had a hand in *Ordination* and *Bishops* did not ordaine alone.

l. 24. *As hollow teeth upon a Lute-string show.* Itinerant tooth-drawers of the sixteenth and seventeenth centuries advertised themselves by displaying their trophies in their hats, on their belts, as necklaces, and on strings hung up where they plied their trade. See Chettle, *Kind-Harts Dreame*, 1592 (*The Bodley Head Quartos*, iv, 1923), pp. 31–34) and Pindborg and Marvitz, *The Dentist in Art*, Copenhagen, 1960, especially pp. 29 and 35.

The first six books of Joseph Hall's *Virgidemiarum*, 1598, were subtitled 'tooth-lesse Satyrs'. When Milton declared 'a toothlesse Satyr... as improper as a toothed sleekstone' (*Animadversions*, 1641, p. 9) the author of *A Modest Confutation* justified it as one that, unlike *satyrae mordaces*, 'doth spare the person but strike the vice'. Milton retorted '... if it bite neither the persons nor the vices, how is it a Satyr, and if it bite either, how is it toothlesse, so that toothlesse Satyrs are as much as if he had said toothlesse teeth' (*An Apology*, 1642, p. 33). To compare Smec's satirical attempts to *pulled* teeth makes an effective rejoinder, but Cleveland apparently agreed with Milton that satire's badger-footed iambics ('The Rebell Scot', 27–28) should bite. Cf. also 'The Rebell Scot', 79–80.

l. 25. *Th' Italian Monster.* Thorn-Drury found this monster in *The Gentleman's Magazine*, 1777, p. 482, for Saintsbury's edition (p. 46).

Lazarus Collondo [in error for Colloredo], a Genoese, had a small brother growing out of his side, with one leg, two arms, &c. &c.

l. 26. *Dyæresis.* The division of one syllable into two, especially of a diphthong into two simple vowels.

l. 29. *Sturbridge-Faire.* All fairs rejoiced in monsters, and Cleveland's point is that Smec would make a prize exhibit at the greatest of all English fairs, that held about two miles from Cambridge market-place, and probably the original of Bunyan's 'Vanity Fair'. See William Addison, *English Fairs and Markets*, 1953, chap. iii.

l. 33. *The Whore of Babylon.* See Revelation xvii. The term frequently applied to the Roman Church by the Puritans was also the title of Dekker's play, published in 1607.

l. 34. *Gavell-kind.* A legal term, used from the sixteenth century on to denote the custom of dividing a deceased man's property equally among his sons. See Giles Jacob, *A New Law-Dictionary*, 1729, s.v. 'Custom of London'.

l. 38. *To thinke of him as of a thorough-fare.* The Soul, having reached 'Smec', will not need to go on to any other body.

l. 40. *The Purlew of a Metempsuchosis.* 'Purlew', here, is 'a place where one has the right to range at large': cf. Browne, *Religio Medici*, i. 51 (Sayle, i. 73):

> Surely though we place Hell under Earth, the
> Devil's walk and purlue is about it:

'Metempsychosis' is the Pythagorean doctrine of the transmigration of souls. 'Smec' looks like the Pythagorean soul carrying all its bodies with it, and having arrived at 'Smec' the soul need go no further, for he contains within himself opportunities for endless transanimation.

l. 41. *Scotch Marke.* Approximately thirteen English pence. The English Mark was worth 13*s.* 4*d.*

l. 43. *Ignis fatuus.* 'Will-o'-the-Wisp', misleading travellers. The 'tripartite' flame may be comparing its flickering quality to Smec's argument that there was no 'imparity' among bishops, presbyters, and deans, all equal parts of one whole.

l. 45. *nine Taylors.* 'Nine Tailors make a man' (Tilley, p. 649) is probably related to the commoner proverb 'The Tailor makes the man', but Cleveland's allusion is simply another example of multiplicity in unity.

l. 48. *the Decalogue in a single penny.* Possibly the 'shorthand' abbreviation of the Decalogue to 'D', which is also the symbol for a penny. It may, however, allude to the custom of trying to write a great deal in a small space. See *Mercurius Anti-Britanicus,* 1645, p. 30: '*What ever* Iohn Fox *hath said to the purpose contracted into the bredth of a penny*'.

ll. 49–50. *See . . . feet.* The dominant image is of hunting. 'Spend' means 'to bark, or give tongue' (cf. 'Upon a Miser', 65), and 'in Quire' here means 'in a pack'. 'Scan'd their feet' must mean, as Saintsbury suggests, 'kept pace', but the hunting significance of 'under a sheet' is not clear. Underlying this is a printing image. The Curs have hunted under the sheets of Hall's pamphlet, and 'given tongue' in the 'Quire' of paper used for their own. 'Scan'd their feet' is then the equivalent of the modern 'kept their noses in the text'.

ll. 51–52. *One . . . litigious.* This seems to mean 'There is one vacant benefice, and five would-be incumbents compete for it, so that title is disputed'. 'Truss' was some kind of sport which involved leaping on to or over something. *OED* cites '1627. W. Hawkins, *Apollo Shroving,* v. iv. The waues . . . play at trusse and at leapfrogge on one anothers backe.' On a 'Cure' which had become 'litigious' see Blackstone, *Comm.,* iii. 246: 'If two presentations be offered to the bishop upon the same avoidance, the church is then said to become litigious.'

l. 53. *The Sadduces.* A Jewish politico-religious sect, opposed to the Pharisees, who repudiated the resurrection of the body. See Matthew xxii. 23–33.

l. 57. *Prentises Petition.* This petition of the Apprentices of London, submitted in December 1641, protested against their recent loss of trade, which they attributed to Papists, prelates, and malignants. There were several later petitions from the Apprentices, but only this one blames the bishops for economic disasters. See Clarendon, *History of the Rebellion* (Macray, i. 449 ff.) and *Catalogue of the Thomason Tracts 1640–1661*, British Museum, 1908, ii, index, s.v. Apprentices.

l. 59. *Robson and French.* Two members of the Corporation of the City of Cambridge. 'Alderman Robson' is concerned, in 1639, with a trivial incident about the straying of a horse (*Calendar of State Papers, Domestic,* 1639–1640, p. 259), but Thomas French was a prominent Parliamentarian; a sequestrator of Royalist estates, a colleague of Cromwell, and a member of the committee which ejected many Royalist clergy, he became Mayor of Cambridge in 1662. See W. M. Palmer, 'The Reformation of the Corporation of Cambridge, July 1662', *Proceedings of the Cambridge Antiquarian Society,* lxv, 1914, pp. 75–136. Cleveland says that had they not been foreordained Assessors, they would have been born with the devil's sign, the cloven hoof; 'Carret-bunch' is slang for 'hand'.

l. 64. *Polemonie.* A levy falling with a graduated scale of payment upon men of different social ranks, passed on 29 June 1641, and given the Royal Assent on 3 July. See S. R. Gardiner, *The Fall of the Monarchy of Charles I,* 1882, ii. 216, 218.

l. 65. *Caligula.* See Milton, *Eikonoklastes* (*Complete Prose Works,* iii, ed. M. Y. Hughes, New Haven, 1962, p. 579):

Grant him [Charles I] this [the right to reject the advice of a free Parliament], and the Parliament hath no more freedom then if it sate in his Noose, which when he pleases to draw together with one twitch of his Negative, shall throttle a whole Nation to the wish of *Caligula* in one neck.

l. 69. *No Eccho* etc. Probably refers to *A Vindication of the Answer to the Remonstrance,* by 'the same Smectymnuus', published in June 1641 (*Thomason Tracts,* i. 19). No 'Eccho' of this kind is needed to add power to an author who can muster five pairs of lungs on his own account.

l. 71. *No Fellon* etc. A felon twice branded cannot compete with Smectymnuus, who is branded ten times.

l. 73. *Some Welch-man.* Cf. l. 4, and note.

l. 75. *Banes.* Banns.

l. 76. *Et cætera.* The '&c' of the famous Oath. See headnote to 'A Dialogue between two Zealots', p. 82.

l. 78. *Convocation.* A provincial assembly of the clergy of Canterbury or York. The former had passed the '&c' Oath in 1640.

ll. 79–80 *The Priest . . . Moseley, or Sancta Clara.* Samson's feat (Judges xv. 4–8) evidently became an emblem for the destructive union of supposedly irreconcilable opposites; in 1644 an anonymous version of Cowley's 'The Puritan and the Papist' appeared under the title *Sampson's Foxes Agreed to fire a Kingdom: Or, the Jesuit and the Puritan, met in a Round, to put a Kingdom out of Square.* Moseley was not Milton's publisher (Saintsbury, p. 48) but Dr. Moseley or Moysley, vicar of Newark, who attempted to keep the peace between Charles's bishops and the Scottish clerics in 1639. Robert Baillie (*Letters and Journals*, Edinburgh, 1841, i. 200) found him 'good and simple', not in sympathy with the Laudians. But when he returned to England with a petition from the Covenanters, Edward Norgate, Coke's secretary in Newcastle, reported on 17 May to Robert Read, Windebank's secretary: '. . . seeing the Doctor in a very formal and canonical priest's coat, I asked him if he durst wear it there [Scotland]. He said he wore it continually and received no affront, though the people took him for a bishop and called him my Lord. Yet his man told me that his master is deaf, and so indeed he is, and heard not when the women said in passing, If thou beest a bishop the Devil hold thy head! A cold cast in thy chops! or My mallison on thee! with such like courteous ejaculations'. *Calendar of State Papers, Domestic* (1639), ccccxxi, 189–91. See also David Masson, *Life of Milton*, 1871, ii. 60–61.

Franciscus a Sancta Clara was the religious name of the English Catholic theologian Christopher Davenport, who entered the Franciscan order at Ypres in 1617, later returned to England (becoming chaplain successively to Queens Henrietta Maria and Catherine of Braganza), and published in 1634 a treatise to show how the Thirty-nine Articles might be interpreted to reunite the Anglican and Roman communions. See John Rushworth, *Historical Collections of the Great Civil War*, iv. 210, and Fr. John Berchmans Dockery, O.F.M., *Christopher Davenport*, 1960.

l. 80. *chuse you whether*. Take your choice. Cf. 'Upon an Hermophrodite', 1.

l. 83. *get a Vestery*. 'Get' means 'beget'. A 'Vestery' is an assembly of parishioners, usually in the vestry of the parish church, to deliberate on the affairs of the parish. Here it means a litter of little Anglicans.

l. 84. *Synod*. An assembly, in Presbyterian churches, of ministers and other elders constituting the ecclesiastical court next above the presbytery. Here a litter of Presbyterians.

l. 85. *stickle*. To strive, or contend pertinaciously.

l. 86. *a Conclave, or a Conventicle*. The Conclave was the assembly of cardinals, met for the election of a Pope; a Conventicle was any meeting of Nonconformists or Dissenters for the purpose of worship. 'Conclave' exaggerates 'Vestery' as 'Conventicle' exaggerates 'Synod'.

l. 90. *The Groome is Rampant* etc. The Groom is eager to mate, but the Bride is incapable of producing offspring. 'Spade', on which CV and the MSS. are agreed despite the variant forms, means 'having the ovaries excised', and presents a simpler and apter sense than D1's 'displai'd' which may perhaps be the result of setting from dictation.

l. 92. *So many Cards* etc. A 'stock' is a 'hand' at cards (cf. ll. 20–21). To 'bilk' is a term in the game of cribbage, meaning to balk, or spoil anyone's score in his crib.

l. 97. *Queen-Mother*. Not Henrietta Maria (Saintsbury, p. 48), but Marie de Médicis. See the Clarendon State Papers (Bodleian MS. Clarendon 19, f. 60ᵛ, dated 6 October 1640):

> There is a greate rumor raised heere in the City, & in most partes of the Country, that the qu: Mother Hath procured a Grante from yoʳ Maᵗʸ concerning an imposition upon lether; & it is so constantly reported & belieued, that the inõcent queene suffers extremely in the opinion of the people, where malignity is straingely increased by this meanes against her.

The Mixt Assembly (*page 26*)

D1–W. Reprinted in *The Rump*, 1662.

The 'Assembly' was the famous 'Westminster Assembly'. In October 1642 the Long Parliament passed a Bill appointing a synod to reform the English Church, but it failed to gain the Royal Assent. Accordingly, on the 12th of June 1643 Parliament issued an Ordinance instead of an Act, and the Assembly met for the first time on the 1st of July. It met frequently until 1649, irregularly under the Commonwealth, and was never formally dissolved. The Assembly is described as 'Mixt' because it was intended to include both clergy (Episcopalian, Presbyterian, and Independent) and laity. It is chiefly famous for drawing up the *Solemn League and Covenant* (1643), the *Directory of Public Worship* (1645), and the *Confession of Faith* (1646). See A. F. Mitchell, *The Westminster Assembly, Its History and Standards*, second ed., Philadelphia, 1897, for a full list of all the Members and Officials of the Assembly, and Thomas Fuller, *The Church History of Britain*, 1655, XI. ix (ed. Brewer, Oxford, 1845, vi. 246 ff.).

Cleveland's title was also inspired by the constitutional controversy of 1642 on. While Royalists argued that the three estates in Parliament were the Lords spiritual and temporal and the Commons—all *under* the Crown, the Parliamentarians were evolving the theory of mixed monarchy, in which the King, Lords, and Commons were three co-ordinate, complementary estates. See Charles Herle, *A Fuller Answer To A Treatise Written by Doctor Ferne*, 1642, p. 3; the Thomason copy of the first edition is inscribed 'Mr. Hearle yt made yᵉ parlemt Sermone. Decemb. 29'. This argument was reiterated in *The Maxims of Mixt Monarchy* which reached Thomason on 'February 6th 1642

[1643]' and ultimately provoked Robert Filmer's *The Anarchy of a Limited or Mixed Monarchy*, April 1648, and Hobbes's *De Corpore Politico*, 1650. For a survey of the early stages of this pamphlet war see Ernest Sirluck's Introduction to *Complete Prose Works of John Milton*, ii, New Haven, 1959, 7–51. Line 30 (see note, p. 110) shows that Cleveland had been following the subsidiary constitutional argument over the King's negative voice in legislation. Cleveland's title, taken with ll. 23–30, implies that the Assembly is only an extension of the fantastic new theory of English monarchy.

l. 1. *Fleabitten*. This pejorative, used of a horse or dog, means 'Having bay or sorrel spots or streaks, upon a lighter ground', an apt description of the 'mixed' quality of the Assembly.

l. 2. *ana*. A term used by physicians and chemists, meaning 'in equal quantities or numbers', from Greek ἀνά.

l. 4. *Woolpack*. *OED*, Woolpack, 3, suggests the meaning 'resembling a pack of sheep' and takes Cleveland's reference to be an extension of the better-documented phrase 'Wool-pack cloud' (see Woolpack, 2, b), 'a fleecy, cumulus cloud'. Berdan (p. 231) points out that Johnson's *Dictionary* cites this line as an example of the definition 'anything bulky without weight', but the definition in *OED* certainly provides the richer sense, suggesting the 'Chaos' produced when the usual 'pastoral' function of the clergy is inverted.

l. 5. *discolour'd*. Differently coloured, the one from the other.

l. 6. *Grottesco*. A common spelling of 'Grotesque', which, in painting or sculpture, is the representation of human and animal forms, combined fantastically with foliage and flowers.

ll. 7–8. *Most . . . bue*. Tick-tack or tric-trac is an old variety of backgammon, played on a board with holes along the edge, in which pegs were placed for scoring. See Charles Cotton, *The Compleat Gamester*, 1674 (reprinted in *Games and Gamesters of the Restoration*, ed. C. H. Hartmann, 1930, pp. 76–77). Tablemen are the pieces used in any game played on a table, and the word was especially applied to backgammon (see *OED*, Tableman). Here it carries an extra charge: the idea of 'Tablemen' as 'committee' men, talkers rather than doers; cf. Marvell's use of this image in 'Last Instructions to a Painter', 105–10. Margoliouth says the game was 'so called from the clattering sound made by the pieces'.

ll. 9–14. *Shee . . . lambs*. Two examples of conception by picture. Browne in *Pseudodoxia Epidemica*, vi. 10 (Sayle, ii. 375) attributes the first to Hippocrates after citing the second (Genesis xxx. 25–43) as due to 'the Power and Efficacy of Imagination'.

ll. 15–16. *Like . . . lin'd*. An Impropriator, one who receives the assignment or annexation of a benefice, might be either a lay proprietor or a corporation.

The 'Scarlet Coat' may refer to scarlet robes worn by the Doctors of the Universities, but more probably to the ceremonial robes worn by councillors and aldermen on civic occasions.

l. 19. *Royston Crowes.* The phrase, derived from the place-name Royston, on the borders of Hertfordshire and Cambridgeshire, is applied to the hooded or great crow, a crow of two colours, like the Assembly.

l. 20. *Friers of both the Orders.* The Black Friars or Dominicans, and the Grey Friars or Franciscans, the two orders dominant in England.

ll. 23–24. *Have . . . Gad?* Of the twelve tribes of Israel, Judah was the most powerful and eventually formed a separate kingdom. A portion of the tribe of Levi was set apart for the service of the sanctuary, in a role subordinate to that of the priests, and the Gadites were famous as warriors (1 Chronicles v. 18–22). To 'part stakes', a fairly common seventeenth-century colloquialism, means to share, or to participate. Thus, Judah represents the King, whose dominion has been usurped, and Levi the Church, whose power is threatened by the Parliamentarian Gadites.

l. 28. *yardwand.* A three-foot rod for measuring, here the symbol of the City of London, just as the Sceptre symbolizes the Royal power, and the Crosier the Church. The City was the stronghold of Puritan and Parliamentarian.

l. 29. *Isaac.* Isaac Pennington, Lord Mayor of London in 1642 and 1643, a staunch Puritan and Parliamentarian. See Clarendon, *The History of the Rebellion* (Macray, index *et passim*) and *DNB*. He was a constant butt of Royalist satire. A fair example of what some thought of him is found in 'The Downfall of Cheapside-Crosse, May 2, 3, 4. 1643.' (*The Rump*, i. 138):

> . . . demolisht, and pluckt down
> By th' warrant of Lord *Isaack Pennington*;
> *London's* chief (*ut vis*) who thinks store of good
> He doth, in prisoning, hanging, shedding blood,
> In robbing, plundering each that's good to's King,
> Because no Plate, nor Mony, they will bring
> Into *Guildhall*. . . .

Cf. also 'To P. Rupert', 79.

l. 30. *Judge of* εἰς Ἄδου *and Elegerit.* Judge of the most subtle cruxes being debated in the Assembly and Parliament. The Greek phrase, meaning 'into [the house] of Hades' refers to the question of Christ's descent into Hell which came up in the Assembly's discussion of the Apostles' Creed and the Third of the Thirty-Nine Articles some time between 6 July and 12 October 1643: did the Greek refer to the place of the dead in general—i.e. to the grave —or specifically to the place of eternal torment. Eventually the Assembly voted to accept the former interpretation of men like Selden (*Table Talk*, ed. Sir Frederick Pollock, 1927, pp. 52–53), Ussher (Edward Leigh, *Critica Sacra*, 1639, pp. 12–13), and Milton (*De Doctrina Christiana*, i, chaps. 5 and 16, *Works*, Columbia University edition, 1933, xiv. 277 and xv. 307) to the dismay of Abraham Cowley ('The Puritan and the Papist', *Poems*, ed. A. R. Waller, Cambridge, 1906, p. 152), and Peter Heylyn (*Respondet Petrus*, 1658, pp. 111–13). For the action of the Assembly see Mitchell, *The Westminster Assembly* . . ., pp. 140 and 153 and S. W. Carruthers, *The Everyday Work of the Westminster Assembly*, Philadelphia, 1943, chapter xi.

The Latin 'Elegerit' from the King's coronation oath was the word at issue in the controversy over the King's right to a negative voice in new legislation. The Royalist *Answer to a Printed Book, Intituled, Observations Vpon Some of His Majesties Late Answers and Expresses Printed by his Maiesties command at Oxford* [c. Nov. 20], 1642, argues that all depends on whether its tense is future perfect indicative or perfect subjunctive, for there is 'as much difference between the Tenses, as betweene Democracy, and Monarchy'. The authors, whom Thomason identified as Falkland, Chillingworth, Digges, '& yᵉ rest of yᵉ University', are sure that 'it was meant of the time past', pointing out that 'the Oath in English is free from all ambiguity rendring *consuetudines quas vulgus elegerit* by rightfull customes which the commonalty of this your Kingdome have. . .'. Despite a declaration from Parliament that the verb had always been rendered in the future perfect, Parliamentarians like Henry Parker, one J. M., author of *A Reply to the Answer* . . . (3 February 1643), and Milton in *Eikonoklastes* (*Prose Works*, iii, ed. Hughes, 414) preferred to argue that either tense would support their case.

l. 31. *in chalk and charcole.* In black and white, i.e. clearly.

l. 32. *The . . . Satyr, and the Fawne.* Examples of 'twisted nature', half man, half beast. 'Faun' (mythological creature) should not be confused with 'Fawn' (animal), though both were spelt 'Fawn'. 'Misselany' here probably means no more than 'miscellaneous' (i.e. half man and half beast), but it may also echo the common phrase 'Miscellany Madam', a trader in miscellaneous articles, chiefly trinkets and ornaments; they had shops in the New Exchange.

l. 35. *Tallies.* The two corresponding halves or parts of anything, counterparts. Members of this 'Mixt' Assembly are not integral parts of one unity, as soul and body are, and so they will not be united at the Resurrection.

l. 41. *The flea that Falstaffe damn'd. Henry V*, ii. iii. 38 ff.

l. 43. *him that wore the Dialogue of Cloaks.* Unidentified.

l. 44. *Iohn a Styles . . . Iohn a Noaks.* Like Richard Roe and John Doe, imaginary characters used by young lawyers in their cases and moots. They were originally John (who dwells) at the stile, and John (who dwells) at the oak. Cf. *Hudibras*, iii. i. 615–16.

ll. 45–48. *Like Jewes . . . nor foot.* The Neck-verse was a Latin verse printed in black-letter (usually the beginning of the 51st Psalm), set before anyone claiming benefit of clergy to save his neck. Since Jews would hardly claim benefit of clergy, it would serve to distinguish them from Christians. The second couplet might be paraphrased 'The Members are as mixed and mongrel as the system of Church Government which they are trying to impose on the nation, or as anything else that has neither head nor foot'. To an Anglican, Presbyterianism would be headless and footless, since it was without bishops and priests.

l. 50. *Sacriledge matcht* etc. 'Codpeece-Symony' is the obtaining of a benefice by marrying into the family in whose gift it lies. Cf. the third of the seven poems, 'Mr. Smith, to Captain Mennis', 27–30, *Wit Restor'd*, 1658:

> Some one Il'e marrie that's thy Neece
> And Livings have with Bellie-peece,
> This some call Symonie oth' smock,
> Or Codpeece, that's against the Nock.

l. 52. *Linsie-Woolsie.* Originally a material woven from a mixture of wool and flax, but later a dress material of coarse, inferior wool, woven on a cotton warp, linsey-woolsey was used figuratively, chiefly with the sense 'giving the appearance of a strange medley'. Cf. *Hudibras,* I. iii. 1224–8:

> This zealot
> Is of a mongrel, diverse kind,
> *Cleric* before, and *lay* behind;
> A lawless linsy-woolsy brother,
> Half of one order, half another.

A Vestryman is a member of a parochial vestry, a layman with an interest in ecclesiastical affairs.

l. 53. *Pembroke.* Philip Herbert, first Earl of Montgomery and fourth Earl of Pembroke, was a lay member of the Assembly, and a staunch Presbyterian. Clarendon in *The History of the Rebellion* (Macray, ii. 539 ff.) said of him:

> There were very few great persons in authority who were not frequently offended by him, by sharp and scandalous discourses and invectives against them behind their backs; for which they found it best to receive satisfaction by submissions and professions and protestations, which was a coin he was plentifully supplied with for the payment of all those debts. . . .

l. 55. *Drum-Major oaths.* The Drum-Major, or Drum-Major-General, was a staff officer who controlled the drummers. Pembroke's own military career was far from distinguished, and Clarendon cites his dominant characteristic as Fear.

ll. 57–60. *Hee that . . . Algernoon.* Algernon Percy, tenth Earl of Northumberland, became Lord High Admiral in 1638, but very soon grew dissatisfied with the King's policies, and in the Long Parliament gradually drew to the side of the Opposition. As Saintsbury says (p. 51), 'By putting the fleet into the hands of the Parliament he did the King perhaps more hurt than any other single person at the beginning of the war'. Clarendon describes him as 'the proudest man alive' (Macray, iii. 495), and mentions at some length his ingratitude to the King (ii. 537 ff.). A man with a name like 'Algernon Percy' ought to have little in common with the fanatic Presbyterians, who chose their names principally from the Old Testament. Later in the century 'Obadiah' became a slang name for a Quaker.

l. 62. *By him in Gath* etc. See 2 Samuel xxi. 20 and 1 Chronicles xx. 6. The allusion is to the practice of scanning verse on the fingers. The Man of Gath is not Goliath, but one of his descendants, and an interesting confusion is recorded in *The Rump*, 1662, i. 275:

> In a loud tone and Publick place,
> Sings *Wisedoms hymnes*, that *trot* and pace,
> As if *Goliah* scan'd 'um.

l. 67. *A Jig*. A term applied in mockery to metrical versions of the Psalms. For further comment on this dance, see p. lxiii.

l. 68. *Fielding and doxy Marshall*. Basil Fielding, the second Earl of Denbigh, fought at Edgehill, and was commander-in-chief of the Parliamentary forces in Warwick, Worcester, Stafford, Shropshire, Coventry, and Lichfield in 1643. He was later suspected of half-heartedness and relieved of his command. After the Civil War he gradually went over to the Royalists.

Marshall is the Stephen Marshall of 'Smectymnuus'. His sermon on Judges v. 23, 'Curse ye Meroz . . .', preached to the House of Commons on the 23rd of February 1641, is one of the most famous of the age (see Clarendon, Macray, ii. 320). He later became chief chaplain to the Parliamentary army. Cf. 'The Rebell Scot', 21.

l. 69. *Twiss*. William Twiss (1578?–1646), the Prolocutor of the Assembly. The 'Scotch pipes' is probably a glancing allusion to the *Solemn League and Covenant*, an agreement between the Scots and the English Parliament accepted by the Assembly on the 25th of September 1643.

l. 70. *Cinqu-a-pace*. A dance, the steps of which were in some way regulated by the number five. It was out of fashion, an 'Antick dance'; *OED* quotes this line as its latest example. There is perhaps a subdued reference here to the five authors of 'Smectymnuus', of whom Marshall was the first.

l. 71. *Say and Seale*. William Fiennes, first Viscount Saye and Sele, was 61 in 1643. Clarendon gives him a poor character (Macray, i. 241), and he receives several slighting references in *The Rump* (1662).

l. 72. *Palmer*. Herbert Palmer (1601–47), the Puritan divine educated at St. John's College, Cambridge; M.A. in 1622; fellow of Queens' in 1623; President of Queens' in 1644; and author of numerous theological works. The verb 'to rumple' meant also 'to squeeze together, to distort', and *OED*, Rumple, *v*. 3 cites '*a* 1661 FULLER *Worthies, Northampton.* II. (1662) 282 He was somewhat rumpled in his Mothers womb (which caused his crooked back)'. Symon Patrick, Bishop of Ely, remembered Palmer in his *Auto-biography*, Oxford, 1839, p. 13, as 'a little crooked man'. In Dr. John Hall's transcript of *Extracts From the Papers of Thomas Woodcock* (ed. G. C. Moore Smith, Camden Miscellany, xi, London, 1907, ser. 3, xiii. 85), Palmer is called 'a Gibbose, had a strange and sonorous voice like a Grasshopper, from his very back'. Woodcock, a Nonconformist, adds: '. . . the famous poet Cleaveland abused him in his poems. . . . He once said of him, See you that Palmer—he is a Puritan and I hate all such; but I would give all the world when I dye to go where Palmer goes.'

l. 75. *Kimbolton*. Edward Montagu, Baron Montagu of Kimbolton, who became the second Earl of Manchester in 1642, one of the Parliamentary leaders during the Civil War. See *DNB* and Clarendon's character of him (Macray, i. 242). Cf. 'To P. Rupert', 180. Here he is 'Boanerges', one of the 'Sons of Thunder'; see Mark iii. 17.

l. 76. *Doctor Burges*. Cornelius Burges (1589?–1665), vice-president of the Assembly, one of the leaders of the Puritans among the London clergy. See *DNB*, and cf. *The Rump*, 1662, i. 15:

> Wee'l break the Windows which the Whore
>   Of *Babylon* hath painted,
> And when the Popish Saints are down,
>   Then *Burges* shall be Sainted. . . .

l. 77. *If Burges get a clap* etc. 'Clap', the slang name for gonorrhoea, may also have been a disease in horses (*OED*, Clap, *sb*¹, 14); a meaning that allows a nice play of implications between 'clap' and 'saddle', which also has a sexual application. For 'Compurgators' see 'The Authour to his Hermophrodite', 34. Wood (*Athenae Oxonienses*, iii. 683) speaks of Burges's 'having been several times put to his compurgators' in the consistory of St. Paul's and of having been considered guilty of adultery in the Court of High Commission.

l. 79. *Nol Bowles*. Oliver Bowles, a Puritan divine, and author of a treatise on preaching, *De Pastore Evangelico Tractatus*, published in 1649. Member of the Assembly, he preached to it on the day of the first Fast (see Fuller, *The Church History of Britain*, ed. Brewer, vi. 254), but seems to have taken little part in the later proceedings and is not mentioned by Clarendon.

Phrases like 'in good sadness', 'in good truth', were the utmost liberty which the Puritans permitted themselves in the matter of swearing.

l. 81. *Her Wharton* etc. Philip, fourth Baron Wharton (1613–96), a lay member of the Assembly and one of the earliest anti-Royalists, fought at Edgehill, but his regiment was routed, and the story goes that he was forced to hide in a saw-pit (see Grey's edition of *Hudibras*, Cambridge, 1744, note to III. iii. 286). After this, he abandoned active service and was not a prominent figure in the Commonwealth. The 'pairing' of male and female in the 'Antick dance' (ll. 67–86) requires 'Nol Bowles' to be presented as a female, and he is aptly described as 'coy'. The 'pairing' is destroyed if we accept the reading of CV and MSS., 'Here'. At all events, the reading of D1 is not likely to be a simple compositorial error, since l. 81 begins gathering E and the catchword on D4ᵛ is also 'Her'.

Saintsbury (p. 52) offers several suggestions as to the meaning of 'Mumping Lidy'—the most likely that it is the name of one of the dances of the period. This would satisfy the demands of the context. The verb 'to mump' is common enough (see *OED*), and has several meanings.

l. 83. *Pym and the Members.* The 'Members' were the famous 'Five Members': Pym, Hampden, Hazlerigg, Holles, and Strode, whom the King attempted to arrest in the Commons on 4 January 1642. See S. R. Gardiner, *The History of England, 1603–1642*, 1894, x. 129 ff. The five of them 'partner' the five authors of 'Smectymnuus'.

l. 85. *truck.* Have dealings with, used especially of sexual intercourse.

l. 86. *Gaole-Deliverie.* Literally a deliverance from imprisonment; legally the clearing of a jail of prisoners by bringing them to trial, especially at the assizes. Cleveland says that the issue of the 'Members' and 'Smec' will be the scourings of the county jail.

l. 87. *Thus every Gibeline* etc. In medieval Italian politics the Ghibellines supported the Emperor against the Pope and the Guelphs. During the Civil War in England the names were used to satirize the jarring sects within the Parliamentary party. Cf. *Hudibras*, III. ii. 683–6.

l. 88. *Selden, hee's a Galliard.* John Selden, one of the most learned men of his age, represented the University of Oxford in the Long Parliament and was a member of the Assembly. A moderate Puritan, whose character and accomplishments combined to make him a figure respected by both sides, he took no active part in politics after 1649. The galliard was an elaborate kind of cinquepace; see *Poems of John Marston*, ed. Davenport, Liverpool, 1961, p. 228 n. and note to l. 70 above. Selden is so great a man that he needs no partner, and indeed no partner could be found to match him, from an Assembly such as this.

l. 90. *Sanhedrim.* The highest court of justice, and supreme council at Jerusalem. The Assembly and the Long Parliament were often sneered at as Jewish. Cf. *The Rump*, 1662, i. 86.

l. 93. *Moses Law*. Deuteronomy xxii. 10.

l. 95. *Brook's Preacher*. Thomas Edwards says (*Gangraena*, Part iii, 1646, sig. Kk 1 that this was '*Spencer* sometimes the Lord *Brooks* Coachman an early Preacher too'. On the title-page of *The Brownists Synagogue*, 1641, 'Spencer, The Coachman' is singled out for special mention, and on p. 5 he is called one of 'the two Arch-Separatists'. He is evidently John Spencer, author in 1641 of *A Short Treatise Concerning the lawfulnesse of every mans exercising his gift as God shall call him thereunto*. There are references to him in *Mercurius Anti-Britanicus*, 1645, p. 23; in 'Mercurius Menippeus' in *Butler's Satires and Miscellaneous Poetry and Prose*, ed. René Lamar, Cambridge, 1928, p. 350 (which calls him both 'Groom and Coachman'); and in *Mercurius Pragmaticus*, 6–13 June 1648, which says Lord Warwick has 'in imitation of my zealous Lord Brooke, converted his *Stable* into a Chappel, that *Christ* might be preached where he was born, and to this end likewise turn'd his *Coach* box to a *Pulpit* . . .'.

l. 98. *Party-per-pale*. A term used in heraldry to describe a shield divided by a vertical line through the middle. Cf. *The Coat of Arms of Sir John Presbyter* (1658), reprinted in *The Harleian Miscellany*, 1810, vi. 524–5:

He bears party per pale indented, God's glory, and his own interest; over all honour, profit, pleasure counterchanged. . . .

The Rebell Scot (*page 29*)

D1–W, CR2–4. Reprinted in *Wit Restor'd*, 1658, *The Rump*, 1662, *Poems on Affairs of State*, iii, 1704, *Poems Relating to State Affairs*, 1705, *Deliciae Poeticae*, 1706, and as illustrative material in *A Journey to Scotland . . . By an English Gentleman . . .*, 1699. For the Latin translation by Thomas Gawen in CR1–4, CV, and W see p. xxx.

The Scottish army entered England to fight against the King on the 19th of January 1644, but the poem may have been written a week or so earlier, since in l. 10 it mentions Pym, who died on the 8th of December 1643. It is possible, of course, that Cleveland is here speaking ill of the dead, but the tone of the passage suggests that Pym is still alive.

l. 1. *Providence*. The battle-cry of the New Model army.

l. 4. *truckles*. Originally, sleeps in a truckle-bed, that is, a low bed which can be pushed under a higher one during the day; later used more generally to mean 'takes a subordinate position'.

l. 5. *Ring the bells backward*. Cf. 'To P. Rupert', 18. Bells were rung backward (i.e. a peal was begun with the bass bell) to give alarm of fire or invasion, or to express dismay.

l. 6. *Not all the buckets* etc. Fire-buckets were customarily kept in the choir of a church. Cf. Dryden, 'Annus Mirabilis', stanza 229: 'Some run for buckets to the hallow'd quire . . .'.

ll. 9–12. *And where's . . . as they.* See discussion on p. lix and cf. Marston's 'Preach not the Stoic's patience to me', *Scourge of Villainie*, Satyre ii. 5.

ll. 10–12. *Pym's . . . they.* According to Clarendon (Macray, iii. 321) Pym died 'with great torment and agony, of a disease unusual, and therefore the more spoken of, *morbus pediculosus*, which rendered him an object very loathsome to those who had been most delighted with him'. Gardiner says he died of an internal abscess (*History of the Great Civil War*, i. 255), but Cleveland is obviously referring to the *morbus pediculosus*. The Scots are invading England as the lice invaded Pym.

The 'Myrmidons' are properly the warlike inhabitants of ancient Thessaly, whom Achilles led to the siege of Troy (*Iliad*, ii. 684). But in the seventeenth century the word was commonly used in the sense of 'a hired ruffian'. 'Pig-wiggin' probably means 'small, petty', though its origin is obscure and its spellings various. It was used by Greene and Nashe as a quasi-proper name, and by Drayton as the name of a fairy knight.

ll. 15–16. *Unlesse . . . poyson too.* Cf. Chapman, *Bussy d'Ambois*, III. ii. 18 (*Tragedies*, ed. T. M. Parrott, 1910, p. 33): 'Worse than the poison of a red-hair'd man'. See also Swift, *Gulliver's Travels*, iv. 8: 'It is observed, that the Red-haired of both Sexes are more libidinous and mischievous than the rest, whom yet they much exceed in Strength and Activity.' Red hair, since Judas, has been taken as the sign of almost every evil quality.

l. 19. *Sir Emp'rick.* A quack.

l. 21. *Marshall.* Stephen Marshall, the famous preacher and Puritan. See note to 'The Mixt Assembly', 68.

l. 23. *to play that prize.* To act that part. Cf. 'Smectymnuus', 7.

l. 24. *mouth-Granadoes.* Violent or explosive speeches. The word is formed on analogy with 'hand-grenade'.

l. 26. *Hocus.* A conjurer or juggler. An abbreviation of 'Hocus Pocus', which Tillotson, in 1694, explained as a corruption of 'hoc est corpus' (see *OED*, Hocus pocus). Brewer, in his *Dictionary of Phrase and Fable*, revised ed., 1895, p. 612, suggests a derivation from Welsh 'hocea pwca', a goblin's trick, and says that Ochus Bochus was the name of a famous magician of the North, whose name was invoked by jugglers. See also *The Character of an Oxford Incendiary*, 1643 (*The Harleian Miscellany*, v. 341):

Here the bishops rack themselves in a pulpit, vomiting up daggers, like Hocus, to amaze the people. . . .

ll. 27–28. *Come keen . . . meet.* For the supposed association of the ancient Greek iambic trimeter with the Greek satirists Archilochus and Hipponax, see 'Iambus' in *OED*; Sir Philip Sidney, 'An Apology for Poetry', *Elizabethan Critical Essays*, ed. G. Gregory Smith, Oxford, 1904, i. 176; and Robert C. Elliott, *The Power of Satire: Magic, Ritual, Art*, Princeton, N.J., 1960, chap. i. The Scorpions in l. 30 suggest that Cleveland also knew of the false derivation of 'iambus' from the Greek ἰός meaning poison (Elliott, p. 23 n.). The 'keen iambicks', borrowed by Dryden for *MacFlecknoe*, 203–4, may be, as Richard Merton suggests (*NQ*, ccii, 1956, p. 505), a translation of Horace's *celeres iambos* (*Odes*, I. xvi. 24). Iambic feet, longer on one side than the other, are like those popularly attributed to the badger; see Browne, *Pseudodoxia Epidemica*, iii. 5 (Sayle, i. 326–8). The badger's bite probably comes from Fuller's life of Scaliger in *The Holy State and the Profane State*, Cambridge, 1642, II. viii. 80: '. . . Erasmus was a badger in his jeeres, where he did bite he would make his teeth meet'.

l. 29. *imp.* In falconry, to engraft feathers into the wing of a bird to make good losses, and to restore or improve the powers of flight.

l. 30. *Scorpions.* See 1 Kings xii. 11: 'my father hath chastised you with whips, but I will chastise you with scorpions.' Perhaps because of Milton's use in *Paradise Lost*, ii. 701–2,

> Least with a whip of Scorpions I persue
> Thy lingring. . .

the idea grew up that a scorpion could be a whip of knotted cords, or cords armed with lead or steel spikes. Cleveland may be using the word in both senses, referring to the satirist's role as both poisoner (see note to ll. 27–28) and whipper.

l. 31. *Scots are like Witches.* A witch had no power over someone who had drawn her blood. Cf. *1 Henry VI*, I. v. 6, 'Blood will I draw on thee, thou art a witch', and *Hudibras*, II. i. 17–18.

l. 33. *Now as the Martyrs* etc. The specific reference is to the Neronian persecution in Tacitus, *Annals*, xv. 44. 'Bait' in l. 35 suggests the underlying image of bear-baiting, with Cleveland as the English bulldog tearing the Scottish bear to death.

l. 36. *A Scot within a beast.* According to John Speed, the *Picti* or painted people (see l. 112) preserved the primitive British custom of painting their bodies with 'diuers shapes of beasts' so tattooed that 'looke how their growth for stature, so do these pictured characters likewise increase'—*The Historie of Great Britaine*, 3rd ed., 1632, p. 21.

l. 38. *Fosters no Venome.* According to tradition St. Patrick cleared all Ireland of snakes. See Browne, *Pseudodoxia Epidemica*, vi. 11 (Sayle, ii. 386), and cf. John

Collop, 'On Thomas Lord Wentworth Earl of Strafford', *Poesis Rediviva*, 1655, p. 33, ll. 10–11.

l. 40. *England hath Wolves.* The legend that wolves were extirpated from England in the reign of Edgar goes back to William of Malmesbury. In fact there were wolves in England in the reign of Henry VI. Cf. 'Satires upon the Jesuits', ii. *Poems of John Oldham* with introd. by B. Dobrée, 1960, p. 103. Dryden uses the wolf to stand for the Presbyterians in *The Hind and the Panther*, i. 153 ff.:

> A fiercer foe the insatiate Wolf remains.
> Too boastful Britain, please thyself no more,
> That beasts of prey are banish'd from thy shore. . . .

l. 41. *The Scot that kept the Tower.* Sir William Balfour, Lieutenant of the Tower, was dismissed from this post by the King in December 1641. See Clarendon, *The History of the Rebellion* (Macray, i. 447) and Gardiner, *History of England, 1603–1642*, x. 108. He commanded the Parliament horse at the battle of Edgehill.

l. 43. *The Leopard and the Panther.* In Cleveland's time the Tower was both prison and menagerie, so that 'the Scot' might well exhibit these animals as part of the collection. But within his own person he can display the 'libidine' or lust associated with the Leopard and the Panther in Cesare Ripa, *Della Novissima Iconologia*, Parte Seconda, Libidine (Padua, 1625, p. 397). The Panther was also regarded as deceptive and treacherous. See Dryden, *The Hind and the Panther*, ii. 228, and P. A. Robin, *Animal Lore in English Literature*, 1932, pp. 53 ff.

l. 44. *What all those wild Collegiats had cost.* 'Collegiate' meant both 'a member of a college' and 'an inmate of an asylum or a prison', and the reference here to the Leopard and the Panther, the animals in the Tower, creates a pleasantly grim picture of the 'College of the Tower'. The general meaning is that when honest country-folk (High-shoes) came to London to do business with their lawyers and see the animals in the Tower, Balfour need only exhibit himself to pocket the takings.

l. 51. *Montrose and Crawfords loyall Band.* James Graham, Earl and Marquis of Montrose, one of the most famous and romantic figures of the age, won a number of notable victories for the King against the Presbyterians in Scotland during 1644 and 1645. Clarendon gives a glowing assessment of his character (Macray, v. 121–2). Ludovick Lindsay, fifteenth Earl of Crawford, fought for the King all through the Civil War. See Clarendon, *passim*, and more detailed but equally scattered references in Gardiner, *History of the Great Civil War*.

ll. 55–56. *As in . . . Saint.* During and after the Reformation, medals with profile effigies of Popes were so contrived as to reveal a devil's features when the medal was turned around. See F. P. Barnard, *Satirical and controversial medals of the Reformation, The Biceps or Double-Headed Series*, Oxford, 1927. The *pictures* referred to were possibly devotional objects, painted on glass, with a saint on one side and devil on other. Cleveland's couplet is echoed in Marchamont Nedham's 'An Epitaph upon James, Duke of Hamilton', in *Digitus Dei*, 1649, p. 30, ll. 44–45, and in Nedham's *The Character of a Rigid Presbyter*, 1661, sig. E3–E4: '. . . his Picture should be taken after the fashion of those squint Italian Pieces, which present a Saint on one side, and a Monster on the other'.

l. 57. *He that saw Hell* etc. Probably not a specific reference; if it were one of the rare allusions to Dante in this period, ll. 58–60 would be a totally irrelevant comment. Cf. Donne, 'Satire IV', 157 ff. (*Poems*, ed. Grierson, Oxford, 1912, i. 164).

l. 60. *Proselite*. Any convert from one faith to another, or even from one sect to another, especially a convert from a Gentile to the Jewish faith.

ll. 63–64. *Had Cain . . . home*. The most famous and frequently quoted lines of Cleveland. See, for example, *Pecuniae obediunt Omnia*, York, 1696, p. 82 and cf. 'The Scots Apostasie', 39–42.

l. 67. *at Rovers*. Originally a technical term in archery for shooting not at the butts but at a mark selected at will. Later it was more generally applied in the sense 'without definite aim or object'.

l. 68. *Rags of Geographie*. Cf. Vaughan, 'The Charnel-house', 6 (ed. Martin, p. 41): 'Fragments of men, Rags of Anatomie'.

l. 70. *Epidemicall*. Cf. 'The Scots Apostasie', 32.

l. 73. *the Spanish shrug*. According to Nashe 'the Neapolitan shrug' had become proverbial (though the *Oxford Book of Proverbs* cites his use of it alone). Cf. *The Rump*, 1662, i. 258–9:

> 'Tis not *France* that looks so smug
> Old fashions still renewing,
> It is not the *Spanish* shrug,
> *Scotish* cap, or *Irish* rug;
> Nor the *Dutch-mans* double jug
> Can help what is ensuing. . . .

l. 74. *the Dutch States*. In Cleveland's day 'the States' often meant 'the men at the head of affairs in the United Netherlands'. Lines 74–75 would seem to mean 'Or which of the Dutch leaders looks most like a quart tankard, either in the shape of his belly or the cut of his beard'.

l. 76. *The Card by which* etc. A summary of the previous five lines: these social graces are the chart (Card) by which the 'social Mariner' finds his way about the world.

The strength of the agreement between CV and D1 (Mariners) against the 'Travellers' of the MSS. is qualified by the fact that 'Travellers' is the reading of D5. 'Travellers' might, possibly, be an authorial revision, but D1's reading is preferred because 'Travellers' would simplify the image, and Cleveland seldom simplifies.

l. 78. *Their Estrich-stomacks* etc. The seventeenth century has many references to the indiscriminate voracity of the ostrich, especially to its alleged habit of eating metals. For its association with the folly and desperation of soldiers see Marston, 'Certayne Satyres', i. 95–101 (*Poems*, ed. Davenport, p. 70); Joseph Hall, *Meditations and Vowes*, 1606, iii. 18; Jonson, *Everyman in his Humour* (*Works*, ed. Herford and Simpson, Oxford, 1927, iii. 343); Enobarbus' speech in *Antony and Cleopatra*, III. xiii. 195–200; Henry Vaughan, 'The Charnel-house', 43–44 (ed. Martin, p. 42).

ll. 79–80. *Nature . . . Belt.* See note to 'Smectymnuus', 24. For a picture of the tooth-drawer with teeth on his belt and in his hat see Pindborg and Marvitz, *The Dentist in Art*, p. 23. Cf. Oldham, 'Satires upon the Jesuits', iv (*Poems*, with introd. by Dobrée, p. 128):

> And of his teeth [relics of St. John the Baptist] as many sets there are,
> As on their belts six operators wear.

l. 83. *Sure England hath the Hemerods.* A Haemorrhoid (spelt in a wide variety of ways) was both the anal affliction and the name of a serpent, whose bite was fabled to cause unstanchable bleeding. Cf. 1 Samuel v; Philemon Holland's translation of Pliny's *Natural History*, 1601, The second Tome, p. 150; Robert Wild, *Iter Boreale*, 99–100 (*Poems on Affairs of State*, i. 8); and Marvell, 'Last Instructions To a Painter', 495–8.

l. 84. *North Posterne.* D1's 'North-posture' is probably a compositor's error. A 'postern' is a back door, or a private door. Cf. *The Character of an Oxford Incendiary*, 1643 (*The Harleian Miscellany*, v. 341):

> But the leeches, not able to draw blood there, betook themselves westward toward Wales; and then fell to sucking at the nether postern of the kingdom. . . .

l. 87. *run o' th' score.* See 'To P. Rupert', 76.

l. 88. *Villanage.* The tenure by which a feudal villein held his land, and so, by extension, a state of servitude or subjection.

l. 89. *When an Act past* etc. On 3 February 1641, after the Army Plot, the two Houses voted the Scots a gratuity of £300,000, over and above the £25,000 a month they were already receiving, as a testimony of 'brotherly affection'.

l. 95. *left.* CV's 'left' and 'quitt' of the MSS. present the same meaning, against 'gave' in D1; CV's reading is preferred, as presenting an apter sense than D1's.

l. 96. *Thus to lard* etc. Exodus xii. 36. The phrase 'to spoil the Egyptians' became proverbial, though no instances of it are recorded in the seventeenth century.

l. 97. *Life-guard*. *OED*'s earliest example of this word, in any sense, is dated 1648; to Cleveland's first readers it probably seemed a novelty.

ll. 99–100. *the Cause* etc. This and 'The Fundamental Laws', cry-words of the Puritans, were greatly mocked after the Restoration. See *The Rump*, 1662, i. 225, and *Hudibras*, I. i. 761–2:

> They fight for no espoused *Cause*,
> Frail *Privilege, Fundamental Laws*. . . .

l. 107. *Shrive*. An extension of the normal ecclesiastical use of the word, with the sense of 'inquire into, investigate'.

l. 108. *Twenty pence*. DI's 'Twenty pound' must be wrong. There were roughly ten Scots pence to an English penny.

l. 112. *Picts*. Berdan suggests a pun on the name of the race, and the Latin 'pictus' in the sense of 'empty, vain'. The more usual sense of 'pictus' is 'painted, ornate', perhaps a better gloss on the 'sophisticate' of l. 106. Cf. Marvell, 'An Horatian Ode upon Cromwell's Return from Ireland', 105–6 (*Poems and Letters*, ed. Margoliouth, Oxford, 1927, i. 90):

> The *Pict* no shelter now shall find
> Within his party-colour'd Mind. . . .

l. 115. *Hyperbolus*. In the last ostracism (417 B.C.) Hyperbolus, a demagogue, tried to remove Alcibiades or Nicias from Athens; they, instead, banished him to Samos, where he was murdered by oligarchical revolutionaries.

l. 117. *The Indian* etc. There are two versions of this story. In one the Indian is told that only good Spaniards go to heaven (see *Bartolomé de las Casas his Booke of cruelties in the Indies*, viii. 4, in *Purchas his Pilgrimes in Five Bookes*, the Fourth Part, 1625, p. 1574, the translations by M.M.S. called *The Spanish Colonie*, 1583, and by J. P. called *The Tears of the Indians*, 1656); in William Lightfoot's *The Complaint of England*, 1587, G4ᵛ, he is told that *all* Spaniards go there 'without question' since they die in the Catholic faith.

l. 120. *Erasmus-like*. Cf. 'The Printer to the Reader', Donne's *Ignatius his Conclave*, 1634, sig. A2ʳ⁻ᵛ; Aubrey's *Brief Lives*, ed. Dick, p. 103; Dryden's 'Epilogue to the Duke of Guise', 33–34; Congreve's *The Double-Dealer*, 1694, iv; and Pope's 'First Satire of the Second Book of Horace', 65–66.

l. 121. *A Voider for the nonce*. A Voider was a tray for carrying the scraps and dirty dishes away from the table. 'For the nonce' is used here without any specific meaning more than 'for the occasion'.

ll. 125–6. *A Scot . . . Soland-Goose.* Cf. Joseph Hall, *Virgidemiarum*, IV. ii. 139–40 (ed. Davenport, p. 58 and notes on pp. 207, 225–6) and *Hudibras*, III. ii. 655–6:

> As Barnacles turn Soland-Geese
> In th' Islands of the Orcades.

The belief that trees in the Orkney Islands bore barnacles that dropped into the water and turned into Soland geese is exhaustively annotated in Grey's edition of Butler and explained in rational, scientific terms. See also Browne, *Pseudodoxia Epidemica*, iii. 28 (Sayle, ii. 107), which suggests that the legend was still widely believed.

To P. Rupert (*page 33*)

D1–W; printed twice in W. PR, an undated broadside, was set up from one of the printed editions, probably between P9 and P17. The variant title 'Rupertismus' appears in D5 and the derivative editions thereafter, P11, CV, and O.

The reference to Wharton's atrocity charges in ll. 42–43 suggests a date some time in December 1642. Saintsbury suggests (p. 62) that the poem 'expresses the earlier and more sanguine Cavalier temper, when things on the whole went well'—i.e. before Rupert's fatal inadequacies as a general had made themselves apparent.

l. 2. *the Legislative knacke.* The Long Parliament was the butt of constant satire, for its ability to legislate its way into, or out of, anything. Cf. Denham, 'On the Earl of Strafford's Tryal and Death', 25–26 (*Poetical Works*, ed. Banks, Yale, 1928, p. 154):

> Their Legislative Frenzy they repent;
> Enacting it should make no President.

l. 3. *the Doctors Militant.* The members of the Church and the Universities who had taken up arms. The 'Doctors Militant' here on earth are the counterparts of the spiritual 'Doctors Triumphant', though by Cleveland's time 'Doctors' had vanished from the Anglican litany.

l. 4. *Verser Banneret.* A Knight-Banneret received his title for valiant deeds done on the battlefield, in the presence of the King.

l. 5. *Cacus.* An Italian shepherd, who robbed Hercules of his cattle and concealed their tracks by dragging them into his cave by their tails. See Virgil, *Aeneid*, viii. 190 ff., cf. *Hudibras*, II. i. 429–30:

> 'Tis like that sturdy *Thief*, that stole,
> And drag'd Beasts backwards, into's Hole. . . .

Grey's edition of *Hudibras* lists a large number of other references, both classical and contemporary. Cf. also 'Upon the Kings return from Scotland', 23–24.

l. 6. *Antipodes*. Originally 'that part of the earth's surface which is furthest away from one's present position'; more generally, 'the exact opposite of any person or thing'. Cf. 'Square-Cap', 19. To 'track the times' is to 'follow the fashion'.

l. 8. *Malignant*. In the adjectival sense, 'disposed to rebel', but as a noun the name applied by the Parliamentarians to the Royalists.

l. 9. *Huntington-colt*. John Phillips's *Montelion, Or, The Propheticall Almanack*, 1660, says it is nineteen years 'since the Colt at Huntingdon was voted a sturgeon'. For evidence that this was the colt of an ass see Richard Lord Braybrooke's note to the Bohn Library ed. of Pepys' *Diary*, 1858, iii. 134. Berdan (p. 222) cites Butler's *Acts and Monuments of our Late Parliament*, 1659 (*Harleian Miscellany*, v. 424).

l. 11. *Elsing*. Henry Elsing, Clerk to the House of Commons. 'Splay-mouth'd' means 'having a wide or a wry mouth', clearly an asset to a man whose words had to keep the peace in the Long Parliament.

l. 16. *Periwigg'd the Phrase*. Cf. Sylvester's translation of Du Bartas, *The Divine Weeks*, 1598, II. i. 4, 187–8:

> To glaze the Lakes, and bridle up the floods
> And perriwig with wooll the balde-pate woods.

l. 18. *Bels which ring backward* etc. See note to 'The Rebell Scot', 5.

l. 20. *The Literall and Equitable Sence*. The 'reviling' would be carried in the hidden or subordinate sense of the words, while the literal meaning would be unexceptionable. Just before 22 April 1642, while Charles was taunting Parliament with its inability to find any fundamental law that would allow it to impose military service on the subject without the King's consent, this phrase appeared in *A Question Answered: How Laws Are To Be Understood, and Obedience Yeelded*, quoted in Ernest Sirluck's Introduction to *The Complete Prose Works of John Milton*, ii, New Haven, 1959, 18–19:

'There is in Laws an equitable, and a litterall sence.' When the 'Letter of the Law shall be improved against the *equity* of it', the subject is at liberty 'to refuse *obedience* to the Letter: for the Law taken abstract from its originall reason and end, is made a shell without a Kernell. . . . Nor need this *equity* be expressed in the Law, being so naturally implyed and supposed in all Laws that are not merely imperiall, from that analogie which all bodies Politique hold with the Naturall. . . .'

l. 24. *with Hebrew Spectacles*. Backwards, from right to left. Cf. 'Upon the Kings return from Scotland', 33–34.

l. 28. *multiply't.* Magnify optically.

l. 30. *squibbing Poetrie.* A squib, apart from being a firework, was the name for a short satirical composition.

l. 31. *Bilbo.* A sword from Bilbao, in Spain, famous for its temper and flexibility.

ll. 35–36. *At that . . . tresses.* The siege of Carthage in 146 B.C. See Appian, *Punica,* 93: '. . . raserunt feminas, quum aliorum pilorum esset inopia.'

l. 39. *white powder.* An object of constant research; supposedly a kind of gunpowder, which exploded without noise. See Browne, *Pseudodoxia Epidemica,* ii. 5 (Sayle, i. 274–5):

That therefore white Powder there may be, there is no absurdity; that also such a one as may give no report, we will not deny a possibility.

l. 41. *the Nuns of Helicon.* The Muses, whose sacred mountain was Helicon.

l. 42. *Wharton.* See note to 'The Mixt Assembly', 81. In the second of *The Two Speeches of the Lord Wharton, Spoken in Guild-Hall, Octob. 27. 1642. In which are contained a full and true Relation of the Battell betweene the two Armies at Kinton,* received by Thomason on 'Novemb. 18th', Wharton said:

. . . the troops under . . . Prince *Robert* . . . killed country-men that came in with their teemes, and poore women, and children that were with them.

An indignant denial, *Prince Rupert his Declaration,* reached Thomason from Oxford on 'Decemb. 2ᵈ'; he dated his copy of *The Parliament's Vindication in Answer to Prince Rupert's Declaration* 'Decemb. 6' and another *Answer* by G. H. 'Decemb. 7'.

l. 44. *Their Generall wants Militia to touch.* Robert Devereux, third Earl of Essex, one of the most prominent generals on the Parliamentary side, was twice divorced on the grounds of impotence. For 'Militia', cf. the Latin word as used by Florus, *Epitome,* II. xvi: 'Semper alias Antonii pessimum ingenium Fulvia tum gladio cincta *virilis militiae uxor* agitabat'.

l. 49. *Green-sicknesse.* An anaemic disease, often characterized by morbid appetite in young women about the age of puberty. Cf. 'The Antiplatonick', 26.

l. 52. *Then to that Asse etc.* Cf. *Whitney's 'Choice of Emblems',* ed. Green, 1866, p. 18; Browne's *Pseudodoxia Epidemica,* vii. 16 (Sayle, iii. 58); Dryden's 'The Medal', 145. 'A Thistle is a fat salad for an ass's mouth' is in the *Oxford Book of Proverbs,* but the earliest example given is 1721.

l. 56. *Superfœtation*. Properly the formation of a second fetus in an uterus already pregnant; here used figuratively in the sense of 'over-plus, epithesis'.

ll. 59–67. *He, who . . . his vertue*. The 'old Philosophie' is the Aristotelian. Image and argument go back to a passage in the *Nicomachean Ethics*, i. 13 (translated by J. A. K. Thomson, *The Penguin Classics*):

> We have, then, this clear result. The irrational part of the soul, like the soul itself, consists of two parts. The first of these is the vegetative, which has nothing rational about it at all. The second is that from which spring the appetites and desire in general; and this does in a way participate in reason, seeing that it is submissive and obedient to it.

'Plurality of soules' refers to the idea of 'Metempsychosis', or the transmigration of souls, a tenet of the Pythagoreans (among others) which finds no place in the Aristotelian scheme.

   'Breaths' in l. 61 takes a direct object and is probably used in the sense of 'creates, or gives life to, by breathing' (see Genesis ii. 7). The faculties of 'growth and sence' are described as 'Soules Paramount' in l. 64 because each one is itself capable of inhabiting and informing a body. 'Reasons Queen' must be simply 'Queen Reason'. D1's punctuation of ll. 59–70 is obviously wrong, and the later editions and MSS. seldom agree in attempts to correct it. A paraphrase of the passage, as punctuated in this edition, might be as follows:

> Rupert, who commands and dominates the Aristotelian philosophy (which rejected the idea of the transmigration of souls), brings to life in his every breath a Pageant of Heroes. And just as the vegetative and appetitive souls are, in man, subsidiary to the rational soul (though in other forms of life they are the only souls) so the Pageant of Heroes is only a subsidiary part of Rupert's greatness. He is himself alone.

l. 68. *the Sweds*. Those of Gustavus Adolphus, whose part in the Thirty Years' War had made him the talk of Europe.

l. 73. *Whatever man winds up*. Whatever man has included in his nature. *OED* comments on this line as a rare use of the phrase 'wind up'.

l. 74. *Publike Faith*. Parliament forcibly borrowed money 'on the Public Faith', and many people doubted whether they would ever see their money again.

l. 75. *Pandora's Brother*. 'Pandora was created by Hephaestus at the command of Zeus and was endowed with beauty, wit, etc. As Rupert has all these, he is Pandora's brother.'—Berdan, p. 225.

l. 76. *to run upon the score*. To run into debt; see note to 'The Rebell Scot', 87.

l. 77. *the Painters Brieve*. The allusion is probably to Apelles. Cf. Carew, 'Obsequies to the Lady Anne Hay', 25–28 (ed. Dunlap, p. 67 and note):

> Shall I, as once Apelles, here a feature,
> There steale a Grace, and rifling so whole Nature
> Of all the sweets a learned eye can see,
> Figure one *Venus*, and say, such was shee?

See also Randolph, 'The Character of a Perfect Woman', 1–4 (ed. Thorn-Drury, p. 165).

ll. 79–80. *Let Isaac . . . State*. Isaac Pennington, the Lord Mayor of London, was empowered to gather money on the Public Faith in London. Clarendon (Macray, ii. 399) dates this collection in the first fortnight of November, 1642. There were other collections and loans, but this particular one would fall within the period suggested by the note to l. 42.

D1's errors are clearly the result of misreading medial 't' as 'c' in the last word of each line, a mistake more easily made from manuscript copy than from print (cf. 'multiply 't', l. 28). The 'Calfe of State' alludes to Aaron's Gold Calf (Exodus xxxii. 1–35).

l. 82. *silver bridge*. The depressed nasal bridge is one of the effects of syphilis; the silver bridge was a false nose.

ll. 83–84. *Yes . . . Christendome*. The godparent's traditional gift was a silver spoon or cup. Though 'Caleb' in l. 84 can be any Puritan child, Cleveland may be alluding to the sermon his former tutor, Richard Vines, delivered on 30 November before the House of Commons at St. Margaret's, Westminster, on *Calebs Integrity In following the Lord fully* [Num. xiv. 24] apparently favouring the new loan and decrying the current peace party.

ll. 85–86. *Rupert . . . commuting pelfe*. 'Sterling' Rupert outweighs the silver given in lieu of personal service by the citizens. To 'commute' is to ransom one obligation by another.

l. 90. *Gods shadow*. Browne does not annotate this paradox in *Religio Medici*, i. 10 or *The Garden of Cyrus*, iv (Sayle, i. 18; iii. 200), but evidently it was a commonplace of neo-Platonic and/or hermetic thought.

l. 95. *I'le pin my faith on the Diurnalls sleeve*. A 'Diurnall', the forerunner of the newspaper, appeared not necessarily daily, but at short periodic intervals. See Cleveland's own satirical definition in 'The Character of a London-Diurnall' (D1, sig. A2):

> A *Diurnall* is a puny Chronicle, scarce pin-feather'd with the wings of time: It is an History in Sippets: the English *Iliads* in a Nut-shell; the *Apocryphall* Parliaments booke of *Maccabees* in single sheets.

l. 96. *the Guild-Hall Creed.* After Wharton, together with Mr. William Strode, had reported the battle of Edgehill to Parliament, they were appointed by Parliament

> to communicate the whole relation with all circumstances to the city, which was convened together at the Guildhall to receive the same.

Clarendon in *The History of the Rebellion* (Macray, ii. 377) goes on to point out that many of the citizens present had heard that these 'trusty messengers' saw little of the battle, and their report was little believed.

l. 97. *the Common-Councell.* The town, or city, council: Isaac Pennington and his brethren.

l. 103. *the quarrell.* The dispute about the location of the soul is age-old. Plato thought it resided in the head (*Timaeus*, 45, a) and Aristotle, in the heart. For the problem in the early seventeenth century see La Primaudaye, *The French Academie*, 1618, II. xxxvi. 446–8. Cf. also 'Upon the Kings return from Scotland', 3–6.

l. 106. *Hatch him, whom Nature poach'd but Half a Man.* 'Poach'd' means 'pushed roughly together in a heap'. The image of the soul hatching from a shell is common in the century. Cf. Donne, *The second Anniversary*, 183–4 (ed. Grierson, i. 256) and Carew, 'Maria Wentworth . . . exhalauit', 4–6 (ed. Dunlap, p. 56).

l. 109. *'Twas the Mount Athos* etc. The sculptor Dinocrates made an offer to Alexander the Great: he would carve Mount Athos into a statue of the King holding a town in his left hand, and in his right a spacious basin to receive all the waters which flowed from the mountain. Alexander admired the idea, but objected that the neighbouring country was not fruitful enough to support the project. See Vitruvius, *De Architectura*, ii, Preface, and Plutarch, *Life of Alexander*, 72.

ll. 117–18. *Vipers thus* etc. See Browne's *Pseudodoxia Epidemica*, iii. 16 (Sayle, ii. 26):

> That the young Vipers force their way through the bowels of their Dam, or that the female Viper in the act of generation bites off the head of the male, in revenge whereof the young ones eat through the womb and belly of the female, is a very ancient tradition.

Cleveland may also have known the legend of the Ibis, *Pseudodoxia Epidemica*, iii. 7 (Sayle, i. 336–7).

l. 120. *gigg.* To spin like a top.

l. 122. *Even his Dog.* See *Observations upon Prince Rupert's white Dog, called Boy* (Thomason's copy is dated 2 February 1643) and *The Parliaments Unspotted Bitch. In answer to Prince Ruperts Dog called Boy and his Malignant She-Monkey.*

l. 123. *Lundsford.* Thomas Lunsford, at one time Lieutenant of the Tower, and later a Colonel in the King's army, though not a very successful soldier. He was captured at Edgehill. See Clarendon (Macray, i. 478) and *The Rump*, 1662, i. 65:

> From Lunsford eke deliver us,
> That eateth up Children.

l. 128. *the sense o' th House.* The general opinion of the House of Commons, a common catch phrase in the Royalist satirical poems.

l. 131. *ceremonious wag o' th taile.* A suspiciously Catholic touch, recalling the Vulgate's account of Tobit's dog in the Book of Tobit: 'Blandimento suae caudae gaudebat'. Protestants maintained that this greeting had no authority in any ancient version of the text.

l. 133. *At least the Countesse will, Lust's Amsterdam.* Probably Lucy, Countess of Carlisle, 'beauty, wit, harlot, and traitress (though, too late, she repented)'— (Saintsbury, p. 66). Clarendon associates her defection with that of the Earl of Holland in the autumn of 1641, and Sir Philip Warwick (*Memoires*, 1701, p. 204) says she 'changed her Gallant from Strafford to Mr. Pym, and was become such a She-Saint, that she frequented their sermons, and took notes'.

Amsterdam, a refuge for any persecuted English sectary, had opened its doors to all religions.

l. 138. *Fox the Finder.* 'The Fox is the finder' was proverbial. It was a common accusation that Pym invented plots in order to discover them. Cf. *The Rump*, 1662, i. 33:

> Nor yet the Grave advice of Learned *Pym*,
> Make a Malignant, and then Plunder him.

l. 144. *Sir Arthur.* Probably Sir Arthur Haselrig, one of the 'Five Members'. Clarendon alludes to him as the tool of others when he acted in the attainder of the Earl of Strafford (Macray, i. 365) when he was used by his party 'like the dove out of the ark, to try what footing there was . . .'.

ll. 147–8. *the mutinous stir* etc. The one Jesuit executed at this time was Father Holland, hanged at Tyburn on the 22nd of December 1642. But Catholics of all kinds were commonly referred to as Jesuits.

l. 151. *Jowler.* Properly, a heavy-jowled dog, but used as a quasi-proper name for any kind of dog.

l. 152. *at a fault.* A hound is said to be 'at a fault' when it has overrun the line of scent.

l. 153. *Glyn and Maynard.* Sir John Glynne and Sir John Maynard, lawyers and members of the Long Parliament, both took leading parts in the trial of

Strafford. One famous couplet was omitted from the early editions of *Hudibras* because they were still alive and influential:

> Did not the learned Glyn and Maynard,
> To make good subjects traitors, strain hard?

l. 157. *S. Peters shadow heal'd.* Acts v. 15–16.

l. 161. *Sure Iove descended* etc. Ovid. *Met.* iv. 610–11. Cf. also 'Fuscara', 77–78.

l. 167. *th' accumulative King.* Probably the 'cumulative, collective' King, describing the 'Five Members' who are dubbed with the nickname of Pym their leader, and referred to in the next line.

l. 169. *Velam-ears.* Cf. the 'leather-eares' of 'Smectymnuus', 98.

l. 170. *Phylacters.* Small leather cases containing passages from the Old Testament, worn at certain times, on the forehead and arm, by orthodox Jews, reminding them of their obligation to keep the Law. Probably because of Matthew xxiii. 5, they were often associated with the Pharisees, as seventeenth-century satirists frequently noted. See, for example, *The Old Pharisee, with the new Phylacteries of Presbytery* (*Harleian Miscellany*, vi. 344–54).

l. 174. *Chin-cough.* An epidemic distemper, especially of children, later known as 'hooping-cough'.

l. 180. *Kimbolton.* See note to 'The Mixt Assembly', 75.

On the Archbishop of Canterbury (*page 38*)

D1–W. Reprinted in Lloyd's *Memoirs*, 1668.

William Laud was executed on the 10th of January 1645 after a long imprisonment and an unspectacular trial. Clarendon's account is not so indignant as one might have expected (Macray, iii. 465–8), and a more partial view is given by Fuller, *The Church History of Britain* (ed. Brewer, vi. 293–305). Gardiner (*History of the Great Civil War*, ii. 99–108) gives a brilliantly balanced account of Laud's trial, and a penetrating assessment of his character and influence. Cleveland's poem was probably written soon after the event, though there is nothing to suggest a precise date.

l. 2. *He brews his teares.* Cf. *Troilus and Cressida*, iv. iv. 6–8.

l. 3. *chymically.* By alchemy.

l. 6. *quaver'd out.* Prolonged in song with trills and quavers.

l. 8. *Bushells Wells.* Thomas Bushell (1594–1674), first the page and later the friend of Bacon, is chiefly remembered as a mining engineer who in 1636 completed a grotto at Enstone, near Woodstock, which included 'all the curious fine water-works and artificial conclusions that could be imagined' (Wood, *Athenae Oxonienses,* iii. 1007 ff.)

l. 9. *hee 'l tune his teares.* Cf. 'Upon the death of M. King', 1–2.

l. 12. *Conduit head.* The reservoir.

l. 14. *Britaines Vespers.* As compared with the Sicilian Vespers of 1282.

l. 15. *expresse.* Represent by drawing or painting.

l. 18. *Seths Pillars.* See Josephus, *Jewish Antiquities,* i. 70–71, where it is said of the descendants of Seth, the son of Adam:

> Moreover, to prevent their discoveries from being lost to mankind and perishing before they became known . . . they erected two pillars, one of brick and the other of stone, and inscribed these discoveries on both; so that, if the pillar of brick disappeared in the deluge, that of stone would remain to teach man what was graven thereon and to inform them that they had also erected one of brick. It exists to this day in the land of Seiris. (Loeb translation)

Cf. Donne's 'The Progresse of the Soule', i. 9 and *An Elegie on the Most Reverend Father in God William, Lord Archbishop of Canterbury,* 179–180 (dated 10 January 1645 in the Thomason Catalogue), reprinted in *The Rump,* 1662, i. 71–79:

> On *Marble Columns* thus the *Arts* have stood,
> As wise *Seth's Pillars* sav'd 'em in the *Flood.*

l. 24. *And by a Law dough-bak't.* 'Dough-baked' means 'half-baked'. The laws of Parliament lack the King's consent. Originally an Ordinance had been a declaration by the King without the necessary concurrence of Parliament; after August 1641 it became a declaration of the two Houses without the necessary concurrence of the King. 'Act' was not used again until January 1649.

ll. 25–26. *The Lyturgie . . . Text.* On the 4th of January 1645 the Lords assented to the Bill of Attainder against Laud and accepted the Commons' amendments to the Ordinance declaring the Book of Common Prayer abolished forever and replaced by the Westminster Assembly's Directory of Public Worship. See *Acts and Ordinances of the Interregnum,* ed. Firth and Rait, 1911.

l. 28. *Nocturnall Lucubration.* Night thoughts. A lucubration is a study or meditation. Cf. Robert Chamberlain, *Nocturnall lucubrations. Whereunto are added Epigrams and Epitaphs,* 1638, and 'The Political Satire of Mildmay Fane', *Harvard Library Bulletin,* xi, Winter 1957, pp. 55–56.

ll. 31–36. *A sight . . . their sin.* The general sense is:

> This is a sight which would convert a Pagan, or make the rabble weep. Just as the Hyena weeps as it eats, so the tears of the rabble serve only to pickle their sins.

Alvin Kernan notes (*Jonson's Volpone*, New Haven, 1962, p. 223) that in emblems the Hyena was associated with the Mantichora, a man-eater with red eyes (see Pliny, *Natural Historie*, trans. Philemon Holland, 1634, i. 206); these eyes may have suggested weeping to Cleveland. Cf. Samson's 'Out, out, hyena' to Dalila who, the Chorus says, enters weeping in *Samson Agonistes*, 748.

l. 40. After l. 40 EG27 inserts six lines, nowhere else attributed to Cleveland:

> The Persians insufficient to dye
> Descend into their dust by Simony.
> Passe not without allowance, but interre
> Their Treasure too, and bribe the Sepulcher.
> Their Gold commutes for man, he payes his fine
> In kind, his body makes his graue a mine.

l. 44. *by Prophecy.* Cleveland is probably thinking of the anonymous *A Prophecie of the Life, Reigne, and Death of William Laud, . . . By an Exposition on part of the 13. and 15. Chapters of the Revelation of Iohn . . .*, 1644, with the MS. date 'Novemb. 23' on the Thomason copy. This judges the acts of Laud to be those of the horned beast.

l. 50. *'Tis height makes Grantham steeple stand awry.* A common proverb. The earliest reference in Tilley is to Lodge, *Wit's Misery*, 1596, p. 14: 'His beard is cut like the spier of Grantham Steeple.'

A Song of Marke Anthony (*page 40*)

D1A, D2A, D4–W. The first stanza was reprinted in *Westminster Drollery*, 1671 ff. For the authenticity of this poem see p. xxxv. Its prosodic interest is discussed by Saintsbury (pp. 10–12). The version in the four MSS., Ash 47, A27, EP25, and RP147, contains five stanzas, while D1A and H35 have only four (Ash 38 has only ll. 1–10). The passage omitted (16–24) runs from the middle of one stanza to the middle of the next. D1A has been taken as copy-text, and the text established by choice between D1A and the reconstructed readings of the hyparchetype of the five-stanza MSS. Copy-text for ll. 16–24 is EP25.

Hyder Rollins, in *Cavalier and Puritan*, New York, 1923, prints a ballad called 'The Flattering Damsel' (pp. 444–50) set to the tune of 'Marke Antony' and calls attention to the following entry in Eyre and Rivington,

A Transcript of the Registers of the Worshipful Company of Stationers. 1640–1708, 1913, reprinted New York, 1950, i. 1:

> 4. Nov. 1640. Entred for his copie under the hands of Doctor WYKES a table called *The Coblers thred is cutt,* and 3 ballads under the hand of Master HANSLEY, viz᷑, *Never marke Anthony, The kind Cuckold, & Englands comfort revived.*

The tune does not seem to have survived at all, but a date of *c.* 1639 seems appropriate for the poem.

l. 6. *complement.* 'That which completes or makes perfect'. Cf. Rollins, *Cavalier and Puritan,* p. 82:

> Our gracious King, our *Charles* the Great,
> Our ioyes sweet complement. . . .

ll. 17–18. *Her moyst . . . palme.* Cf. Donne, 'The Extasie', 5–6 (ed. Grierson, i. 51).

l. 35. *Eyes humour Chrystaline.* The crystalline humour, part of the focusing equipment of the eye, was situated immediately behind the iris. The line means that the lady peeped into the depths of the poet's eye.

l. 39. *Mysticall Grammer* etc. Harris F. Fletcher in *The Intellectual Development of John Milton,* Urbana, Ill., 1961, ii. 263, paraphrases the Oration of one Praevaricator at Christ's College in 1651 whose mistress and 'her amorous toils, *arte amandi,* were the true logic, poetry, natural philosophy, speculation, contemplation, the true *physica,* even the true mathematics'. The oration was printed in *Seventeenth Century News,* Summer 1955, xiii. 27–28 and discussed by William T. Costello in 'A Cambridge Prevaricator in the Earlier Seventeenth Century', *Renaissance News,* Winter 1955, viii. 179–84.

l. 45. *ingeny.* Cleverness, ingenuity.

The Authours Mock-Song to Marke Anthony (*page 42*)

D1A, D2A, D4–W.

For discussion of 'mock-songs' see George Kitchin, *A Survey of Burlesque and Parody in English,* Edinburgh, 1931, chap. iii.

l. 3. *pattins.* A name given to many different kinds of shoes, but especially overshoes.

l. 7. *gume.* EP25's 'gume' (supported by 'Gom' in O) is a variant of 'gome', an archaic word meaning 'man'. D1A's 'Groom' is probably a sophistication.

l. 8. *Su. Pomfret.* Probably, as Berdan suggests (p. 215), some lady of easy virtue well known to a Cambridge audience.

l. 10. *Sus.* A slattern, or slut; a variant of Soss, which meant 'a sloppy mess or mixture'.

l. 15. *Dun in the mire.* Originally a dun-coloured horse, a 'Dun' was also used as a quasi-proper name for a horse of any kind. As early as Chaucer (*Manciple's Prologue*, 5) 'Dun is in the mire' was proverbial for 'things are at a stand-still, a deadlock'.

ll. 23–24. *Uglier . . . taile.* Envy (Invidia) was frequently depicted with snakes instead of hair. See Cesare Ripa, *Della Novissima Iconologia*, Padua, 1625, Parte Secunda, p. 333.

l. 26. *Mandrake.* See Browne, *Pseudodoxia Epidemica*, ii. 6 (Sayle, i. 285).

l. 28. *Epicæne.* Common to both genders. See 'Upon an Hermophrodite', 62 and note.

l. 37. *Frost, Pond, and Rivers.* See 'A young Man to an old Woman Courting him', 13–14. Frost was a third famous astrologer and almanack-maker.

Square-Cap (*page 43*)

D5–W.

'Square-Cap' is related in some way to the ballad 'Blew Cap for me', entered to Thomas Lambert on the 22nd of March 1634 (Arber, *A Transcript of the Registers of the Company of Stationers of London*, 1877, reprinted New York, 1950, iv. 289) and printed in *An Antidote Against Melancholy*, 1661, and *The Roxburghe Ballads*, ed. Hindley, 1873, i. 100–6. J. W. Ebsworth in his note on the ballad (*Choice Drollery*, Boston, Lincs., 1876) argues that it was probably written between 1633 and 1648. A comparison of the striking similarities between the ballad and Cleveland's suggests that his is the later. Strode's 'The Capps' (ed. Dobell, 1907, p. 107) does not resemble Cleveland's poem in form or phrase, but lists a very large number of 'Capps' and provides some useful points of comparison.

l. 1. *Come hither* etc. Cleveland's 'bouncing Girle' may be a reference to Thalia, Muse of comedy, whose name in Greek means 'luxuriant, blooming'. Or she may be compared to Terpsichore, Muse of the dance (N.B. 'round' in l. 3 and 'pipes' in l. 4).

l. 2. *Hippocrene.* A fountain on Mount Helicon. See note on 'To P. Rupert', 41.

l. 6. *Barley broth.* Strong ale. Cf. *Bacchus Bovntie* (*Harleian Miscellany*, ii. 273):

Goody Goodale . . . standing stoutly in this opinion, that the barley-broath, above all other, did beare away the bell, and neither grape nor berry might in any respect be compared to the maiestie of the mault.

l. 8. *Square-cap.* A University graduate. The square cap required of all gradu-ates since 1588 had been objected to by Beza and the Puritans as 'Romish in origin and an invention which contravened the natural shape of the head, . . . borrowed from the priests of Baal'. Replaced by the undergraduate's round pileus under the Commonwealth, it reappeared at the Restoration (J. B. Mullinger, *The University of Cambridge*, Cambridge, 1884, ii. 195 n. and iii. 555–6).

l. 9. *And first for the Plush-sake the Monmouth-cap coms.* 'Plush-sake', not in *OED*, seems to mean 'looking for comfort'. A 'Monmouth-cap' is a soldier. Cf. *Henry V*, IV. vii. 99, and Strode's 'The Capps', 30–31:

> The souldiers that the Munmoth weare,
> On castle toppes theyr ensignes reare. . . .

l. 10. *Shaking his head* etc. Cf. Jonson, *Every Man in his Humour*, IV. ii. 51 (ed. Herford and Simpson, iii. 365):

> S'light, he shakes his head like a bottle, to feele and there be any braine in it!

l. 12. *pottle.* Originally a liquid measure equal to two quarts; here 'a bottle of wine'.

l. 15. *La-bee.* A contraction of 'let-a-be', i.e. let me alone.

l. 16. *If ever I have a man* etc. Cf. the refrain of 'Blew cap for me':

> Yet still she reply'd, Good Sir, La be,
> *If ever I have a man, blew cap for me.*

l. 17. *Calot-Leather-cap.* The serjeant-at-law. The 'Calotte' was the plain skull-cap, or coif, worn over the wig.

l. 19. *Antipodes.* See 'To P. Rupert', 6; and Marvell, 'Upon Appleton House', 771–2 (ed. Margoliouth, i. 83).

l. 22. *St. Thomas his Lees.* A decree of the 29th of October 1632 ordains that scholars and students of Corpus and Pembroke shall play football only 'upon St. Thomas Layes', which later became the site of Downing College. See J. W. Clark, *Memories and Customs*, Cambridge, 1909.

l. 24. *wrought-Cap.* A knitted or woven cap. Cf. Strode's 'The Capps', 78–79:

> The cruell Cappe is knitt, like hose,
> For them whose zeale takes cold i' th' nose. . . .

l. 25. *a long-wasted conscience.* An easy, or loose conscience. Cf. *The Rump*, 1662, i. 161:

> From two hours talk without one word of sense,
> From Liberty still in the future tense,
> From a Parliament long-wasted Conscience,
> *Libera nos, &c.*

l. 32. *Sattin-Cap*. A clerk in holy orders. Cf. Strode's 'The Capps', 69–70:

> The Sattin and the Velvett hive
> Unto a Bishopric doth drive. . . .

ll. 34–35. *He told . . . did carry*. Parish clergy were permitted to marry, but Fellows of colleges were not. 'Closely did carry' means 'concealed, kept disguised'.

l. 40. *The Lawyer's a Sophister by his round-cap*. The sophister was 'one who makes use of fallacious arguments, a specious reasoner', and at Cambridge a student in his second or third year, still required to wear the undergraduate's round cap. For the 'round-cap' of the Lawyer, cf. Strode's 'The Capps', 39–42.

l. 45. *livery and season*. Delivery and possession (seisin) of lands and tenements.

l. 46. *Iohn-a-Nokes*. See 'The Mixt Assembly', 44.

l. 47. *Impropriation*. Something appropriated to a private owner, a property.

The Hue and Cry After Sir John Presbyter (*page 45*)

H1–3, P1A–W. Reprinted in *The Rump*, 1662. H1 is dated by Thomason 4 May 1649. H2 (7 August) was printed from it, as was P1A, and the MS. L22 was copied from it. CV and H3 derive from the printed editions after P1A. H1 is taken as copy-text and repunctuated throughout.

The poem must be dated later than June 1646 because of the reference in l. 7 to the Negative and Covenanting Oath, never mentioned together before this date (see *Calendar of the Proceedings of the Committee for Compounding, General Proceedings*, 1889, pp. xi, 39). 'Madams Confession' (l. 11) may reflect the Westminster Assembly's discussion of Public Confession in September 1646. Possibly, the poem was not written until after Oxford University's protest in June 1647 against the Negative and Covenanting Oath; a date as late as this would explain why the poem did not appear in D1–6.

'Sir John Presbyter' derived his name from the cant phrase ('Sir John') for priest and from Presbyter (or Prester) John, the legendary potentate of a Christian sect in Ethiopia or the East who took his title in all Christian humility since, as he wrote to the Pope, he had a bishop and king for his chamberlain and an abbot and king for his cook ('Prester John', *Encyclopedia Britannica*).

l. 1. *With Hair in Characters* etc. With short hair and large ears. 'In characters' means 'in shorthand' and 'in text' means 'in text-hand' (i.e. longhand). Cf. *The Rump*, 1662, i. 42:

> What Creature's this with his short hairs,
> His little band and huge long ears,
> That this new faith hath founded. . . .

. 2. *With a splay mouth* etc. 'Splay' (cf. 'To P. Rupert', 11) means 'twisted, wry', and 'circumflext' means 'bent, twisted round'.

l. 3. *With a set Ruff* etc. He has a long, thin neck. Supply 'he' before 'wears'.

l. 4. *Like Cartrages* etc. Cf. *Times Alteration or A Dialogue betweene my Lord Finch and Secretary Windebancke at their meeting in France the eight of Jan. 1641:*

> *Windeb.* What becomes of the man i' th great ruffe?
> *Finch.* Why faith I know not, but if I were his Judge, I would have the sets fild with gunpowder, and fire set to it, and if that blow not off his head, hee should be hanged.

l. 6. *Bomball.* 'Related to bomb' (*OED*). Probably either 'bomb-ball' (Saintsbury, p. 76) or 'bomb-all', referring to Sir John's random pulpit-fire.

l. 7. *The Negative and Covenanting Oath.* Two Oaths; one subscribing to the Solemn League and Covenant, the other swearing *not* to 'adhere unto or willingly assist the King in this War, or in this cause against the Parliament, nor any Forces raised without the consent of the two Houses of Parliament...'. (*Acts and Ordinances of the Interregnum*, ed. Firth and Rait, i. 665–6.)

ll. 9–10. *The Bush . . . Directory.* The *Directory for the Publique Worship of God*, 1645, replacing the Book of Common Prayer, laid down detailed instructions for the conduct of public worship, though not, as Cleveland mockingly claims, for the styling of the communicant's beard. Sir John's beard is like a box hedge, cut by the topiarist to illustrate the details of a story.

l. 11. *Madams Confession hanging at his eare.* '. . . every man . . . ought to be willing by a private or publique confession, and sorrow for his sinne, to declare his repentance to those that are offended. . . .'—*The Confession of Faith and Catechisms Agreed upon by the Assembly of Divines at Westminster*, chap. xv, article vi, 1649. The *Confession* alone had been privately printed for the Parliament shortly after 7 December 1646.

l. 15. *Jump.* A short coat, often worn by Presbyterian ministers (as opposed to the long cassock).

l. 18. *Divine right of an Ordinance.* For the term 'Ordinance' see note for 'On the Archbishop of Canterbury', 24. When tradesmen of the City objected to Parliament's Erastian provisions for Church reform, a Committee of the House asked the Assembly to answer with scriptural documentation a list of embarrassing questions—among others whether 'parochial and congregational elderships appointed by ordinance of Parliament or any other congregational or presbyterial elderships' could be of divine right. See Gardiner, *History of the Great Civil War*, iii. 77–79, 93–95, 105, 126. For the whole conflict between Erastian and *Iure divino* Presbyterians in Parliament and Assembly see Ernest Sirluck's Introd. to *Complete Prose Works of John Milton*,

ii. 92–107 and *Minutes of the Sessions of the Westminster Assembly of Divines*, ed. Alex. F. Mitchell and John Struthers, Edinburgh, 1874.

l. 26. *Lops and Lice*. Fleas and Lice. Cleveland, however, seems to be referring to some kind of cloth or material.

l. 30. *Like to a Sergeant*. Cf. *The True Character of a Rigid Presbyter*, 1661, F2ᵛ, attributed to but disowned by Marchamont Nedham: 'He has trimm'd the Cavalier worse then the angry Barbers of Grays-Inn use to do a Bayliff of Middlesex.'

l. 32. *Made up of Ears and Ruffs, like Duckatoons*. See Aloiss Heiss, *Descripción General de las Monedas Hispano-Cristianas*, Madrid, 1865–9, iii. 173, and plates 191. 8, and 192. 28. Cf. *Hudibras*, I. iii. 147 ff.

ll. 33–34. *That Hierarchie . . . Religion*. i.e. instead of the old order of bishops, priests, and deacons, a new Presbyterian one elected, according to the Ordinance of 9 June 1646, to Elderships in the City—money-changers again in the Temple. See Mark xi. 15–18.

l. 35. *Antick heads*. Gargoyles.

l. 38. *now both are gotten in*. Both those outside the Church and those outside the Commons House.

ll. 39–40. *Then what . . . rebounds*. Whatever seemed arrogant in the Bishop appears equally so in this new Scotch dispensation.

l. 41. *stating Prelacy*. The Presbyterian pseudo-prelacy, which 'states it'. Cf. Fuller, *The Church History of Britain*, v (ed. Brewer, iii. 49): '*Wolsey* began to *state it* at *York* as high as ever before, in proportion to his contracted revenues.'

Classick Rout. Cleveland's adjective, like Milton's (cf. 'On the new forcers of Conscience under the Long Parliament', 6–7 and in *Tenure of Kings and Magistrates, Prose Works*, iii. 196) derives from the Westminster Assembly's plan to organize the English Church by 'provinces' subdivided into classical assemblies or 'classes'.

l. 42. *That spake it often* etc. That had formerly reiterated its ambitious ideas in the guarded language of compromise and diplomacy (see note to 'The Scots Apostasie', 11–12), but was now expressing them openly.

ll. 43–46. *So by an Abbyes* etc. Probably an allusion to the Assembly of Divines, a voice emanating first from Henry VII's Chapel in Westminster Abbey and later from the Jerusalem Chamber, in the Deanery there. Its continuous attempts to establish Presbyterianism in England had all been false starts (hicops) which Cleveland could attribute to the imperfection of a 'Mixt' assembly (see pp. 26–28 and notes). Ironically, the *Confession of Faith* declared in article iv of chap. xvi that 'They, who in their obedience, attain to the greatest height, which is possible in this life, are so far from being able to supererogate, and to doe more then God requires, as that they fall short of much which in duty they are bound to doe'.

ll. 47–48. *Since . . . Discipline.* 'They' refers to the new prelacy in ll. 41–42. Upon the old Episcopal diocese and parishes of London, Ordinances from August 1645 to June 1646 (*Acts and Ordinances of the Interregnum*, ed. Firth and Rait, i. 749 ff. and 833 ff.) superimposed the province and classes of Presbyterian Church government in which discipline was to be maintained by ministers and lay elders acting together in synods convoked, attended, and supervised (see *Confession of Faith*, chap. xxiii, art. iii) by the Civil Magistrate. The best Episcopal pun for these mixed ecclesiastical and secular authorities was 'diocesans', which could mean 'bishops' or 'the clergy or people of a diocese'. Lay and clergy, State and Church were both to ride the one horse of Church discipline, or—another meaning of ride—tyrannize twice over in the new system.

l. 49. *That Paul's.* Demonstrative (i.e. the Presbytery). The Committee of the Presbyteriall Province of London met in the Convocation House of St. Paul's until 1648.

l. 50. *Weavers-Hall.* See note to ll. 33–34.

l. 51. *Ordinance.* In all its political and religious senses.

l. 53. *Dagon.* The national god of the Philistines. Cf. 'The Mixt Assembly', 1–4.

l. 57. *Pray for the Miter'd Authors.* Prayers for the dead were regarded as unprofitable in the Homily 'On Prayer' and ignored by the Book of Common Prayer after 1552. They were expressly forbidden by the Assembly's *Larger Catechism* and *The Confession of Faith*, chap. xxi, art. iv.

l. 58. *Demicasters.* False bishops. 'Demicastor' was an inferior quality of beaver's fur, or a mixture of this and other fur, used in hats.

l. 60. *His Finger's thicker.* Cf. 2 Chronicles x. 10.

To the State of Love (*page 47*)

P1–W. The text of P1 has been repunctuated, since the compositor frequently produced nonsense by stopping too heavily.

l. 2. *sate.* P1's 'tempt' is weaker than either 'sate' (CV) or 'feast' (MSS.), and the context requires the strongest hyperbole.

Seekers. A general name for many sects. See Ephraim Pagitt, *Heresiography*, 1647, p. 145.

l. 3. *Shaker.* A sectary whose devotional exercises were accompanied by shaking or convulsions; later synonymous with 'Quaker'. Cf. *The Quakers Shaken*, 1653, *The Quakers Shakers*, 1655, and many others.

l. 6. *Adamite.* See Ephraim Pagitt, *Heresiography*, 1645, p. 85:

An old heresie, of which St. *Augustine* maketh mention, but renewed by the *Anabaptists.* In the assembly of the *Adamites* men and women pray naked, celebrate the holy Communion naked, heare Sermons naked. These Hereticks had their Conventicles in subterranean places, called *Hypocausta*, because that under the place of their meetings a furnace of fire was kindled to warm the place of their Conventions; for they uncloathed themselves when they entered into it, and stood naked both men and women, according to the similitude of *Adam*, and *Eve* before their Fall. They call the place of their meeting *Paradice.*

l. 11. *the fair Abbess of the skies.* Probably Diana, goddess both of chastity and of the moon. Her 'Nunnery of eyes' would be the stars.

l. 19. *Deals out.* 'Dazzles', the reading of P1, spoils the point made by 'reflection' in the previous line. The lady is brown because her eye is the source of the Summer's light and heat, and she is sunburnt by the light she creates. This image is developed in ll. 20–24. Cf. 'The General Eclipse', 1–5.

l. 20. *dormant.* Dormer.

l. 34. *With Drake, I girdle in the world.* In *Whitney's 'Choice of Emblems'* (ed. Green, p. 203), an emblem celebrating Drake's circumnavigation of the world depicts the hand of Providence issuing from a cloud and holding a girdle which encompasses the globe. The other end of the girdle is attached to a ship resting on the globe, and the motto is *Auxilio diuino.* The emblem is reproduced in Henry Green, *Shakespeare and the Emblem Writers*, 1870, p. 413.

l. 37. *How would thy Center take my Sense.* Cf. Donne, 'Elegie XVIII', 35–36 (ed. Grierson, i. 117):

> So we her ayres contemplate, words and heart,
> And virtues; but we love the Centrique part.

l. 44. *Inspir'd like Mahomet* etc. Mahomet fed his dove with wheat out of his ear. When hungry, it would light on his shoulder and thrust its beak into his ear, inducing the Arabs to believe that the Prophet was inspired by the Holy Ghost in the shape of a dove. See, for example, *Merry Drollery*, 1661 (ed. Ebsworth, Boston, Lincs., 1875, p. 192); *The Rump*, 1662, i. 190; Dryden's *Hind and Panther*, iii. 1095–1110.

l. 47. *squeezing wax.* Wax used to seal documents.

l. 49. *Privie Seals.* Documents to which the Privy Seal was attached, especially a warrant demanding a loan.

l. 52. *Salley-port.* An opening in a fortified place for the passage of troops when making a sally.

l. 54. *Twin-conserves.* Two stores, or hoards.

ll. 59–60. *No sooner . . . Ear-rings worn.* As soon as her words issue from her ruby lips they become jewels in the ears of the hearer. Cf. Chapman, *Bussy D'Ambois,* III. ii. 6 (*Tragedies,* ed. Parrott, 1910, p. 33):

> Truth's words, like jewels, hang in th' ears of kings.

l. 62. *It is a kiss* etc. A 'venter', here, is probably 'one or other of the three chief cavities containing viscera, consisting of the abdomen, thorax, and head' (though see Saintsbury, p. 21). Berdan's anatomical explanation (p. 203), 'Her speech is, then, a kiss of the heart', seems preferable to Saintsbury's because it transfers the hitherto purely physical love to a deeper level.

l. 64. *Rosomond.* Rosamond Clifford, surnamed 'The Fair', daughter of Walter de Clifford and mistress of Henry II. According to legend in later medieval chronicles, the King built a labyrinth or maze at Woodstock to conceal her from Queen Eleanor.

l. 67. *pickearing.* Scouting or skirmishing in front of an army. The word also came to mean 'flirting'. Cf. Shadwell, *The Virtuoso,* v (*Works,* ed. Montague Summers, 1927, iii. 171):

> There's a Lady hovering about you, and longs to pickeer with you.

l. 74. *That Baron Tell-clock.* In seventeenth-century usage freemen of the City of London, York, and the Cinque Ports were styled 'Baron', and at law the term still survived in the sense of 'Husband'. See Giles Jacob, *A New Law-Dictionary,* s.v. Baron, and Baron and Feme. Thorn-Drury noted in his copy of Berdan (now owned by Dr. Harold F. Brooks) an analogue in *The Foure Ages of England,* 1648, p. 15, attributed to, but repudiated by, Cowley in the Preface to his *Poems,* 1656:

> Justice, the junior Judge, sate like a block,
> Or puisne Baron, but to tell the Clock.

Samuel Wesley remembered this phrase as Cleveland's in *Maggots,* 1685, p. 87.

l. 75. *Boot-esel.* A trumpet call, from French *bouter,* to put, and *selle,* saddle, warning knights or cavalry to saddle up.

The Hecatomb To His Mistresse (*page 50*)

P1–W. L22 was probably copied from a printed text, and its readings are recorded only when they agree with H18 and O. Several passages in P1 have been repunctuated. A few garbled lines appear in B.M. Add. MS. 47111, p. 24.

A hecatomb is literally the sacrifice of a hundred oxen (ἑκατόμβη), but even in Homer the meaning had become simply 'a great public sacrifice' and was not necessarily confined to oxen. Here Cleveland offers up a hundred lines of bombast against bombast. For this poem's relation to Donne's 'Negative Love' and the courtly tradition of the unknown or unknowable mistress see H. M. Richmond, 'The Intangible Mistress', *MP*, lvi, May 1959, pp. 217–23.

l. 2. *splaid*. Cf. 'Smectymnuus', 90.

l. 7. *fantastick Postillers*. Commentators or annotators. The 'text' in the following line is the poet's mistress, whom no commentator can properly annotate.

l. 9. *pelf*. Trumpery, frippery, rubbish.

l. 11. *As Spiders travel* etc. Cf. *Hudibras*, III. i. 1461–2 and 'Upon the Kings Return from Scotland', 21–22.

l. 17. *soaring Quill*. It soared when it belonged to the bird, and now will soar again in verse.

l. 18. *Jacobs staff*. An instrument for taking distances and heights. Cf. Overbury, 'An Almanacke-maker' (*The Overburian Characters*, ed. Paylor, The Percy Reprints, xiii, Oxford, 1936, p. 37):

His life is upright, for he is alwaies looking upward; yet dares beleeve nothing above *Primum mobile*, for 'tis out of the reach of his *Jacobs Staffe*.

See also *Hudibras*, II. iii. 783–6.

l. 21. *Intelligence*. i.e. the angel.

l. 22. *Sunday-suit*. Best clothes. *OED* has no example before 1738.

l. 29. *blazon*. Describe in proper heraldic language.

ll. 31–36. *As then . . . others are*. The distinction between sensible and non-sensible substance, discussed at length by Aristotle (*Metaphysics*, xii), was one of the great concerns of medieval philosophy.

l. 40. *The Almanacks mishap'd Anatomie*. Medical astrology, still preserved in Almanacks, referred the affections of various parts of the body to the predominance of particular constellations. Cf. *Twelfth Night*, I. iii. 138–43.

l. 43. *brief.* List or catalogue.
are. As opposed to 'seem', l. 39.

l. 48. *common Sensibles.* Those sense-objects which are proper to no one sense, but common to all. Aristotle (*De Anima*, 425ª27) gives movement, rest, number, shape, and dimension as examples. See also Foster and Humphries, Aristotle's *De Anima . . . And the Commentary of St. Thomas Aquinas*, 1951, pp. 252–3 and 353 ff.

l. 58. *well-tun'd face.* Cf. Lovelace's 'Orpheus to Beasts', 8–14 (*Poems*, ed. Wilkinson, Oxford, 1930, p. 37):

> Oh could you view the Melodie
> Of ev'ry grace,
> And Musick of her face,
> You'd drop a teare,
> Seeing more Harmonie
> In her bright eye,
> Then now you heare.

l. 66. *Oh now that Scaliger would prove his sixt.* The sixth sense (sensus communis) is discussed by J. C. Scaliger in *Exotericarvm Exercitationvm Liber Qvintvs Decimvs, De Svbtilitate, Ad Hieronymvm Cardanvm*, Paris, 1557. See *Exercitatio* lxvi, and *Exercitatio* ccxcviii. 15.

l. 72. *the long disputed Paradice.* In patristic, medieval, and Renaissance literature there was great speculation as to the location of the primeval Paradise and great dispute about the distinction between an earthly and a heavenly paradise, and whether Paradise was, or was not, an intermediate state between earth and heaven. See Raleigh's *The History of the World*, 1614, I. i. 3.

l. 75. *breath a vein.* Give vent to a vein, lance it so as to let blood.

l. 82. *Quartans.* Fevers recurring every fourth day.

l. 89. *Alas poor Gotham* etc. The version of this proverbial story in which the cuckoo is kept *out* of a wood by means of a wall seems to be the most common, but Berdan (p. 206) quotes *Thoroton's History of Nottinghamshire*, 1677 (ed. Throsby, Nottingham, 1790–7, i. 42–43): King John, intending to pass through Gotham on his way to Nottingham, was refused by the inhabitants, who feared that the ground over which a king passed would become a public road. The King sent servants to inquire about this incivility, but the villagers heard of their approach. When the servants arrived they found some inhabitants trying to drown an eel in a pool; others dragging carts on to a barn, to shade the wood from the sun; and others building a hedge around a cuckoo, which had perched on a bush. The servants reported to the King that the village was a village of fools. See also J. B. Colman, 'The Wise Men of Gotham', *NQ*, lxi, 28 December 1850, p. 520.

l. 100. *Periphrasis.* An amplification, or larger expression of something; a development of the more usual meaning of 'circumlocution'. Cf. Lovelace, 'The Toad and Spyder', 137–8 (ed. Wilkinson, p. 166):

> Till he but one new Blister is,
> And swells his own Periphrasis. . . .

Upon Sir Thomas Martin (*page 53*)

P1–W. P1's text is repunctuated throughout.

On the 27th of March 1643 an Ordinance was passed for 'sequestering notorious Delinquents Estates' to raise money for the Parliamentary cause. The archbishops and bishops were the principal targets, but anyone who opposed the will of Parliament could be reduced to beggary without recourse to law. Committees were appointed in each county, and among the Sequestrators for the county of Cambridge are 'Sir Dudley North, Sir John Cuts, Sir Thomas Martin Knights'. According to the Ordinance, any two or more of the Sequestrators constituted a tribunal, so that Sir Thomas Martin, sitting with one of the 'Esquires', could issue a warrant in the name of the Committee for Sequestration in the county of Cambridge. See *Acts and Ordinances of the Interregnum,* ed. Firth and Rait, i. 106–17, and Gardiner, *History of the Great Civil War,* i. 100 ff. In view of the date of the Ordinance, the poem, probably Cleveland's last at Cambridge, must have been written after the 27th of March 1643.

In the Trinity MS. of Anne Sadleir's Letters (CT5), a poem 'Upon the memorable Modell of King Charles the 1st. Throwne from the West-end of Paules, by the mallicious Souldiers; wch did light upon its feete and stood upright' contains a reference to Martin:

> The sad examples of those desp'rate wights
> Hoyle, Venne, and Martin (alias Thomas Knights).

l. 1. *gather pence! A piece.* Saintsbury's emendation (p. 24). P1 reads 'Hang out a flag, and gather pence apiece'.

l. 3. *timpany.* A disease which caused distending of the stomach, but also, figuratively, 'a swelling of pride or arrogance, the condition of being puffed up'.

l. 4. *No Lecturers wrought cap, nor Bartlemew Fare.* 'Lecturers' were preachers in the Church of England, usually chosen by the parish, to deliver afternoon or evening 'lectures'. They were frequently Puritans, and Cleveland's 'wrought cap' (cf. 'Square-Cap', 24) suggests that a Puritan is meant. For 'Bartlemew Fare' see William Addison, *English Fairs and Markets,* 1953, pp. 50–58.

l. 6. *Tredeskin.* John Tradescant, who died *c.* 1637, established a physic garden and museum, 'Tradescant's Ark', on the east side of South Lambeth Road in London. His collection was handed down to his son, and then to Elias Ashmole, who made it the basis of the Ashmolean Museum at Oxford.

l. 7. *Gog and Magog.* See Revelation xx. 8. The two great effigies of the Giants, which had stood in the Guildhall since at least the time of Henry V, were destroyed in the Fire of London in 1666.

l. 11. *Issachar Couchant.* Genesis xlix. 14: 'Issachar is a strong ass couching down between two burdens.' Cf. Milton, *Eikonoklastes* (*Prose Works*, iii, p. 446 and note).

l. 14. *Valentine and Orson.* A romance attached to the Carolingian cycle, first published in Lyons in 1489, about twin brothers who were abandoned in the woods in infancy. Valentine is brought up as a knight in the court of Pippin; Orson grows up in a bear's den, a wild man of the woods tamed by Valentine, whose servant and comrade he becomes. The romance was translated into English, and first published *c.* 1565. A second edition 'Newly corrected' appeared in 1637.

l. 16. *Voider.* A servant who clears away the dishes after a meal. Cf. *The Character of a London-Diurnall* (D1, sig. A4ᵛ):

> O brave *Oliver!* Times voyder, sub-sizer to the Wormes. . . .

l. 18. *Windsors Hospital.* The 'Poor Knights of Windsor' were military pensioners residing within the precincts of Windsor Castle. Martin, in his plurality of being, incorporates them.

l. 19. *Pair-royal.* A set of three cards of a kind.

ll. 23–26. *But can . . . Heraulds vote.* 'Mettal on Mettal', or the juxtaposition of the two heraldic metals gold and silver, was objected to, as Saintsbury points out, because the two colours were difficult to distinguish *in the field*. The arms of Godfrey of Boulogne, a leader of the First Crusade, who died at Jerusalem in 1100 and who gave his name to a Romance printed by Caxton in 1481, were an exception to the heraldic rule: five golden crosses on a silver shield.

l. 29. *Priscan bleeds.* 'To break Priscian's head' was proverbial (see Tilley). The phrase meant 'to speak false Latin'.

l. 30. *one Julius.* The consulship of Julius and Caesar. See Suetonius, *Caesar*, xx.

l. 33. *oaded.* 'Dyed in woad'. Woad was often used as a ground for another colour, which explains the 'twice dipt' and 'double dy' of the next line.

l. 37. *Amphibious.* 'Having two lives, occupying two positions, combining two classes or ranks'. Cf. Browne, *Religio Medici*, i. 34 (Sayle, i. 50):

> we are onely that amphibious piece between a corporal and spiritual Essence, that middle form that links those two together. . . .

The Antiplatonick (*page 54*)

P1 A–W. Also in Beaumont's *Poems*, 1653, and Thomas Jordan's *Claraphil and Clarinda: In a Forest of Fancies*, n.d. The copy in Bodleian MS. Add. B. 109 (f. 99) was taken from a printed text.

The vogue for poems on Platonic and Antiplatonic love is discussed by J. B. Fletcher, 'Précieuses at the Court of Charles I', *The Journal of Comparative Literature*, i, April–June 1903, pp. 120–53, and by F. O. Henderson, 'Traditions of Précieux and Libertin in Suckling's Poetry', *ELH*, iv, December 1937, pp. 274–98. The earliest use of the word 'Antiplatonic' recorded by *OED* is Suckling's in the *Dramatis Personae* of *Aglaura*, 1638, where Orsames is described as 'A young Lord antiplatonique . . .'. There is an 'Answer' to Cleveland's poem in Jordan's *Claraphil and Clarinda*.

l. 7. *Y'are Salamanders of a cold desire.* See Browne, *Pseudodoxia Epidemica*, iii. 14 (Sayle, ii. 18–21).

l. 10. *The Widow of Pigmalion.* Ovid, *Met.* x. 243 ff. The idea that Pygmalion's *widow* returned to stone (or ivory) on the death of her husband may well be original with Cleveland.

l. 12. *the new-crusted Niobe.* Ovid, *Met.* vi. 146–312.

l. 18. *Cease for to Candy up your selves.* To 'candy' is to sweeten, or give a pleasant appearance to something, but Cleveland is probably using the phrase 'to Candy up' in the sense of 'to preserve in syrup'.

ll. 19–20. *No more . . . calcining flame.* Berdan's note (p. 206) reads: 'The Platonic lovers, thus forming a sect apart, calcine love, i.e. reduce it to nothing but dust'. But 'to calcine' can also mean 'to purify, or refine, by consuming the grosser part'. Both meanings are present.

ll. 21–22. *Women Commence . . . a Hart.* Women take their degrees by Cupid's dart, as a King ennobles a Hart by the act of hunting it.

l. 24. *Paroll.* 'Something spoken, a statement or declaration', and 'the undertaking given by a prisoner that he will not escape'.

l. 26. *green-sicknesse.* See note on 'To P. Rupert', 49. Morbid appetite accounts for the 'Charcoal' in l. 28.

l. 32. *As skilfull Gamesters are to seek at Sharp.* A 'sharp' was a small sword, or duelling rapier. The line means 'As skilfull fencers are found wanting in a real duel'.

ll. 37–38. *Let a Magnetick . . . Cuiraseer.* A 'cuirass' was a piece of body armour, originally of leather, but later of metal. Wearing this, he would be irresistibly attracted to the 'Magnetick' lady.

l. 40. *Turn-pikes.* Spiked barriers fixed in or across a road or passage, as a defence against sudden attack, especially an attack by cavalry.

How the Commencement grows new (*page 56*)

P2–W. P2's text has been repunctuated. C42's copy of the poem is headed (f. 31) 'Mr. Cleuelands verses w^c were sung at Sidney colledg at coṁencemt night 4 Julii 1636 wch he retracted 1° Augusti in the consistory'. The poem's local notoriety is suggested by the exchange it provoked between John Salt-marsh of Magdalene and Robert Wild of St. John's (see p. lv); partial con-firmation of Cleveland's recantation is found in Saltmarsh's final couplet:

> What glory's this unlesse the poet vaunts
> his fidlers barely singe, but he recants.

Very likely the novelty of the Commencement in the plague year of 1636 was that there was none; the Midsummer Fair in Cambridge was cancelled, and when the plague had closed the Fair in 1630 the Commencement had also been postponed from 6 July until October. See Charles Henry Cooper, *Annals of Cambridge*, Cambridge, 1842, iii. 226, 275–8. Cooper quotes Fuller's *History of the University of Cambridge* on how the plague of April 1630 to January 1631 'served to cheapen degrees and lower the standard of attain-ment':

> . . . this corruption of the air proved the generation of many doctors graduated in a clandestine . . . way, without keeping any Acts, to the great disgust of those who had fairly gotten their degrees with public pains and expense. Yea, Dr. Collins being afterwards to admit an able man doctor, did . . . distinguish *inter cathedram pestilentiae, et cathedram eminentiae*, leaving it to his auditors easily to apprehend his meaning therein.

l. 1. *Curranto-news.* A Coranto is a letter or paper containing public news, a forerunner of the modern newspaper. See Joseph Frank, *The Beginnings of the English Newspaper*, chap. i.

l. 2. *New teacher of the town.* Apparently a catch phrase for Puritan. See p. 144.

l. 3. *New England voyage.* The original New England Company founded in 1628 drew most of its support from Puritans dissatisfied with Laud's ecclesiastical policy. See Godfrey Davies, *The Early Stuarts,* Oxford, rev. ed., 1952, p. 337.

l. 8. *Symony-Doctours.* An apt use of 'Simony'. See Acts viii. 18–19.

l. 11. *Without any need of an Argument draper.* The word 'draper' probably means no more than 'seller' (see *OED*, Ale-draper, and cf. 'Declamation Draper', l. 16 of 'No Hubbub surnamd Hue & cry'). The 'argument-draper' provided candidates with 'ready-made' arguments.

l. 15. *Gaffer.* 'Master, or governor'; it refers here to parsons.

l. 16. *Easter book.* The account book recording the 'Easter-dues' paid to the incumbent by his parishioners. 'To chaffer' means 'to trade'; the parson uses his Easter-dues to pay the fee for his degree.

l. 17. *steeple.* By synecdoche, 'Parish'. Cf. 'The Authour to his Hermophrodite', 15. The reference is probably to those sectarian ministers whose church was a gathered community rather than a parish organization.

l. 18. *placets.* Affirmative answers used in the Universities when a question was put to the vote. The form was 'Placetne vobis, domini doctores ? Placetne vobis, magistri ?', to which the answer was either 'Placet' or 'Non placet'. Cf. Marlowe, *The Massacre at Paris*, 866–8 (*Works,* ed. C. F. Tucker Brooke, Oxford, 1910, p. 470). The 'means' of the sectarian minister come from the approval given him by his congregation.

l. 20. *Toll-man Barnaby.* Unidentified.

l. 26. *the Margaret Professor.* The Lady Margaret Professorship of Divinity, founded in 1502 by Lady Margaret, Countess of Richmond and mother of Henry VII, was held from 1623–43 by Dr. Samuel Ward, master of Sidney Sussex and, according to Trevor-Roper (*Archbishop Laud,* 2nd ed., 1962, p. 206), a leader of the Puritan majority at Cambridge.

l. 29. *Inceptor.* One about to enter formally into the degree of Master or Doctor.

l. 30. *Grogoram.* A coarse fabric of silk, or mohair and wool mixed with silk.

ll. 31–32. *With like . . . beyond-Trent-beleif.* The strange 'invention' of roasted beef might well 'pose' or puzzle the North-countryman, who was used to salted boiled beef.

l. 33. *Who should he but hear* etc. See Fuller, *The History of the University of Cambridge,* 1655, p. 167:

Now began the University to be much beautified in *buildings.* . . . But the greatest alteration was in their *Chappels,* most of them being graced with the accession of Organs.

l. 34. *Sallingers round*. A contraction of St. Leger's round, an old country dance.

l. 43. *Prevaricators wit*. The 'Prevaricator' or 'Varier' was an orator who made a jocose or satirical speech at the Commencement. Cf. George Peacock, *Observations on the Statutes of the University of Cambridge*, 1841, Appendix A, p. xxv:

> It was one of the complaints of Archbishop Laud, when proposing to visit archi-episcopally the University of Cambridge, that 'St. Mary's Church at every great commencement is made a theatre, and the praevaricator's stage, wherein he acts, and sets forth his profane and scurrilous jests, besides divers other abuses and disorders'.

l. 45. *no serious Oxford man comes*. Probably a reference to Archbishop Laud's failure to exercise the right of visitation he had won from the King in Council on 21 June, 1636, over the protest of the University. See Cooper, *Annals*, iii. 275–8.

l. 46. *Hums*. Students at both Universities were accustomed to express approbation by humming. Cf. Mildmay Fane's second poem to Cleveland, in G. Thorn-Drury's *A Little Ark containing Seventeenth-Century Verse*, 1921, ll. 3–4 and note.

l. 48. *Mun*. A contraction of Edmund. For Edmund Salter (Jesus) and John Martin (King's) see Venn and Venn, *Alumni Cantabrigienses*.

Fuscara (*page 58*)

P2–W. P2's text is repunctuated. Both MSS. omit 63–78; CV was printed from a manuscript of the complete poem. The title shows that the lady of the poem is of a dark complexion (Latin *fuscus*), like the mistress of 'The Heca-tomb'.

l. 2. *suckets*. Sweetmeats.

l. 11. *distreins*. Makes a seizure for debt.

l. 13. *tinckture*. Hue or colour.

ll. 17–18. *That Pulse . . . or no*. Cf. 'To P. Rupert', 71–72.

l. 20. *transpiring*. Emitting as vapour through the surface of the body, exhal-ing. Cf. Crashaw, 'Hymn to the Name . . . of Jesus', 211–14 (ed. Martin, p. 245):

> What did Their weapons but with wider pores
> Inlarge thy flaming-brested Louers
>   More freely to transpire
>   That impatient Fire.

l. 22. *Tender as 'twere a Jellie glov'd.* 'The jelly'd Philtre of her lips', l. 41 of 'To the State of Love', is only just saved from mawkishness by its context. Nothing could save this famous line.

l. 23. *drone-pipe.* The bass pipe of a bagpipe, which emits only one continuous tone.

l. 34. *Inoculate Carnation.* To 'inoculate' is to yield a bud to another stock, to engraft. Cf. 'A young Man to an old Woman Courting him', 6, and *Hamlet*, III. i. 117–19:

> You should not have believed me, for virtue cannot so inoculate our old stock, but we shall relish of it. . . .

'Carnation' is the pale colour of human flesh. The point of ll. 33–34 is that the dark lady (Fuscara) has freckles on her wrist.

l. 50. *Had suck'd the Toll of all her span.* Had taken his toll from her whole hand.

l. 52. *As Danes carowse by Kettle-drums.* Cf. *Hamlet*, I. iv. 10–12.

l. 60. *Fraught both with East and Western prize.* Laden with the riches of 'both the Indias'. Cf. 'The Hecatomb to His Mistresse', 4.

l. 61. *assayd.* The technical, mining sense of 'to test the composition of an ore or alloy, or to determine the degree of purity in precious metals'.

ll. 62–63. *Arm'd like . . . a pore.* A 'Lancepesade' (the more common spelling) was a non-commissioned officer of the lowest rank. Cf. Henry More, 'To the Young Authour [John Hall] Upon his Incomparable Veine in Satyre and Love-Sonnets' (*Philosophical Poems*, ed. Geoffrey Bullough, Manchester, 1931, p. 164):

> With phansies queint and gay expressions pat,
> More florid then a Lanspresado's hat   (55–56).

A 'Spanish pike' is a needle. Cf. Ford, *The Sun's Darling*, II. i (*Works*, ed. Gifford-Dyce, 1869, iii. 125):

> A French gentleman, that trails a Spanish pike; a tailor.

l. 70. *Ravilliack.* François Ravaillac, the assassin of Henry IV of France, executed in Paris on 27 May 1610. Cf. *The Rump*, 1662, i. 26:

> The flame lockt up in bold *Ravillacks* urne,
> Is snatcht from thence, and in their hearts does burn.

l. 78. *Danaes golden showre.* An inappropriate use, since it was Jove, not Danaë herself, who produced the golden shower. See 'To P. Rupert', 161.

To Julia to expedite her promise (*page 60*)

P6–W. RP84 probably derives from a printed text, since it omits l. 35 with P9, P11–P17, but P6, CV, and O seem to descend independently from the archetype. P6 has been taken as copy-text because its readings are superior to those of CV or O, which never agree against it. The *apparatus criticus* lists only departures from P6.

Johnson, in the *Life of Cowley*, quotes ll. 1–4 and 10–18 as if they formed one complete stanza, saying of them, 'Who would imagine it possible that in a very few lines so many remote ideas could be brought together?'

l. 1. *under-Shreive*. Under-Sheriff. Cf. 'A young Man to an old Woman Courting him', 35.

l. 3. *She-Advowson*. The 'Advowson', the right of presentation to a living or benefice, is used loosely here to signify 'future possession'. Cf. 'Square-Cap', 36–37.

l. 6. *Anticks*. Both 'antiques' (enforced by 'benighted' and 'withered') and 'clowns' (made appropriate by 'Panting Expectance' and 'Monkeys'). The lovers are not only fools, but ancient fools.

l. 8. *Hymens Monkeys*. The 'fettered ape', a common figure in medieval and Renaissance art, represents the 'Voluntary captive' who has exchanged native freedom for material pleasures. See H. W. Janson, *Apes and Ape Lore in the Middle Ages and the Renaissance* (Studies of the Warburg Institute, xx), 1952, chap. v. The ape was also traditionally a figure of Lust, and perhaps Cleveland refers to both simian emblems.

l. 9. *Rebated Foynes*. Blunted or dulled foils. Such a combat is not (unfortunately) a genuine fight.

l. 11. *By Candle end*. By auction, in which bids are received as long as a small piece of candle burns, the last bid before the candle goes out securing the article. Cf. 'The Elegy offered to the Memory of that Incomparable Son of Apollo, Mr. John Cleveland', 51–52 (W, p. 283):

> The Cause by Candles-end he did not rate,
> When others Pens did Truth assassinate. . . .

ll. 17–18. *The Sober Julian . . . Gregorian*. The difference between the calendar introduced by Julius Caesar in 46 B.C. and that instituted by Pope Gregory XIII in 1682 amounted to ten days in over sixteen hundred years. In Cleveland's conceit, the 'fleet Gregorian' is some ten minutes a year faster than the 'Sober Julian'.

l. 26. *Ostend*. When the Spaniards finally occupied Ostend on 20 September

1604 after a famous three-year siege, little was left. See J. L. Motley, *History of the United Netherlands*, 2nd ed., 1869–70, iv. 201:

> There were no churches, no houses, no redoubts, no bastions, no walls, nothing but a vague and confused mass of ruin.

l. 32. *woe*. Woo.

l. 36. *Furlowes*. Passports, licences, or permits.

l. 41. *recruited*. Renewed, restored.

l. 42. *Pelops*. Ovid, *Met*. vi. 411 ff.

l. 44. *Herriot*. In English law, a feudal service consisting, originally, of weapons or horses, restored to a lord on the death of his tenant; later the render of the best live beast or dead chattel of a deceased tenant. See Giles Jacob, *A New Law-Dictionary*. As l. 45 goes on to explain, even if Julia should live for ever, she is no more than a Heriot, to be rendered back to Love, on the death of the poet.

l. 48. *regealing*. Melting, unfreezing. *OED* quotes this line as its only example. The prefix 're-' has the same force as the English 'un-', implying the undoing of some previous action.

ll. 52–54. *Else pious . . . maladies*. See John v. 2–4, and cf. Carew, 'The tooth-ach cured by a kisse', 13–16 (ed. Dunlap, p. 110):

> That Angell sure that us'd to move
> The poole, men so admir'd,
> Hath to her lip the seat of love,
> As to his heaven retir'd.

On Princess Elizabeth (*page 62*)

P11, CV, W.

Both Berdan's date, 28 December 1638, and Saintsbury's, 26 December 1638, are wrong. The Princess was born on 28 December 1635. Although the date in *Burke's Peerage, Baronetage & Knightage* (ed. L. G. Pine, 101st ed., 1956, p. lxxvii) is a day later, the *DNB* and several poems in *Carmen Natalitium ad cunas Illustrissimae Principis Elisabethae decantatum intra Nativitatis Dom. solennia per humiles Cantabrigiae Musas*, the volume of Greek and Latin congratulatory verse from the University, all agree that it was Holy Innocents' Day. The title of Richard Sterne's poem (sig. A4ᵛ), '. . . Elisabetham . . . natam ad crastinum S. Innocentium', suggests that the Princess was born late at night on 28 December, but the title of Cleveland's poem could never be correct. When it came to be printed more than twenty years later, few people would have recalled the exact date of the unfortunate Princess's birth.

l. 2. *Hesperus and Lucifer*. The evening star or Venus when she appears before sunset, and the morning star or Venus when she appears in the sky before sunrise. Cf. Donne, *The Second Anniversary*, 197–8, and Problem 9 of his *Paradoxes and Problems*.

l. 3. *Antitype*. That which is shadowed forth or represented by the 'type' or symbol. Here Venus the star shadows forth Venus the goddess, and Cleveland equates the goddess with Princess Elizabeth.

l. 5. *Her Brother*. Charles II, born on 29 May 1630. A star was said to be visible during daylight on the day of his birth. Cf. Dryden, 'Astraea Redux', 288–90:

> That star, that at your birth shone out so bright,
> It stain'd the duller sun's meridian light,
> Did once again its potent fires renew. . . .

See also Dryden's 'Annus Mirabilis', stanza 18; Herrick's 'A Pastorall on the birth of Prince Charles', 20–22; Waller's 'On St. James's Park', 127–30; Cowley's 'Ode upon His Majesty's Restoration and Return', 11–16.

l. 7. *vie*. Match one thing with another, by way of rivalry or comparison.

Parting with a Freind upon the Rode (*page 63*)

O, P11–P12. RP84 and L22 are probably copied from the printed text, which derives independently from the archetype. Some punctuation has been added.

This farewell is probably earlier than 25 November 1641, the approximate date of 'Upon the Kings return from Scotland', which elaborated many of these conceits.

l. 2. *Hippoletus*. For Hippolytus' death see Euripides' *Hippolytus* or Seneca's *Phaedra*. Ἱππόλυτος or 'loosed horse' implies a driver unable to control his steed.

l. 4. *Lud to Bishopsgate*. Ludgate was the western entrance to the old City, Bishopsgate the northern. A traitor, after being hanged and drawn, was quartered.

ll. 5–8. *thy . . . west*. 'Thy', like 'his' in ll. 7–8, is impersonal. Cf. 'Upon the Kings return from Scotland', 13–16 and note.

ll. 9–10. *Peace fond Philosopher . . . Reflection*. Possibly a reference to the search for perpetual motion.

l. 16. *Principles*. Elements.

ll. 17–20. *Reluctance . . . child*. An unwilling death, unlike Falstaff's peaceful expiration (see *Henry V*, II. iii), is a sign that the dying man despairs of salvation.

ll. 21–22. *But Loue . . . goe.* Cf. 'Upon the Kings return', 23–24.

l. 23. *foundered Rhyme.* Lame verse with defective feet. The epithet derives from 'founder', an inflammation of a horse's foot.

l. 24. *Hunts counter.* Follows the scent or trail of game in the reverse direction —the *right* way (see next lines) to track Cacus' cattle.

l. 25. *splay-foot.* Clumsy-footed; like 'foundered', used figuratively of the verse or 'rhyme'.

l. 26. *Backwards . . . tongue.* Cf. 'To P. Rupert', 24 and note.

ll. 27–28. *Then since . . . with mee.* Cf. 'Upon the Kings return', 41–42 and note.

Epitaphium Thomae Spell (*page 64*)

CV, W. Since the 'editors' of CV were both members of St. John's College and in residence during the time that Spell was President and Cleveland a Fellow, there is little doubt that this epitaph is genuine. For what is known of Thomas Spell and for the species of composition known as 'Carmina Lapidaria' to which this epitaph belongs see pp. xxxiv and xxxviii–xxxix.

l. 4. *Fuit nomen, erit Epitheton.* He was a name, he will be a household word. 'Epitheton', a grammatical term meaning 'adjective, or epithet', cannot be understood here in its strict sense. An alternative translation, 'That was his name, his title awaits him in the future', is less defensible.

l. 12. *Mitionem.* See Terence, *Adelphoe*, where Mitio (or Micio) is the typical mild, lenient, kindly old man, contrasted with his severe, crabbed brother, Demea. Terence describes Mitio as *clemens, urbanus, placidus*, which probably suggested Cleveland's '*Omine pacis*' (l. 14) and '*Urbanitas*' (l. 15).

l. 13. *Alcedo.* The Kingfisher, or Halcyon. Cf. Browne, *Pseudodoxia Epidemica*, iii. 10 (Sayle, i. 350):

> For at that time, which happeneth about the brumal Solstice, it hath been observed even unto a proverb, that the Sea is calm, and the winds do cease, till the young ones are excluded; and forsake their nest which floateth upon the Sea, and by the roughness of winds might otherwise be overwhelmed.

l. 22. *Et Pastor gregis in cruce providus.* And shepherd of his flock, caring for them in time of trouble. This sense of 'crux' is frequent, especially in Plautus and Terence. With 'Pastor gregis', 'in cruce' seems to invite the meaning of 'an instrument of execution, a cross'. But the religious interpretation—'And shepherd of his flock, caring for them on the cross'—makes very little sense.

Elegy on Edward King (*page 65*)

J, PII–12. PII may have been carelessly printed from J, but more probably derives from a manuscript. Its readings are, in all but one case, inferior to those of J, which has been taken as copy-text and repunctuated.

For Cleveland's probable authorship see p. xxxviii. See also the notes for 'Upon the death of M. King', pp. 79–80.

ll. 5–8. *Till thou . . . the Universe.* These lines, appended to the 'Epitaph on the Earl of Strafford' in H35, clearly belong here. The 'Athenian owls' in l. 7, wise birds that flew only after dark and the emblem of the city of Athens, represent the Cambridge poets of the day. 'Taking owls to Athens' was equivalent to 'carrying coals to Newcastle'.

l. 9. *Thy death makes Poets.* Cf. 'Upon the death of M. King', 5–8.

ll. 11–14. *Now the . . . as it gains.* The death by water is a central concern of the elegists in *Justa Edovardo King*. See Williamson, *Seventeenth Century Contexts*, 1960, pp. 134–6, and cf. 'The Authour to his Hermophrodite', 7–10 and note.

ll. 21–25. *As night . . . highest heav'ns.* This image, with variations, is found in nearly all the elegies. See Williamson, pp. 144–5. For 'close-mourner' in l. 21 see 'The Kings Disguise', 24.

Epitaph on the Earl of Strafford (*page 66*)

D1–W. Reprinted in *Poems on Affairs of State*, iii. 1704. Probably written shortly after Strafford's execution on 12 May 1641. For Cleveland's claim to authorship see p. xxxiii. Of the many poems on this subject this is the best, though those by Denham and Fanshawe contain some good lines.

l. 6. *A Papist, yet a Calvinist.* C. V. Wedgwood in *Poetry and Politics under the Stuarts*, Cambridge, 1960, pp. 66–67, argues that Cleveland, a Fellow of Strafford's college, St. John's, might well have picked up the information that the Earl, described by the populace as 'Papist', was in his personal religion a Calvinist.

ll. 7–8. *His Prince's . . . Reliefe.* The manuscripts punctuate these lines variously, usually attempting to make the couplet one sentence.

l. 10. *The People's violent Love, and Hate.* Cf. Denham's early version of 'On the Earl of Strafford's Tryal and Death', 17–18 (ed. Banks, p. 153):

> The enimy and martire of the state,
> Our nations glory and our nations hate.

l. 12. *Riddles lie here.* Cf. 'The Kings Disguise', 89–90.

l. 14. *Speechlesse still.* Cf. Vaughan, 'Abels Blood', 33–35 (ed. Martin, p. 524):

> I, may that flood,
> That proudly spilt, and despis'd blood,
> Speechless and calm, as Infants sleep!

The Scots Apostasie (*page 67*)

S, D5–P17, W. Reprinted in *The Rump*, 1662. The question of authorship is discussed on p. xxxv. The poem appeared as a broadside in 1647 (Thomason dates his copy 'March 10th 1646', i.e. 1647), and possibly predates by a week or so its appearance in D5. S exists in two states (B.M. 669. f. 10, uncorrected, and B.M. Lutt. ii. 200, corrected). The uncorrected state has 'banded' for 'bawded' at l. 34 and 'Ships' for 'steps' at l. 38. Because both states of S omit ll. 67–68, D5 has been taken as copy-text.

In 1646, while the King was held by the Scots at Newcastle, John Campbell (1598–1663), first Earl of Loudoun and Lord Chancellor of Scotland, tried unsuccessfully to persuade him to accede to Parliamentary demands. Thomason dates his copy of *Severall Speeches, Spoken by the Right Honourable the Earle of Loudoun* . . . Edinburgh, 1646, 'Nou: 6th London by Rob: Bostock' and crosses out the Edinburgh imprint. The speeches were printed again on 9 November, and had appeared separately several times in the past weeks. Cleveland's 'again' (l. 3) suggests that the poem was written after 9 November 1646, and the date of S that it was topical in the early weeks of 1647, after the departure of the Scots army and the handing over of the King to the English Commissioners (see ll. 37–38). Bostock's answer, *The Scots Constancy* (see p. xxxv), shows that he regarded the satire as a reflection on his publication:

> . . . what of Loudons speech? 'tis writ in Gold
> With admiration honest men behold
> His Loyalty. . . .

l. 3. *flag'd.* Made limp or flaccid.

l. 6. *tinctures.* The (supposed) essential principle of any substance, obtained in solution. Like the alchemist's tincture, Loudoun's eloquence looked impressive, but closer examination showed it to be no more than political trickery.

ll. 11–12. *Who reconcil'd . . . Pence?* The doubtful sense of the Solemn League and Covenant caused it to be several times amended. In the end the door was left open for Independency or Presbyterianism in England, the Covenant pledging reform of the Church of England 'according to the word of God' and defence of the Church of Scotland; then the usual forced loan was levied, which, as far as the City was concerned, was reconcilement enough.

ll. 13–16. *Or did . . . hammering?* The Scots are asked: 'Did you believe your continued loyalty to Charles would wreck the Scottish–English alliance (that construction forged in sin, and fit to be hammered out only by Satan)?' 'Fabrick' here means 'engine, contrivance, or appliance'.

l. 20. *Your sixty Kings. A brief Chronicle of all the Kings of Scotland*, Aberdeen, 1623 (*Harleian Miscellany*, iii. 462–75) lists fifty-three Scottish kings who were murdered, slain in battle, or suicides. Bostock, in *The Scots Constancy*, asks:

> What sixty Kings were murder'd by the Scots?
> 'Tis but a fable. . . .

l. 28. *flee.* A variant spelling of 'fly'.

l. 32. *Epidemick curse.* A wide-spread, universal curse. Cf. 'The Rebell Scot', 70.

l. 36. *Reproach the Traytors* etc. A variation on the common proverb 'A King loves the treason but hates the traitor' (see Tilley). Cf. Middleton, *Women Beware Women*, II. ii. 446–8 (*Works*, ed. Bullen, 1885, vi. 291).

ll. 41–42. *Till forc'd . . . at home.* Cf. 'The Rebell Scot', 63–64.

ll. 53–54. *And such . . . to you.* 'Such' refers to the 'banisht Men' in the previous line, and 'send' has a double object, 'such' and 'them'.

ll. 63–65. *Untill . . . sav'd.* Cleveland, in cursing the Scots, was obliged to be tactful in the matter of Charles's Scottish ancestry. Cf. 'The Rebell Scot', 49–50.

The General Eclipse (*page 69*)

CV, W. The first four stanzas appear in Ash 78, and stanzas one, two, and four are set to music as 'Beauties Eclyps'd' in AD, with a few variants probably produced by the composer.

The poem is one of the many variations on Wotton's 'You meaner beauties of the Night'. Saintsbury and Berdan dated it 1645, but J. B. Leishman ('You meaner Beauties of the Night: A Study in Transmission and Transmogrification', *The Library*, 4th ser. xxvi, September–December 1945, p. 116) thought it was written after the King's execution. 'The King's Goodnight' (l. 10) seems appropriate to Charles's surrender to the Scots, and a date of May–June 1646 would not be contradicted by any other reference in the poem.

l. 2. *mend.* Supplement. Cf. 'To the State of Love', 18–26.

ll. 3–4. *Whose Beauty . . . Easter-day*. See Browne, *Pseudodoxia Epidemica*, v. 22 (Sayle, ii. 272).

ll. 6–7. *Courageous Eagles . . . Light*. 'For in the Eagle the spirit of sight is most temperate, and most sharpe in act and deede of seeing and beholding the Sunne in the roundnesse of his circle, without anye blemishing of eyen . . . . Also . . . ther is one mañer Eagle that . . . is ful sharpe of sight, and shee taketh her owne birdes in her claws, and maketh them to looke euen on the Sunne, and . . . ere their wings bee full growen, and except they looke stiflye and steadfastly against the Sunne: shee beateth them, and setteth them euen before the Sunne . . . and though she sette her sight neuer so straight and steadfast on the Sunne, yet she casteth her eie to waite and espie after her praye, as Gregorye saith.'—Stephan Bat[e]man, *Batman vppon Bartholome*, London, 1582, xii. 1.

l. 17. *Cuts the Intail off* etc. Breaks the succession.

ll. 22–23. *whose Pæan . . . after it*. A Paean is a song of praise or thanksgiving, and a Psalm of Mercy is the psalm sung or recited on the scaffold before an execution. Thus, the 'psalm-singing' Roundheads could praise God and cut off a man's head without even changing the chant. See also 'The Kings Disguise', 44.

l. 25. *mew'd*. Moulted.

ll. 26–27. *See how . . . Captive Turk*. Cf. the fate of Bajazeth in Marlowe's *Tamburlaine*, Part I, iv. ii.

l. 32. *al-a-mort*. Sick to death, dispirited. Cf. 'Smectymnuus', 27.

l. 35. *John Lilburn*. The political agitator and pamphleteer (1614?–57), who fought for Parliament from 1642 to 1645, and then left the service, refusing to take the Covenant. Thereafter, a constant embarrassment to the party of Cromwell, he was sent to the Tower in 1649 and brought to trial, but acquitted. He later settled down and became a Quaker.

Mr Cleauelands reply from Belvoir (*page 70*)

EG27, Berdan. See also p. xl.

During the Civil War both Belvoir Castle, in Leicestershire, and the town of Newark, fifteen miles away in Nottinghamshire, were Royalist garrisons. Belvoir, the seat of the eighth Earl of Rutland, a Parliamentarian, was captured for the King by Colonel Gervase Lucas in January 1643. It was the stopover where Prince Rupert refused to confine himself when in late October

1645 he came with Prince Maurice to plead for a reconciliation with his uncle after the fall of Bristol. In the same month it was besieged by Colonel Pointz, but the garrison held out until the spring of 1646, when Lucas surrendered (see *Victoria County History, Leicester*, ii. 110 ff.). The title suggests that Cleveland spent some time at Belvoir after his appointment as Judge Advocate at Newark in May 1645 and before the fall of the Belvoir garrison. But the '3 Newarke Poets' remain mysterious. Were they members of the Royalist garrison or the besieging Parliamentary force? What work of theirs occasioned this 'Reply'?

l. 1. *Gleeke.* A set of three Court cards of the same rank in one hand, in the game of gleek; more generally, 'a set of three, a trio'.

l. 3. *Terse.* A variant of 'tierce' which can mean 'a band or company of soldiers' or 'three cards in any suit in the game of piquet', although its commonest meaning is merely 'a third part'. Possibly Cleveland is also thinking of tercet, the term in prosody.

l. 5. *The very Jeoffryes of the times.* Professor D. J. Gordon has suggested that the reference is probably to Jeffery Hudson (1619–82), a dwarf in King Charles's court, whose capture by Flemish pirates in 1630 is celebrated by Davenant. See Enid Welsford, *The Fool*, 1935, pp. 179–80, and cf. 'Vpon Lee & Owens Fencing, a Dᖟ Roan & a Jeffray', 6.

l. 9. *Poets of the Dale.* Belvoir stands on a prominence, Newark on the plain.

l. 10. *take the finger.* Perhaps 'to be weaned', as calves and lambs are sometimes weaned from their mothers by giving them a finger which has been dipped in milk or water to suck.

l. 11. *Clarretteeres. OED* lists 'Clareteer' only as a nonce-word in the sense of 'a drinker of claret'. If the manuscript reading is correct, it must be interpreted in some such sense as 'claret-drinking bouts'.

ll. 13–14. *Wee are . . . the game.* 'Birds of fame' leads one to expect that 'tonies' and 'high comers' will be terms connected with falconry. The word 'Tony' appears in some dialect compound words as an adjective meaning 'bullfinch'. See Wright, *English Dialect Dictionary*, which gives as examples 'Tony-hood' and 'Tony-hoop', and says that the word is found principally in the North Country and in Somerset. 'High comers' probably refers to a hawk flown 'at the high mountee', when the hawk pursues its quarry into the clouds, where the fight takes place. At Belvoir, the fighting takes place on the heights, whereas at Newark the battle is on the plain.

l. 17. *to play at Wasters.* To fence with single-stick or cudgel.

A Translation of Lovelace's 'Song' *(page 71)*

RP147. Lovelace's poem and Cleveland's translation appear on pp. 135–6, the former headed 'Songe', the latter 'The same done into Latine'. The Latin version transposes stanzas two and three, which are here restored to their proper position. The following transcript of RP147's text of the 'Songe' (collated against the text in *The Poems of Richard Lovelace*, ed. Wilkinson, pp. 26–27) is offered to facilitate comparison with the translation:

> Why shouldst thou say I am forsworne
>   Since thine I vow'd to bee
> Lady it is already morne
>   And twas last night I swore to thee
> That fond impossibility.
>
> Haue not I lou'd thee much & long;
>   A taedious twelue houres space?
> I should all other beautyes wrong,
>   And rob thee of a new imbrace
> Could I still doate upon thy face.
>
> Not but all ioy in thy browne haire
>   By others may be found
> But I must court the black & faire
>   Like skillfull Minerallists y^t sound
> For treasure in unplow'd-up ground.
>
> But if w^n I haue lou'd my round
>   Thou prou'st y^e $\begin{smallmatrix}\text{pleasant}\\\text{constant}\end{smallmatrix}$ shee
> With spoyles of meaner beautyes crown'd,
>   I laden will returne to thee
> Eu'n sated with variety.

| 1 shouldst thou say] should you sweare | 6 not I] I not | 8 should] |
| must   13 court] search   16 But] Then | 17 $\begin{smallmatrix}\text{pleasant}\\\text{constant}\end{smallmatrix}$] pleasant | |

l. 11. *In nitidis.* 'Nitidus' usually means 'shining, glittering', but there are examples of its use to describe a woman's hair.

ll. 13–14. *est . . . amor.* In reading l. 13 of the 'Songe' Cleveland presumably contrasted 'black' very strongly with the 'browne' of l. 11, and translated 'Nevertheless even a black love is beautiful and comely'. In l. 14 the manuscript reads 'decorq' where one would expect 'decorusque'.

l. 17. *firmam.* Translating the 'constant' rather than the 'pleasant' of the original.

To his Mistress (*page 71*)

Fol. Punctuation has been added. For Cleveland's claim to authorship see p. xl.

l. 2. *Posthume*. Probably an aphetic form of 'Imposthume', meaning here 'a gathering cloud, or its contents'. The two eyes of heaven are defective in vision, by comparison with the lady's eyes.

ll. 5–8. *The Chrystall . . . body glorifyed*. For this idea, that the rays of the sun redouble their power by reflection from a lady's eyes, see 'To the State of Love', 18–26, and 'The General Eclipse', 1–2. Lines 7–8 are also a variation on the 'pupilla' theme, used in 'Upon an Hermophrodite', 31–32.

l. 20. *ordiall tryall*. Trial by ordeal was not abolished until the reign of Henry III. Ordeal by fire, which was limited to persons of rank, required that the accused should hold hot metal or burning wood in his hands, and walk upon heated ploughshares. If his flesh was not burnt, he was declared innocent.

On the Pouder Plot (*page 72*)

L.22. For Cleveland's claim to authorship see p. xl.

This treatment of the subject could be, like Milton's, a school exercise, but the conclusion and the vision in ll. 18–20 would be pertinent to a period after the fall of Laud and the defeat of the King's forces when Charles seemed for the first time in physical danger. Perhaps the poet added these touches to an early piece, thinking to use it in one of the Royalist mercuries.

l. 1. *miterd Hill*. The cleft top of Mount Parnassus.

ll. 5–14. *Satyres . . . hot expression*. The conventional emblem from the days of Joseph Hall and other Elizabethans for the shafts of the satirist. Cf. 'Smectymnuus', 12–13.

ll. 23–25. *Poore infant Roome . . . Experience*. Probably a reference to Romulus' slaying of Remus. Parricide, Clarendon's word for the execution of Charles I, meant the slaying not only of a parent but of any venerated person, such as a king.

l. 26. *The Viper . . . Parricide*. In ancient Rome parricides were drowned in a sack with a viper. For the reason why vipers became emblems of filial impiety see 'To P. Rupert', 117–18 and note.

ll. 33–34. *The auncient Stagarite . . . a flitting soul*. Cf. 'To P. Rupert', 59–60 and note.

l. 36. *Cethegus & those hayr-braynd men.* C. Cornelius Cethegus, in league with Catiline, was condemned to death in 63 B.C. for the attempted murder of leading senators. 'Hayr-braynd' may derive from *vesana* in Lucan's famous 'manus vesana Cethegi'.

l. 40. *in blood . . . Cateline.* Cf. 'A Dialogue between two Zealots . . .', 57–58.

l. 43. *Whether in ayre* etc. The syntax would be clearer if the parenthesis began at 'Whether'.

l. 44. *Might in their vault . . . the locall Hell.* The cellar under the Parliament House where the powder was stored could be the local hell, as opposed to the hell each plotter carried in his own breast.

ll. 46–47. *Outvy'd Joues cannon . . . . black hall.* Excelled Jove's thunderbolt, turning Whitehall into Hades. Natural law seems defied, but the poet is also thinking of the law attributed to Hippocrates in Browne's *Garden of Cyrus,* chap. iv (Sayle, iii. 199): 'Lux orco, tenebrae Jovi, tenebrae orco, lux Jovi'.

l. 48. *Phlegethon.* In Greek and Roman myth, the flaming river of Hades.

l. 59. *Then.* Thus the MS. There is no reason to suppose a line or couplet has been omitted.

Εἰς τὸ δεῖν πίνειν—Anacreon (*page 74*)

O. The sixteenth-century Latin translation from which this and other contemporary English versions of the Greek were derived is noted on p. xl. For extensive commentary on the Greek text, its Latin analogues, and French translations, especially for ll. 3–4, see Thomas Stanley, *Poems,* 1651, pp. 96–97.

l. 7. *Skinkers. OED: arch.* or *dial.* Tapsters or servers of liquor.

News news News (*page 74*)

O. The date must be shortly after the fall of Newcastle-upon-Tyne to the Scots, 19–21 October 1644. A pro-Scottish prose satire, *The Pigges Corantoe: Or Newes From the North,* dated by the Thomason Catalogue 26 March 1642, is not related in content, but suggests the existence of a northern news-sheet for which Cleveland's doggerel would be an appropriate beginning. Almost all punctuation has been supplied.

l. 2. *chopping.* Whopping.

l. 7. *Lesley the Pedler.* Alexander Leslie, Earl of Leven, took Newcastle twice: after Newburn in August 1640, and after Marston Moor in 1644. After the first capture, John Newport reported of Leslie on 11 September 1640:

> . . . there are 4,000 soldiers in the town, and where they lie look what any of the townspeople bring in for their own provisions, they . . . give the people what they ask for anything they take, but will not suffer any of the town to dress any meat for themselves or their servants but what they buy of them; and so the townsmen sell them meat at one rate, and they make them give double the price for it again. . . .
> *Calendar of State Papers, Domestic,* 1640–1, cccclxvii, p. 49.

l. 10. *Rabbyes.* Scotch Presbyterian elders, supposed to consider organs part of Laud's programme to return to Rome. Cf. 'How the Commencement grows new', 33–34 and note.

l. 11. *Pigs.* Bagpipes, often made of pigskin or a pig's bladder; the forerunner of the organ, they had been a substitute for it in small Scottish churches. See William H. Gratton Flood (*The Story of the Bagpipe,* 1911, pp. 4, 50), who also cites (pp. 48–49) sculptures and carvings in Melrose Abbey and elsewhere of hogs playing on and dancing to the pipes. For the association of their stomach-shaped bag with gluttony and lechery see Edward A. Block, 'Chaucer's Millers and Their Bagpipes', *Speculum,* xxix, January 1954, pp. 239–43. See also 'The Pigg', in *The Loves of Hero and Leander . . ., and other choice Peices of Drollery,* 1651, stanza 5, pp. 49–50, and the saying in Howell's *English Proverbs,* 1659: 'I think thou wast born at Hoggs-Norton where piggs play upon the organs.'

Jiggs. Cf. 'The Mixt Assembly', 67.

l. 12. *Sow-Babyes.* Possibly a reference to Jupiter who, in Cretan legend, was suckled by a sow; see Browne, *Pseudodoxia Epidemica,* iii. 25 (Sayle, ii. 81).

l. 13. *The Bishoprick.* The diocese of Durham.

l. 17. *told al in.* Cleveland exploits both meanings of this phrase; the Scots have (1) allured and decoyed all the citizens to be their customers (see ll. 4, 6–7) and (2) summoned all to a (Presbyterian) service.

l. 19. *wrote on his sleeue.* Probably related to 'pin on one's sleeve' (cf. 'To P. Rupert', 95) meaning to pin one's faith on or adopt for one's arms. One who wrote his own name there would be for himself alone.

l. 20. *John Blakston.* The regicide John Blakiston (1603–49), M.P. for Newcastle in 1641 and its Mayor after Leslie's second victory. Denzil Lord Holles says (*Memoirs,* 1699, p. 65) that Blakiston was really in sympathy with 'the Army party'—i.e. the Cromwellians—and 'thrust on' by them to prove that the Scots did not need more compensation from Parliament than what they had already 'rais'd upon the Country'.

l. 21. *of the mother*. The phrase goes with the verb and means 'of their hysteria'. Cleveland is thinking of Presbyterians like Janet Geddes who precipitated a riot by throwing her stool at the Dean of St. Giles Cathedral when he attempted to read the new Scottish Liturgy there on 23 July 1637.

l. 24. *stoole of Repentance*. *OED*: A stool formerly placed in a conspicuous position in Scottish churches for the use of offenders (esp. against chastity) making public repentance.

No Hubbub surnamd Hue & cry (*page 75*)

O. The date might be early in Cleveland's days at Cambridge were it not for the allusions to journals of the mid-40's and early 50's. Possibly these are later additions. Punctuation has been added.

l. 1. *Hue & cry*. Cf. 'The Kings Disguise', 72 and note.

l. 2. *o yes*. 'Oyez' was often written as it was then pronounced.

ll. 2–4. *Spy . . . Noone*. Joseph Frank, *The Beginnings of the English Newspaper*, mentions several journals that would fit these lines: *The Spie*, an anti-Royalist sheet by Durant Hotham, a Cambridge graduate who purported to communicate 'Intelligence from Oxford' from February to June 1644; *The Dutch Spy*, probably edited by Daniel Border in the spring of 1652; the Leveller-rousing, pro-Royalist *Man in the Moon*, edited by John Crouch from April to November 1649 and January to June 1650; *Mercurius Democritus, A True and Perfect Nocturnall Communicating Wonderfull News Out of the World in the Moon, . . .*, also edited by Crouch from April 1652 to February 1654; and *Mercurius Cinicus*, whose issue of 4 to 11 August 1652 says of *Democritus*: 'You stole so much out of poor *Diogenes* as furnished thy Pamphlets three weeks.'

ll. 5–6. *Lithgow . . . Tom: of Odcombe*. For the travel literature by William Lithgow (1582–1645) see the *DNB*, and for that of Thomas Coryate of Odcomb, Somerset, see Douglas Bush, *English Literature in the Early Seventeenth Century*, Oxford, 1962, pp. 183–4. 'Word of Creed' must mean 'believable word' and 'for a need', 'at a pinch'.

l. 7. *Siquis*. See 'The Kings Disguise', 83 and note.

l. 12. *Triptolemus*. Inventor of the plough and, in some legends, son of Ocean and Earth. Cleveland confuses his birth with that of Pluto, god of wealth, begotten when Demeter lay with Iasion in a thrice-ploughed (τρίπολος) field; see *Odyssey*, v. 125 ff. and Hesiod, *Theogony*, 912–13. Cf. *A Character of the New Oxford Libeller*, 1645, which seems to be punning on Cleveland's name and accusing him of squandering some inherited lands: '. . . he turned Alchemist, and made projection of his Land, to give a tincture to his brain.'

l. 18. *by rebound.* By confirming after another.

l. 24. *White Rose . . . Crickett.* Perhaps, by synecdoche, neither on crucial matters of state (York vs. Lancaster) nor on sporting events.

l. 25. *to nick it.* To drink heavily. See Nick, v. in Farmer and Henley, *Dictionary of Slang and Colloquial English,* 1905.

l. 27. *Quotation.* Here used in two senses: (1) 'observation', introducing the direct discourse in the last half of the line and (2) 'price' or 'wager', though this last is not in *OED.* Cf. *Hudibras,* II. i. 297–8:

> . . . I've heard old cunning *stagers*
> Say Fools for *Arguments* use wagers.

ll. 28–29. *Sweares not by's Wine . . . oath.* Cf. 'A Dialogue between two Zealots . . .', 55–56. To 'take an oath' meaning to 'drink liquor' is listed in Partridge's *Dictionary of Slang and Unconventional English,* 1961, as 'c. 19' and 'mostly U.S.', but Ben Jonson must have known it when he wrote the second line of 'Drink to me only with thine eyes'.

l. 30. *Rides no set stage of wordes.* Does not travel the same course every day in his conversation.

l. 39. *The Goose of non plus . . . mouth.* He finds himself at a loss for a retort. Cf. *Mercurius Anti-Mercurius,* no. 2, 26 September–2 October 1648, p. 4, which speaks of General Munro 'who came into the North as feirce as a Gander, but waddled out as quiet as a Goose'.

On an Alderman who married a very young wife (*page 77*)

O. All punctuation has been supplied.

l. 8. *eighty-eight.* Cf. 'A young Man to an old Woman', 44 and note.

ll. 21–22. *Like Hocus . . . throat.* Cf. 'The Rebell Scot', 18–19, 26 and notes.

Vpon Lee & Owens Fencing, a Dʳ Roan & a Jeffray (*page 78*)

O. Lines 13–14 would date this doggerel after Cromwell's victories in August–September 1648, if not after those at Dunbar in September 1650 or Worcester in September 1651. The title may refer not to a fencing match but to some defensive alliance of incompatibles. In Scottish law, 'to fence' meant 'to open the proceedings of (the Parliament or a Court of Law) by the use of a form of words forbidding persons to interrupt or obstruct the proceedings unnecessarily', and the Tables were the Committees of the Four Estates assembled at Edinburgh when the Scottish Parliament was not in session. In Scottish Presbyterian churches 'to fence the tables' was 'to deliver an exhortation calculated to deter unworthy persons from communicating', though *OED* gives no example of this usage before 1709. Lee seems to be either a Scot or one favouring the Presbyterians; Owen, a Cromwellian Independent. Such affiliations would be appropriate for Edward Leigh (Wood, *Athenae Oxonienses*, iii. 926 ff.), a victim of Pride's Purge, and John Owen, D.D., Dean of Christ Church, Oxford. But physically Owen does not qualify; *DNB* says he was 'tall and strong', whereas 'a Dr Roan & a Jeffray' would be a fat giant and a dwarf; cf. 'The Authour to his Hermophrodite', 35, 'A Dialogue between two Zealots', 47, and 'Mr Cleauelands reply from Belvoir to the 3 Newarke Poets', 5 and note. As the speculation indicates, the subject here is even more a mystery to the editors than that of 'Mr. Cleauelands reply'. All punctuation has been supplied.

l. 3. *The Banes are askt.* Cf. 'Smectymnuus', 75.

l. 5. *In a Familiar stile.* Cf. 'A Dialogue between two Zealots', 51. The phrase may also imply a shot-gun wedding, as would 'in a familiar way'.

l. 6. *I Godfray . . . Jeffray.* Lee may be cast in the role of Godfrey of Bouillon, liberator and protector of the Holy Sepulchre in *Jerusalem Delivered*; see 'Upon Sir Thomas Martin', 25 and note. Owen may be the resourceful hero captured by pirates in Davenant's mock-epic 'Jeffereidos'; see 'Mr. Cleauelands reply', 5 and note.

l. 8. *The Scotch Hobby & Bucephalus.* The scrubby little Scotch horse that could be the steed of Alexander should be that of the short, deformed, but energetic Alexander Leslie; see 'News news News', 7 and note. After Cromwell's victory at Preston, Leslie, who had refused to be a party to the Engagement unless Charles accepted the Covenant, raised an army in Edinburgh to defend Scotland. He installed Argyle's party in power and then welcomed Cromwell with a great banquet in Edinburgh Castle.

ll. 9–10. *How Davids pibble . . . Beame.* Cf. 'A Dialogue between two Zealots', 23–24. Probably a reference to 'Crumwells handful' in l. 13.

l. 11. *shuffeled & packt.* The phrase originally referred to a stacked deck of cards, then to an assembly, jury, or committee selected or manipulated to serve party ends.

l. 12. *foyling.* The word may be 'fayling'.

l. 15. *The Italian monster.* Cf. 'Smectymnuus', 25–28, and note. According to J. Greene's translation of Gaspar Bartholine (*Gentleman's Magazine*, 1777, p. 482), Lazarus's little brother had the larger head.

APPENDIX

Portraits of Cleveland

No authenticated seventeenth-century painting of Cleveland is known to exist. The engraving by J. Basire used as a frontispiece for J. Nichols's *A Select Collection of Poems*, 1781, vii, has on its circular frame the words:

THIS, THIS IS HE, WHO IN POETIC RAGE WITH SCORPIONS LASH'D THE MADNESS OF THE AGE. JOHN CLEIVELAND ESQ. AET. CIRC. 32.

Nichols says (frontispiece and p. 10 n.) it is from an original 'in the possession of the Dean of Carlisle', a portrait by Isaac Fuller of Cleveland during his 'attendance on the King at Oxford'. The 'Dean' was the future Bishop Percy, great-great-grandson of Cleveland's brother William, and this plus the fact that the figure in the portrait is holding a scroll of the 'Rebell Scot' explains why Berdan reproduced a later engraving[1] of the same painting then in the possession of Mrs. Isted and why another reproduction accompanied a recent article by C. V. Wedgwood ('A Metaphysical Satirist', *The Listener*, lix, 8 May 1958, pp. 769–71) after the Tate Gallery acquired the portrait in 1955. However, a cleaning of the painting in 1961 removed the title on the scroll, revealing underneath a drawing which may be, according to Sir John Summerson, the plan of a triumphal arch and on the figure a lace collar of the period after 1657. David Piper of the National Portrait Gallery suggests that the portrait is Vertue, i. 52: 'The Picture of . . . Architect a half lenght [*sic*] by. Fuller. in poseš. Kerey-chaser.'[2] Possibly connected with Restoration celebrations, it was retouched and faked into a Cleveland portrait for Lord Oxford, who was buying portraits of poets for his new library at Wimpole in 1730.[3]

[1] R. Rhode's, drawn by T. Unwin in 1822. Berdan's is a Grafton Press copy. A print published by W. Walker, 8 Gray's Inn Square, London, 1 Jan. 1822 is in the library of the National Portrait Gallery.

[2] *Vertue Note Books*, The Walpole Society, xviii, Oxford, 1930.

[3] Pope, mentioning this portrait in a letter to the Earl of Oxford in June 1730, associates his own unpopularity at the time with Cleveland's: 'I advise; that two Poets Heads, which I see in another room, be always kept together, as being both

A painting by William Dobson on canvas, 30″ × 25″, in Bridgewater House has also been called a Cleveland portrait. The silver print of it in the library of the National Portrait Gallery shows a man with bust to the right in black dress with white collar and long fair hair. On the back it is marked 'P. Lely, H. R.' The same painting at Corsham in the collection of Lord Methuen is said to represent J. Ash (see notes on file in the library of the National Portrait Gallery). It is certainly not the man painted by Fuller, though it might just possibly be the original for the anonymous engraving of Cleveland in the Hoe copy of P2 (1651) in the Beverly Chew collection now in the Huntington Library, the first to appear in any of his editions.

This engraving, frontispiece of the present edition,[1] depicts Cleveland in what has been called a 'clerical habit' but may be the robes of a lawyer or judge advocate, holding a book. It reappears in this state in individual copies of P5–9 (1653–6), P13 (1659), P15 (1662), and P16 (1665). A second state with different tassels and ornamentation on the band and book appears in individual copies of P7 (1654), P10 (1657), and P14 (1661). A smaller derivative of the 1651 engraving in copies of *The Idol of the Clownes* (1654, Wing, 4673) and *The Rustick Rampant*, 1658, is set in a new oval wreath cut off at the sides; it makes the expression less smiling and the hair less curly. In individual copies of CR1–3 (1659–62) and P15 (1662) the head of 1651 is removed from its oval wreath, set on a pedestal within a rectangle, and crowned with laurel; this bust is given a white collar, no tassels, six buttons, and the inscription:

> Vera Effigies J: Cleaulandi.
> For weighty Numbers, sense, misterious wayes
> Of happie Wit, Great Cleauland claimes his Baies.
> Sepultus Colleg: Whitintonis. 1. May Anᵒ: 1658.

In copies of P14 (1661) and CV (1677) the head of 1653 without hand or book but with the white collar and ten buttons is set in a rectangle in an oval on a pedestal on which is printed 'Vera Effigies IOHANNIS CLEAVELAND' over the imprint. This, without the imprint, is also the frontispiece for W (1687).

Oddheaded fellows (Cleveland and Another) & kept at a convenient distance from the Library, not to be of ill Example to those who shall come to study there.'— *Correspondence of Alexander Pope*, ed. George Sherburn, Oxford, 1956, iii. 114–15.

[1] Reproduced by permission of the Huntington Library, San Marino, California.

INDEX OF FIRST LINES

INDEX TO INTRODUCTION
AND COMMENTARY

This index is selective and lists primarily *people* mentioned in the Introduction and *subjects* treated in the Commentary.

PRINTED IN GREAT BRITAIN
AT THE UNIVERSITY PRESS, OXFORD
BY VIVIAN RIDLER
PRINTER TO THE UNIVERSITY

THE POEMS OF
John Cleveland

EDITED BY

BRIAN MORRIS

AND

ELEANOR WITHINGTON

OXFORD
AT THE CLARENDON PRESS
1967

Oxford University Press, Ely House, London W.1

GLASGOW NEW YORK TORONTO MELBOURNE WELLINGTON
CAPE TOWN SALISBURY IBADAN NAIROBI LUSAKA ADDIS ABABA
BOMBAY CALCUTTA MADRAS KARACHI LAHORE DACCA
KUALA LUMPUR HONG KONG TOKYO

© *Oxford University Press 1967*

PRINTED IN GREAT BRITAIN